Teaching Labor History in the United States, 1850–2020

TEACHING CRITICAL THEMES IN AMERICAN HISTORY

Caroline R. Pryor, Erik B. Alexander, James M. Mitchell,
Whitney Blankenship, Michael E. Karpyn, and Jenice L. View

General Editors

Vol. 9

The Teaching Critical Themes in American History
series is part of the Peter Lang Education list.
Every volume is peer reviewed and meets
the highest quality standards for content and production.

Adam I. Attwood (ed.)

Teaching Labor History in the United States, 1850–2020

PETER LANG

New York · Berlin · Bruxelles · Chennai · Lausanne · Oxford

Bibliographic information published by the Deutsche Nationalbibliothek.
The German National Library lists this publication in the German National Bibliography; detailed bibliographic data is available on the Internet at http://dnb.d-nb.de.

Library of Congress Cataloging-in-Publication Data
Names: Attwood, Adam I. editor
Title: Teaching labor history in the United Sates, 1850-2020 / editor, Adam I. Attwood.
Description: New York, NY: Peter Lang, [2026] | Series: Teaching critical themes in American history, 2576-0718; volume 9 | Includes bibliographical references and index.
Identifiers: LCCN 2025038684 (print) | LCCN 2025038685 (ebook) | ISBN 9781636678924 hardback | ISBN 9781636678917 paperback | ISBN 9781636678894 pdf | ISBN 9781636678900 epub
Subjects: LCSH: Labor--United States--History--Study and teaching
Classification: LCC HD8066 .T43 2026 (print) | LCC HD8066 (ebook) | DDC 31.0973--dc23/eng/20250828
LC record available at https://lccn.loc.gov/2025038684
LC ebook record available at https://lccn.loc.gov/2025038685

Cover image: Marchers carrying labor union banners, March on Washington, 1963. Courtesy of the Library of Congress. Public Domain.

ISSN 2576-0718
ISBN 978-1-63667-892-4 (Hardback)
ISBN 978-1-63667-891-7 (Paperback)
ISBN 978-1-63667-889-4 (ePDF)
ISBN 978-1-63667-890-0 (ePUB)
DOI 10.3726/b23326

Published by Peter Lang Publishing Inc., New York (USA)

info@peterlang.com

This publication has been peer reviewed.

www.peterlang.com

Table of Contents

List of Figures

Preface

The story of labor in the United States is a story of the nation's identity and lived experience—a dynamic and evolving narrative of resilience, progress, and collective struggle. Yet, despite its profound significance, labor history remains a marginalized topic within the standard social studies curriculum for grades 6–12. This volume, *Teaching Labor History in the United States, 1850-2020*, is an effort to address this gap and to bring this multifaceted history into the classroom in a way that is both scholarly rigorous and deeply practical for educators.

The motivation for this work arises from two primary ideas. First, labor history encompasses far more than industrial strikes and legislative milestones; it is an interconnected web of social, cultural, and economic forces that have shaped the American experience. Second, in an era where social studies curricula are often constrained by standardized expectations, teachers need both accessible scholarly resources and adaptable pedagogical strategies to enrich their lessons. This volume is an invitation to expand the narrative of U.S. history education by integrating labor history as an essential lens through which students can understand the past and grapple with the complexities of the present.

This book gathers the work of dedicated scholars and educators, each contributing a chapter that merges historical analysis with actionable classroom tools. Each chapter presents a substantive essay grounded in rigorous research and scholarly citations, providing readers with an academic foundation for understanding key themes and events in labor history. Following the essay, contributors offer pedagogical strategies tailored to 6–12 classrooms, including lesson plans that align with educational standards while encouraging critical thinking and engagement. Chapters conclude with integrative summaries that bridge the gap between scholarly insights and their classroom application.

Among the topics explored in this volume are labor rights movements led by historically underrepresented populations, the evolution of unionization, the sociocultural forces influencing labor policies, and the transformative effects of technology—from the early internet to modern computerization—on labor dynamics. These themes are presented not as isolated moments, but as interconnected processes that reveal the continuous thread of labor's impact across time. This work is particularly significant for its commitment to amplifying voices and stories often omitted from traditional narratives. By examining the contributions and struggles of underrepresented groups within the labor movement, this volume seeks to foster a more inclusive and nuanced understanding of U.S. history. It also underscores the interplay of labor with broader societal factors, such as media representation, sociocultural perceptions, governmental policies, and technological change.

Teaching students with the tools to critically analyze history and to draw connections between the past and their own lived experiences is of foundational importance to this volume. The chapters in this volume aim to empower teachers to not only teach content knowledge but also practical strategies for fostering inquiry, discussion, and reflection in their classrooms. The interconnected history of labor in the United States is a story worth telling and worth teaching. It is my goal that this volume serves as both a resource and an inspiration for educators, helping to ensure that labor history is woven into the education of future generations. By doing so, the struggles and triumphs of the past are illuminated and provide students with the historical lens to navigate the complexities of their own futures.

Adam I. Attwood
Austin Peay State University
Clarksville, TN

Acknowledgments

Thank you to the peer reviewers for reviewing the individual manuscripts for this volume and for reviewing the complete volume. Thank you to Series Editor Dr. Caroline R. Pryor (Southern Illinois University Edwardsville) for chairing the Editorial Advisory Board of the Teaching Critical Themes in American History Series that reviewed this volume and provided constructive critiques at each step of the process for this book project.

Introduction: Teaching Labor History

Adam I. Attwood

This volume addresses labor history across time as an interconnected process. The teaching of labor history in secondary schools seems to have a renewed sense of urgency as artificial intelligence (AI) emerges as a major change factor in how society envisions labor and people's relationship to their labor. In thinking about the First Industrial Revolution and the Second Industrial Revolution, there was a social process at work in which more and more individuals moved from small rural communities into more concentrated living conditions that formed ever larger urban communities. As the factory system emerged and employed more people than in rural agriculture, labor unions emerged in larger numbers. Though guilds had existed for many centuries, the nineteenth-century labor union concept was a new economy of scale. Labor union expansion and retraction cycles continued throughout the twentieth century and into the twenty-first century. New technologies are just one of several factors affecting people's conceptualization of labor and the organization of labor. Throughout these strands of labor history has been something of a "social algorithm." This concept is adapted from a historical analysis of industrialization in the context of labor trends analysis (De Vries, 2003). When teaching high school students about industrialization, the factors affecting labor must be referenced. In discussing labor then, marketable goods must be referenced, which requires an explanation of market dynamics. As shown in Figure A, illustrative explanations may be required to explain complex dynamics affecting labor. As such, this could be called a social algorithm. The purchased goods should be thought of as ranging from items requiring very little household labor before they are transformed to the consumable *Z* commodities (e.g., textiles), to those (e.g., wool) that require extensive household labor before the transformation to a *Z* commodity is complete.

As shown in Figure A, an interpretation of De Vries' (2003) explanation of industrialization suggested a social algorithm in which cause-and-effect relationships are theorized as part of continuity and change over time. In this example interpretation, rural agricultural labor might have had many jobs but low relative efficiency when trying to feed a growing population. As industrialization started, technologies affected labor efficiencies. Workers could go from a one-to-one laborer to finished product unit ratio, to a much higher ratio with the factory system; but for that to occur, people needed to centralize which led to the substantial growth of urban centers. As rural laborers relocated to

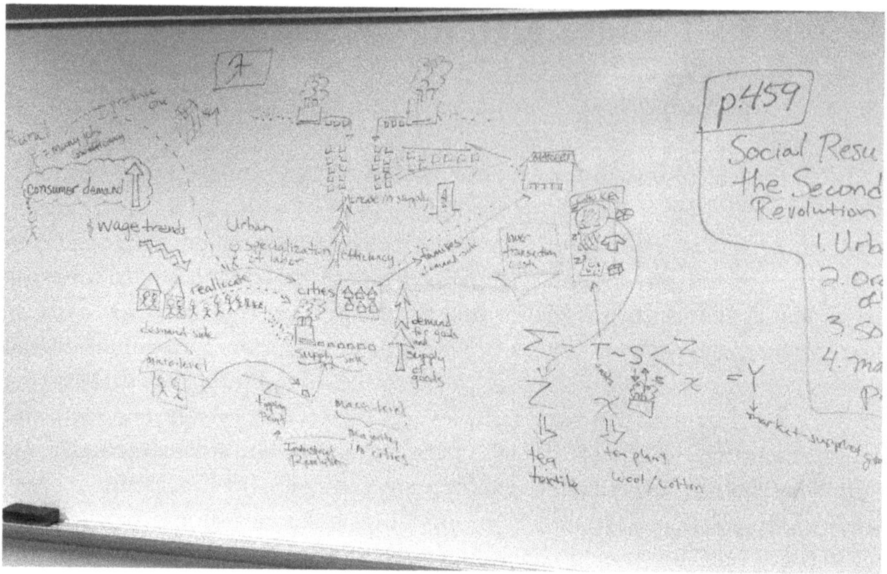

Figure A: An Infographic of a Social Algorithm of Industrialization on the Board in a High School Classroom.

Note: Social algorithm of the First Industrial Revolution based on De Vries (2003). Photo courtesy of Adam I. Attwood.

towns, which then became cities, wages were part of the enticement to relocate. However, for factories to maintain their economic efficiency, wages were lower than the input unit costs to produce a finished product for markets as consumable goods. The factory laborers were also consumers, and so the concentration of people in cities increased microeconomic demand affecting macroeconomic pressures on the supply-side, reaching a tipping point triggering the Second Industrial Revolution. The increase in supply through more technologically efficient use of labor in producing consumable goods for the market lowered per-unit costs, increasing affordability for more people which increased demand. As transaction costs also lowered, the cycle continued upward and expanded. The *Z* commodity is an algebraic symbol here for a finished product, but it must be at a market for consumer access transforming *Z* in the consumable product also known as *Y* (e.g., $\sum = T \sim S +/- Z = Y$). This is using algebraic notation to signify social processes and is not strictly a mathematical formula. In a way, this is adapting fuzzy logic to social processes that may not be replicable from a technical social science methodological perspective (Freese & Peterson, 2017); rather, this explanation is a social science-informed historical logic puzzle. The explanation here is an example of replicating a discussion of historical process using the same sources.

After explaining a social algorithm of industrialization, a quiz prompt or discussion prompt could be developed. In a paragraph, explain the framework for the Industrial Revolution based on the excerpt read in class with the infographic on the board. Explanation must include an understanding of the social algorithm using all the following terms/words: purchased goods, household labor, consumable commodities, raw materials, tastes, relative prices, supply-side, demand-side, market-supplied goods, urban, rural, division of labor. These vocabulary terms are all in the infographic explained by the teacher.

In addition to the social algorithm concept, archeophisomorphic theory posited to explain how social values that may seem anachronistic or outdated may persist (Attwood, 2018). The emergence of the common school movement during the Second Industrial Revolution of the late nineteenth century was indicative of the standardization of time as a finite resource. The factory model regimented time in a way not previously seen at such a level of integration and standardization across nations. That concept of time was implemented into the public and private schools with the bell system that standardized time into units that students progressed through at regimented intervals (Attwood, 2024).

This volume features chapters by scholars who are analyzing and evaluating historical trends in labor that feature continuity and change over time. Each chapter interconnects across time and place on the topic of labor history as a process of culture, social policy, and cultural continuity and change. Lesson plans illustrate how these complex topics may be taught in ways that advance knowledge of labor history and foster social studies skills. Topics proceed chronologically from the 1850s up to 2020 and thematically from the Industrial Revolution to the Emerging Artificial Intelligence Revolution.

References

Attwood, A. I. (2018). *Social aesthetics and the school environment: A case study of the chivalric ethos*. Palgrave Macmillan. https://doi.org/10.1007/978-3-319-60345-2

Attwood, A. I. (2024). Time as a finite resource in education: Theorizing temporality in school culture. In D. R. Cole, M. Mirzaei Rafe, & G. Y. A. Yang-Heim (Eds.), *Educational research and the question(s) of time* (pp. 209–29). Springer. https://doi.org/10.1007/978-981-97-3418-4_12

De Vries, J. (2003). The Industrial Revolution and the Industrious Revolution. In S. M. Beaudoin (Ed.), *The Industrial Revolution* (pp. 81–8). Wadsworth Cengage Learning.

Freese, J., & Peterson, D. (2017). Replication in social science. *Annual Review of Sociology, 43*(1), 147–65. https://doi.org/10.1146/annurev-soc-060116-053450

Exploring the Complexity of the Pullman Strike Through Causal Mapping

Alex Honold

All historical figures are shaped and constrained by the culture, laws, politics, and technology of their time. In popular historical accounts in books and film, individual-agentic explanations of events tend to overshadow the *structural* conditions and contexts surrounding those events. This is not surprising. Stories of "heroes" and "villains" make for more compelling narrative accounts than do details about faceless, sociopolitical structures, such as public opinion, inflation, or budget deficits. However, for students to develop as critical consumers and creators of historical narrative, they must be able to contextualize agentic action. This chapter and lesson about the 1894 Pullman Strike offer a chance for students to grapple with the choices and legacies of historical actors while investigating and representing the complex social, political, and economic structures that shaped those actions and their outcomes.

Taken together with other nineteenth-century strikes, the story of Pullman is a familiar one. Deteriorating economic conditions caused businesses to lay off workers and lower wages. Corporate leaders refused to bargain with aggrieved workers. The workers went on strike where they clashed with strikebreakers and private guard forces. As the violence and destruction of property escalated, business owners sought the help of the federal government to shut down the strike (Currarino, 2011).

Still, the situation at Pullman differed in several ways. Many Pullman workers lived in Pullman's eponymous company town where rent and utility prices were set by the company. An upstart, ambitious labor leader and union in Eugene V. Debs and the American Railway Union elevated what might have been just a local strike into a national railroad strike (Currarino, 2011). The nationalization of the strike would also not have been possible without the massive expansion of rail lines in the late 1800s. To counter the strike, corporate lawyers were now armed with a new legal tool in the Sherman Anti-Trust Act, passed just four years before the Pullman Strike (Bassett, 1997). Newspapers also began to turn against unions who they increasingly saw as disruptive and politically radical (Rondinone, 2009). Ultimately, the Pullman Strike ended in failure for the rail workers and represented a significant setback for the labor movement. However, several of the union's demands influenced the populist and progressive movements in the ensuing decades.

So how do we make sense of what happened at Pullman? Why did workers strike? How did it become a national strike? What were the real consequences of worker's and Pullman's actions? To answer these questions, we need to "zoom-in" to the event itself. We need to understand the people at the heart of the action—their character, motivations, and power. We also need to "zoom out"—to analyze the layers of social, political, and economic contexts surrounding the strike and its outcome.

Post Civil War Industrialization and Labor Unrest

The seeds of American industrial growth and economic integration were planted well before the Civil War. Expansions in the U.S. rail system and inventions like the steam-powered engine and telegraph dramatically increased the efficiency and reach of American manufacturing. After the Civil War, with the legal and financial backing of the federal government, railroad companies expanded their tracks from 45,000 miles in 1871 to well over 200,000 miles by the end of the 1800s (Library of Congress, n.d.). These railroads carried both consumer goods and the raw materials needed for further industrialization: oil, coal, iron—extracted from the earth at a dizzying pace.

By the end of World War I, the United States was the world's leading industrial power—a development enabled by geographics, demographics, laws, and politics. Plentiful farmlands and seemingly endless supplies of energy and metals ensured a steady stream of inputs for American factories. To secure these resources, the U.S. government irreparably altered the environment and forcibly removed native peoples from their lands. The great human cost of industrialization and expansion was also borne by Asian and European immigrants who supplied the enormous manpower needed to build U.S. railroads and operate its dangerous factories. Finally, such massive, industrial capitalism would not have been possible without the business-friendly stances of all three branches of the U.S. government. Congress and state governments passed laws that empowered monopolists, sometimes inadvertently. Courts frequently sided with the growth-minded corporations over workers' and tribal rights. And, presidents routinely dispatched troops to enforce court injunctions against striking workers.

Industrialization expanded the managerial class and elevated a new group of ultra wealthy entrepreneurs, whose riches would have been inconceivable 50 years prior. These ultra wealthy, such as John D. Rockefeller, Andrew Carnegie, and J. P. Morgan amassed their fortunes through anti-competitive practices, such as buying out competitors (horizontal integration) or buying out all their production inputs (vertical integration). The monopolization of major industries also meant workers had less choice about where to work and, therefore, less power to demand fairer wages or safer working conditions (Dubofsky & McCartin, 2017).

As a result, workers started to organize into labor unions, such as the Knights of Labor. Many of these early union leaders sought not only material improvements for their workers, but a fundamental change in the relationship between work and capital. They argued that workers, as an integral part of production, deserved more control over the means of that production. The ideology and demands of the labor movements in the industrial north coalesced in many ways with the growing populist sentiments in the agricultural south and west, whose power threatened the interests of the new corporate and managerial classes.

It is estimated that in 1894 alone, a total of 750,000 workers went on strike (Rezneck, 1952). Often the federal and state governments turned a blind eye as corporations used private guard forces to crush strikes. When violence got out of hand, federal troops often joined with businesses to quell strikes and protect private property. One such event, the Haymarket Square Riot, ended with the death of seven police officers and a handful of pro-worker protesters. The violence at Haymarket hurt public support for unions and the Knights of Labor (Currarino, 2011). Meanwhile conditions and wages for workers continued to deteriorate across the country.

The Panic of 1893 and The Pullman Strike (1894)

The increasing interdependence of the industrial economy meant that businesses were more vulnerable to financial downturns in other sectors and countries. From the 1870s to the 1890s, the U.S. experienced semi-regular recessions and economic panics (1870, 1873, 1882–85, 1887, 1890, 1893, 1896) (National Bureau of Economic Research, 2023). These downturns led to reduced demand for goods and labor. With fewer job opportunities available, workers saw their bargaining power diminish as working conditions worsened.

The Panic of 1893, lasting until 1897, was perhaps the worst of these financial downturns. The panic was caused by, among other factors, a reduction in railroad investment, agricultural overproduction, and issues in foreign markets and land speculation (Whitten, 2001). The effects were dramatic. Hundreds of banks and tens of thousands of businesses failed. The national unemployment rate ballooned to 12 percent and stayed near there until the end of the decade (Currarino, 2011).

Just months before the Panic began in May, Eugene V. Debs, then a 37-year labor activist, helped to found the American Railway Union (ARU). Unlike other rail unions, Debs sought to organize both skilled and unskilled workers (though ARU members voted to exclude non-white workers). This coalition helped to rapidly increase the size and power of the ARU which soon outstripped all other rail unions (Salvatore, 1982). In April of 1894, the ARU and Debs initiated a successful strike against the Great Northern railroad, resulting in a rare labor victory amid an economic downturn (Currarino, 2011). Debs would later try to repeat that success in a strike against the Pullman railcar company in the same year.

The Pullman Strike

George Pullman founded the Pullman Company in 1862. The company grew rapidly with the expansion of the U.S. rail system, but their focus on luxury train cars made them vulnerable to economic recessions. The Panic of 1893 hit the company particularly hard (Bassett, 1997).

Prior to the panic, work conditions at Pullman were comparable to other industries at the time. Pay for unskilled labor was relatively low. The work was tightly controlled and could be quite monotonous (Montgomery, 1989). However, unlike other companies, Pullman's influence over workers reached beyond the shop floor. In 1880, Pullman had purchased 4,000 acres of land outside of Chicago which he developed into Pullman Town, a company-owned town designed to house workers and provide for their basic needs (Bassett, 1997). Although the town was sanitary and aesthetically appealing, Dubofsky and McCartin (2017) write that,

> The employees had little choice but to live within this feudal domain, rent their homes or apartments from the company, buy their water and gas from the company, pay the company for such other services as garbage removal and the daily watering of streets, buy supplies from the company store, and subscribe to the company's rental library (p. 145).

Charitable reviews of Pullman Town at the time hailed it as an innovative improvement on the slums and tenements which housed other factory workers across the city (Smith, 2007). Critics, however, assailed Pullman Town as paternalistic, controlling, and undemocratic (Addams, 1902).

Dubofsky and McCartin (2017) found that workers complained about the cost of living in Pullman Town well before the Panic of 1893. After the Panic, life in Pullman became untenable. As demand for train cars decreased, Pullman decided to lay off two-thirds of the company's workforce and cut remaining wages by an average of 33 percent (Currarino, 2011). At the same time, Pullman refused to lower rent or prices in the town, claiming a need to fulfill an obligation to the town's investors. As a result, many workers ended up forfeiting their paychecks back to Pullman, sometimes taking home little more than a few cents each paycheck (Dubofsky & McCartin, 2017). On top of that, foremen began to push workers harder to make up for lost crewmen. They also prevented workers from speaking to each other on the job or assembling into groups (Montgomery, 1989).

Things turned around relatively quickly for the company in the following year. The company hired back most of the workers it had laid off. Yet, Pullman still refused to increase pay or decrease rents in the town (Smith, 2007). In mid-May, 1894, several frustrated Pullman workers formed a committee and presented a list of grievances to the company's Vice President. The company had assured these committee members that there would be no retributions for their action. Nevertheless, three of the members were summarily fired after the meeting (Dubofsky & McCartin, 2017).

Wasting little time, the ARU locals representing Pullman workers called for a strike. Ninety percent of Pullman workers walked off the job. Pullman responded by firing all remaining workers and shutting down the plant (Currarino, 2011). Debs, an idealistic but pragmatic leader, sought to settle with Pullman through arbitration, to which Pullman allegedly responded, "there is nothing to arbitrate" (Smith, 2007, p. 235).

Debs and the ARU countered by threatening to detach Pullman cars from all the trains operated by ARU members, not just the trains running through Chicago (Bassett, 1997). Still refusing to compromise, Pullman sought help from the General Managers Association (GMA), an industry group representing all the rail lines passing through Chicago (Salvatore, 1982). The GMA ordered the firing of any worker accused of detaching a rail car. The tactic backfired. Whole train crews of ARU members began quitting, causing rail disruptions from the Midwest throughout the rest of the country (Salvatore, 1982). Detractors in the GMA and press publicly derided Debs as an opportunist, a foreigner, and an anarchist (Rondinone, 2010; Smith, 2007). Debs turned the same rhetoric back on Pullman, calling his paternalistic control "foreign" to American democracy (Smith, 2007, p. 241).

The GMA issued an order that all Pullman cars be attached to mail cars, so that anyone detaching a Pullman car could be accused of disrupting the mail service—a federal crime. They also hired strike breakers from Canada to operate the trains (Dubofsky & McCartin, 2017). Tensions grew between union workers and the strike breakers. Perhaps hoping to stoke a violent confrontation, the GMA convinced U.S. Attorney General Richard Olney, a former railway company lawyer, that violence on the rails was eminent. Olney then deputized thousands of men (paid by the railroad companies) to keep the trains running. This move sparked violent clashes between union members and the newly deputized workers, including widespread property damage (Dubofsky & McCartin,

2017). Debs and the ARU leadership continued to call for nonviolence, which ARU members heeded. Most of the violence that occurred, Smith (2007) argues, resulted from "unemployed and discontented workers with no connection to the strike" (p. 237).

Nevertheless, the GMA used the riots and rail disruption as a pretext to seek a court injunction against the strikers. Lawyers representing the GMA pointed to a provision of the recently passed Sherman Anti-Trust Act which made illegal any "conspiracy ... in restraint of trade or commerce among the several states" (Sherman Anti-Trust Act, 1890, Sec. 1). They argued that the strikers were preventing the free flow of interstate commerce and were, therefore, violating the law. Although the framers of the law intended it to curb monopoly power, corporations were now using it turn to the courts against strikers (Bassett, 1997).

Sensing impending defeat, Debs and the ARU once again sought to negotiate an end to the strike, asking simply for the right of union members to return to work. Pullman and the GMA refused (Bassett, 1997). Armed with a court injunction, the GMA sought federal intervention. The governor of Illinois protested, but President Grover Cleveland dispatched the troops anyway, justifying the use of force under the guise of promoting the free flow of mail (Smith, 2007). The strike ended in July 1894.

The aftermath of the strike was largely seen as a failure for the ARU and rail workers. The ARU collapsed (Montgomery, 1989). Debs and 200 others were charged with, in most cases, violating court injunctions. Debs served six months in prison. While there, he would develop more radical views about capitalism and ultimately become a socialist (Salvatore, 1982). His work on the Pullman Strike and imprisonment also launched him to national political prominence. Upon his release from prison, he spoke to an enthusiastic crowd of over 100,000 fervent supporters (Dubofsky & McCartin, 2017). Nevertheless, the union movement as a whole suffered an enormous setback just like it had at Haymarket. In the last decades of the 1800s, union membership fell by half (Dubofsky & McCartin, 2017). Corporations like Pullman also began looking to further kneecap union power by specializing and routinizing formally high-skilled, craftsman jobs (Montgomery, 1989).

Out of the smoldering ruins of the Pullman Strike emerged some hope for labor reforms. The largest labor union, the American Federation of Labor, which had been critical of the ARU's actions during the Pullman Strike, began lobbying against the use of injunctions on striking workers (Dubofsky & McCartin, 2017). Populist politicians also took up many of the causes of the union movement, though political and racial divisions in the movement stifled much of their electoral power (Dubofsky & McCartin, 2017).

Despite his seemingly heavy-handed support of the railway companies, Cleveland decided to create a commission to investigate the causes of the Pullman Strike. The commission ultimately condemned Pullman for his overbearing control on workers' lives and his refusal to negotiate with workers during the strike (Smith, 2007). The commission also recommended that Congress create a law (eventually passed in 1898) requiring that railway companies deal with worker disputes through mediation (Bassett, 1997). Pullman Town would eventually be stripped from the company and incorporated into the city of Chicago (Smith, 2007).

Contextualizing and Framing the Pullman Strike

What is the story of the Pullman Strike really about? It depends, as with all historical narratives, on evidence and historical interpretation. We have the words of Debs and Pullman from letters and newspaper interviews. We have records from the inquiry conducted by the Cleveland administration. And we have accounts from the workers themselves. Using the same or similar set of facts, a historian can frame the story in multiple ways. A historian could fit the events at Pullman into the common narrative frameworks of the Gilded Age, where greedy monopolists frequently took advantage of workers, corrupted the government, and destroyed the environment. The story could be told as an inspiring, though ultimately tragic, tail about individual workers and activists who took on a formative corporate power. The Pullman Strike could also be told as a single episode of a much bigger story about workers' struggles within a capitalist system.

Historical narratives are useful because they impose coherence and meaning on what could otherwise be a confusing flurry of facts and documents. Including *all* pieces of evidence or explaining *all* the structural conditions that influenced any one historical event or action would make for a long, confusing story. Historians must make interpretive choices. A historian, for instance, might include as part of their narrative Pullman's decision to keep rent prices the same. Pullman's decision, however, was influenced by an uncountable number of structural conditions, such as the nature of corporate profit-motivation, the laissez-faire attitude of the U.S. government, and the dehumanizing ideas of Social Darwinism. When framed in the context of these structural conditions, Pullman's "decision" may come across less like a personal choice and more like a reflection of how capitalism operated in the late 1800s.

A historians' process of deciding what to include or exclude is not usually transparent in their final, polished accounts. This might lead readers to the false assumption that historical inquiry and writing are simply a matter of finding out what happened and putting it down on paper. In the upcoming lesson on the Pullman Strike (Appendix), students will explicitly grapple with the complex and tenuous nature of causal reasoning and historical interpretation. To aid in this, students will work with causal maps, which are a non-narrative, visual way to represent complex historical events.

Causal Mapping as An Instructional Tool

This lesson will introduce students to the practice of historical causal mapping. These maps can be created using any concept mapping software, such as Cmap and Lucidchart, or they can be created using chart paper and index cards. All student names used are pseudonyms.

There are multiple frameworks students and teachers can use for mapping causal relationships. In the map shown in Figure 1.1, created using Cmap, the student identified potential factors and outcomes of the Pullman Strike. They then plotted these factors and outcomes with respect to their distance from the event in space and time (X axis as time, Y axis as geographic distance). They connected the factors using different kinds of causal relationships. The dotted lines represent conditions that enabled or constrained certain events or actions. The solid lines represent factors that more directly influenced or led to an outcome. Finally, each factor is labeled as being primarily agentic ("A") or structural ("S").

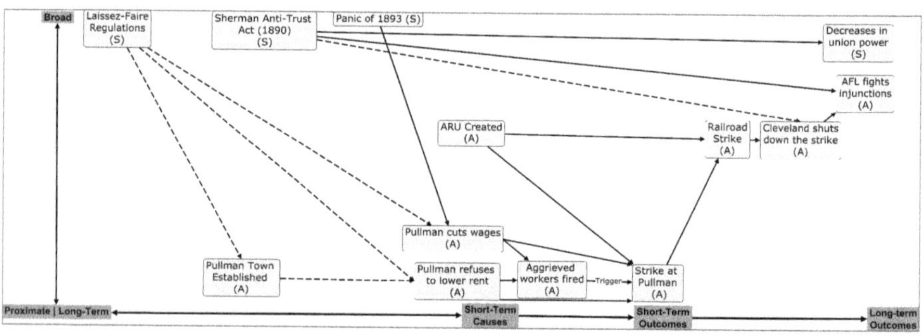

Figure 1.1: Example Student Causal Map of the Pullman Strike created using Cmap.

Note: X axis represents time before and after the Pullman Strike. Y axis represents spatial distance from the Pullman Strike. Lines represent different causal roles (e.g., enabling and influencing). "A" stands for agentic factors. "S" stands for structural factors.

Causal mapping can serve several purposes. Students can use maps as brainstorming tools for writing historical accounts. For instance, a student could create a map of the Pullman Strike and use the map to identify the most important causal relationships. The process of creating the map itself may also reveal further needed areas of inquiry. A student may look at a factor on their map (e.g., "the Panic of 1893") and wonder, *what caused that?* Or, a student might look at two plotted factors and wonder, *is there any connection between these two things?*

Students can also compare their completed maps with other students' to see similarities and differences in how they represented the event. One student might see that they focused more on short-term, proximate causes than another student. Additionally, they may see that their map focused on the actions of multiple historical actors while another student's map focused on broader social, political, or economic structures. Doing these comparisons can spark metacognitive reflection about what one representation offers over another. This kind of comparison can also reinforce the interpretive, constructed nature of historical representation.

Finally, teachers can use causal maps as scaffolds to help students analyze primary or secondary source accounts. A teacher could provide students a complete (or partially complete) map to help them visualize how one account frames a historical event. Or, they could provide completed maps to help students compare how different accounts frame the same event. Students could also create their own map representations of written historical accounts to better understand how an author represents causes and effects.

Overall, causal mapping offers students the chance to see the complexity of historical cause and effect and the interpretive decision-making needed to transform complex causal relationships into coherent historical accounts.

Mapping the Pullman Strike

Step 1: Identifying and Brainstorming Causes and Effects. In order to create a useful causal map, students will need some background knowledge of the Pullman Strike. This could be delivered through a lecture, video, secondary text, or a series of documents. In the provided lesson (Appendix), students will use a secondary narrative text of the Pullman Strike. Using that text, students will begin by identifying known causes, consequences, and conditions of the strike. The narrative in the pages earlier identifies a host of factors to consider, such as . . .

1. The expansion of the U.S. rail system
2. U.S. Native American Policy
3. Industrial innovation
4. Availability of industrial inputs
5. Immigration

6. The Sherman Anti-Trust Act
7. Court Injunctions
8. Newspapers and public sentiment
9. Anti-competitive business practices
10. Union movements (1860s–)
11. Strikes (1880s–)
12. The nature of the U.S. economy (1870–)
13. The Panic of 1893
14. The Leadership of George Pullman
15. The Leadership of Eugene V. Debs
16. The founding and principles of the ARU
17. The founding of the GMA
18. The establishment of Pullman Town
19. Pullman's decision to lay off workers
20. Pullman's decision to keep rent the same
21. Investors in Pullman Town
22. Improvements in Pullman's business (1894)
23. The firing of three Pullman workers
24. The ARU strike and boycott at Pullman
25. Pullman's refusal to arbitrate
26. GMA's decision to fire striking workers
27. GMA's hiring of strikebreakers
28. GMA's decision to attach Pullman cars to mail cars
29. Debs call for nonviolence
30. U.S. Attorney's connection the GMA
31. U.S. Attorney's use of deputized workers
32. Worker clashes with strikebreakers
33. The court injunction against ARU
34. Cleveland's federal intervention
35. The arrest and trial of strikers
36. The de-skilling of labor

The passage earlier, however, only provides one narrative of the Pullman Strike. The narrative begins with U.S. industrialization in the 1800s and ends around the turn of the century. But, as John Lewis Gaddis (2002) points out, "[t]here's no precise rule that tells historians where to stop in tracing the causes of any historical event" (p. 96). There are many additional factors, conditions, or outcomes that exist beyond the scope of the narrative. After students have identified causes and outcomes from the passage, a teacher may ask them to brainstorm additional factors that might be relevant to the Pullman Strike. For instance, to what extent did ideas about scientific management or "Taylorism" influence labor practices at Pullman?" Can the theory of Social Darwinism help to explain Pullman's actions against workers or the public's response to the strike? What role did the political divisions and realignment within the two major parties play?

With a complex event like the Pullman Strike, the number of known and potential causal factors can balloon quickly. Students may have to make decisions about what factors to include and exclude on their maps by asking themselves *what is the most relevant and significant factors for explaining the causes and outcomes of this event?* (e.g., does the weather on the day of the strike really need to be included?).

Step 2: Plotting Factors. The student will then plot their causal factors on the map relative to the factors' time and distance from the event. The timing and spatial scale may be clear for some events and less clear for others. The Panic of 1893, for instance, has a specific start date an obvious nationwide impact. In contrast, a factor like the "expansion of the U.S. rail system" has no specific start date. Therefore, plotting the factors on the map will always be, to some extent, an interpretive and relative process. To help students get started, it may be helpful to pre-plot several common events or developments on the students' maps (Figure 1.2).

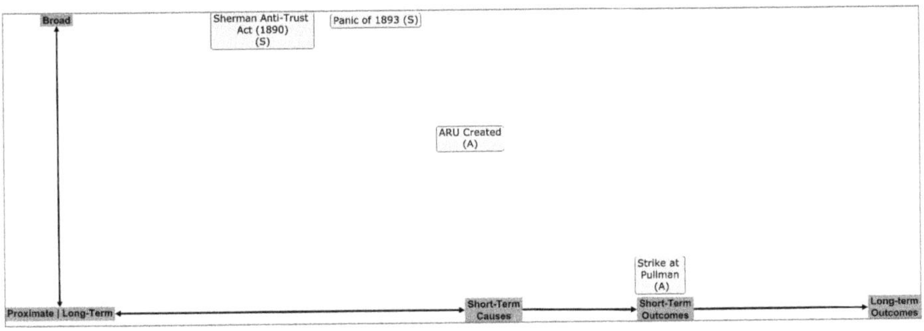

Figure 1.2: Example of Teacher Pre-Plotted Causal Factors on Students' Maps.

Note: X axis represents time before and after the Pullman Strike. Y axis represents spatial distance from the Pullman Strike.

Step 3: Categorizing and Connecting Factors. There are many different ways students can categorize causal factors and causal relationships on their maps. Students can identify causes as being primarily *agentic* or primarily *structural.* An agentic cause is one in which a historical figure or group makes a decision or takes an action. Pullman's refusal to lower rents (although influenced by multiple structural factors) is primarily an agentic action. Structures, which lack clear human actors or intention, can influence, enable, or constrain actions. In the Pullman

Strike, the structure of U.S. courts and laws (e.g., the Sherman Anti-Trust Act) enabled the GMA to seek an injunction against striking rail workers. Structural factors can be further categorized as political, economic, geographic, social, etc.

Determining whether to frame a factor as agentic or structural is sometimes an interpretive process. For example, it was ultimately a judge who issued an injunction against the striking workers. So should the court's action be seen as primarily agentic or an instantiation of a legal structure? Such questions might initially confuse or frustrate students, but grappling with these gray areas may help students to see the types of choices historians have to make when representing history.

There are also many ways to describe the relationships between causal factors. Certain events or actions might *trigger* an outcome given a certain set of conditions. For instance, the firing of the three Pullman workers likely "triggered" the strike but only because other conditions were present, such as the previous wage cuts, the high rents in the town, and the founding of the ARU. Other events or developments may *influence* the likelihood of an outcome. The Panic of 1893 and its effects on businesses certainly seemed to influence Pullman's decision to lower wages. Other developments might be described as *enabling* or *constraining* certain actions or outcomes. The laissez-faire attitude of the U.S. government likely enabled corporations, like Pullman, to severely mistreat and underpay their workers. Figure 1.3 shows how these relationships might be depicted on a causal map.

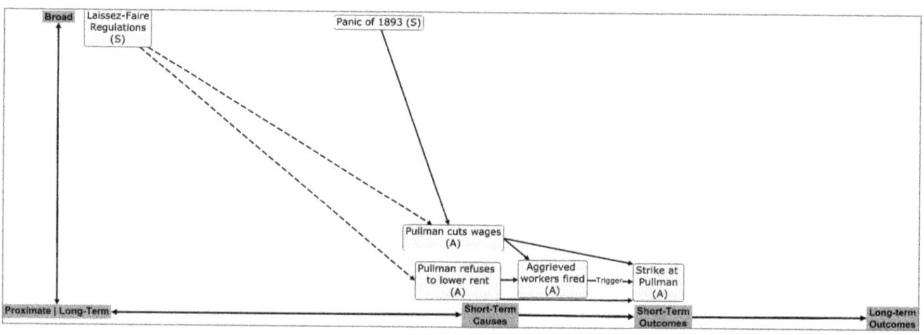

Figure 1.3: Example of Causal Relationships on a Map.

Note: Solid lines represent influencing factors and dotted lines represent enabling factors.

Identifying causal relations is not an exact science. Students may have different interpretations of what factors are connected and how.

Step 4: Reflecting on and Comparing Completed Maps. The process of creating these maps can be iterative, as students will likely continue to identify or inquire into additional factors and causal relationships. When students feel satisfied with their completed map, they may benefit from reflecting on their representation and comparing it with other students'. Seeing other approaches may help students understand the affordances and constraints of different ways of framing the event. The following is a student named Jessica's representation of the Pullman Strike (Figure 1.4).

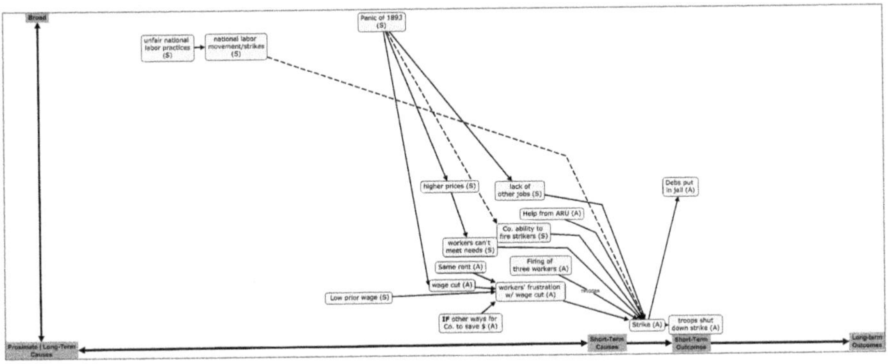

Figure 1.4: Jessica's Map of the Pullman Strike.

In framing the strike, Jessica focused on the workers' and company's intentions and the short-term conditions influencing their actions, such as the availability of other jobs and an increase in prices. She also focused on short-term outcomes, such as Deb's imprisonment. Working within a relatively small problem space, she drew multiple, complex interconnections between conditions, actions, and outcomes of those involved in the Pullman Strike.

In comparison, David focused more on larger, structural forces in his representation of the strike (Figure 1.5).

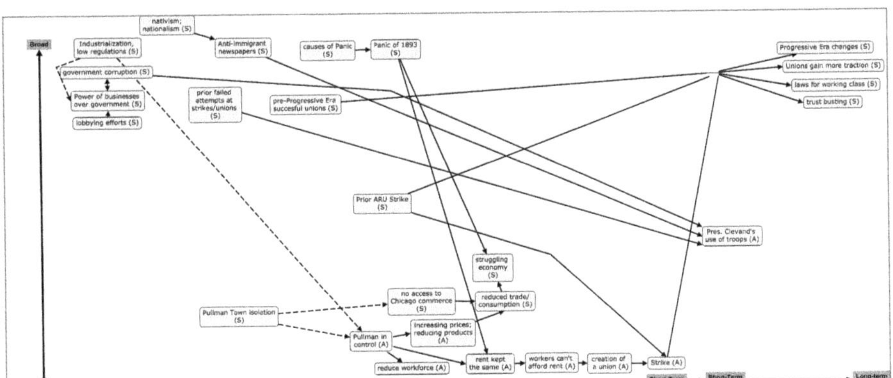

Figure 1.5: David's Map of the Pullman Strike.

He considered how a lack of regulations on businesses enabled those businesses to assert further control over government. He also saw the lack of government regulations as enabling Pullman's ability to control workers. He identified prior failures and successes of the union movement as influencing the outcome of the Pullman Strike and later Progressive Era developments.

Li framed the strike somewhere in between Jessica and David's framing of the strike (Figure 1.6).

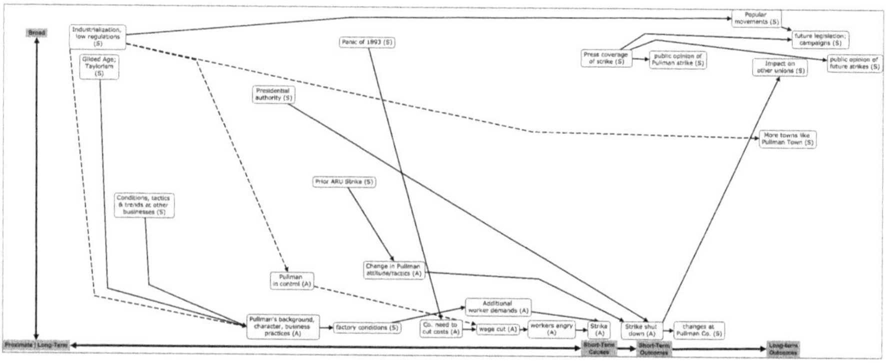

Figure 1.6: Li's Map of the Pullman Strike.

Like David, Li also identified a lack of regulations as enabling Pullman's total control over his business and workers. And, like Jessica, Li considered the characteristics of Pullman as a business owner and the intentions behind his decision-making.

Neither of these three representations of the Pullman Strike is necessarily better or worse. Each framing offers certain affordances and constraints. For instance, by "zooming in" on the details of the strike, Jessica was able to represent the complex interconnections between agents and their local structures. By "zooming out," David was able to represent a broad narrative about nineteenth and early twentieth-century labor movements. Li did a little of both.

By comparing maps, students can engage in critical reflection about their own inquiry process and better understand the constructed and interpretive nature of representing complex historical events like the Pullman Strike.

Student Support

This kind of activity calls on students to engage with historical concepts and thinking skills that they may not yet be familiar with. To support students success in this lesson, teachers may need to incorporate direct instruction on causal reasoning concepts (e.g., "triggers," "long-term causes") and may need to model and scaffold the creation of causal maps.

Teaching about Causation Through Analogies. One way teachers can communicate causal concepts is through familiar analogies. The World History Project website provides an instructional activity where students investigate the death of a camel named "Alphonse" (an activity originally conceived by Chapman, 2003). In the story, Alphonse dies shortly after his owner places one final straw on his back (the "trigger" cause). Students then learn about several underlying conditions of the camel's demise, such as years of difficult labor in harsh terrain, changing economic demands, and political disagreement between other camels. Franchi and Honold (2023) provide a similar analogy activity where students identify the trigger and underlying causes of a wildfire in California. By using a familiar causal story or event, teachers can help students master causal concepts like agency, structure, long-term causes, short-term causes, and underlying conditions.

Modeling and Scaffolding Causal Maps. When teaching historical writing, a teacher might model how to outline a paragraph or provide sentence stems as a scaffold. Likewise, teachers can model and scaffold causal mapping. To model, a teacher might display a completed causal map and then do a "think-aloud" where they verbalize their interpretation of the map. Here is how that might sound:

> Looking at this causal map, I see there is a dotted arrow from "low regulations" to "Pullman's control." What I think this means is that there is not many rules on businesses at this time. This then enabled people like Pullman to have total control over how they run their businesses.

Teachers could also use "think-alouds" to model creating a causal map. Here is how that might sound:

> I know that the Panic of 1893 hurt Pullman's business which led him to cut wages. So, I am going to put a solid line to show that the Panic influenced Pullman's business decision. Because Pullman was the person making the decision, I am going to put an "A" for agent. I know that no one was in control of the Panic of 1893, so I am going to put an "S" to identify that factor as a structure.

It's also important for teachers to model the tenuous, interpretive nature of historical representations. A teacher might think-aloud through a tough decision about whether to label a factor as influencing or enabling, or whether to label a factor as structural or agentic.

There are several ways teachers can scaffold the maps themselves. When students are first working with maps, teachers can reduce the complexity of the map by limiting the number of options for categorizing causes and causal relationships. Teachers can also provide partially completed maps as scaffolds. For instance, a teacher may provide a map with all the causal factors plotted and simply ask students to brainstorm the connections between the different factors.

As students become more comfortable using causal reasoning terms and creating causal maps, these models and scaffolds should be faded out to let students have more interpretive control over their representations.

Pedagogical Strategies

The paper provides the historical content knowledge for the lesson plan (see Appendix) focused on teaching causation in historical contexts. It emphasizes the importance of engaging students with historical concepts and reasoning skills through analogies, such as the death of Alphonse the camel or the California wildfire scenario, which simplify complex ideas like long-term causes and structural or agentic factors. Additionally, it advocates for modeling and scaffolding causal maps as instructional tools, offering practical examples like "think-alouds" to interpret and construct connections. These strategies help students grasp nuanced historical interpretations while progressively developing independent analytical capabilities. By integrating these methods, lesson plans can foster deeper understanding and active engagement with causation concepts, ensuring that students build a solid foundation for historical inquiry and critical thinking.

References

Bassett, J. (1997). The Pullman Strike of 1894. *OAH Magazine of History, 11*(2), 34–41.

Chapman, A. (2003). Camels, diamonds and counterfactuals: A model for teaching causal reasoning. *Teaching History, 112*, 46–53.

Currarino, R. (2011). *The labor question in America: Economic democracy in the Gilded Age*. University of Illinois Press.

Dubofsky, M., & McCartin, J. A. (2017). *Labor in America: A history*. John Wiley & Sons, Incorporated.

Franchi, R. & Honold, A. (2023). Causation, the long and short of it: A year-long instructional focus. *Social Education*, *87*(4), 241–7.

Library of Congress. (n.d.). *Railroads in the late 19th century* [Web page]. U.S. History Primary Source Timeline. Retrieved May 30, 2024, from https://www.loc.gov/classroom-materials/united-states-history-primary-source-timeline/rise-of-industrial-america-1876-1900/railroads-in-late-19th-century/

Montgomery, D. (1989). *The fall of the house of labor: The workplace, the state, and American labor activism, 1865–1925*. Cambridge University Press.

National Bureau of Economic Research. (2023). *US business cycle expansions and contractions*. https://www.nber.org/research/data/us-business-cycle-expansions-and-contractions

National Council for the Social Studies (2013). *The college, career, and civic life (C3) framework for social studies state standards: Guidance for enhancing the rigor of K-12 civics, economics, geography, and history*. NCSS.

National Council for the Social Studies. (n.d.). *The themes of social studies*. Retrieved May 13, 2024, from https://www.socialstudies.org/national-curriculum-standards-social-studies-chapter-2-themes-social-studies

Rezneck, S. (1953). Unemployment, unrest, and relief in the United States during the Depression of 1893–97. *Journal of Political Economy, 61*(4), 324–45.

Rondinone, T. (2009). Guarding the switch: Cultivating nationalism during the Pullman Strike. *The Journal of the Gilded Age and Progressive Era, 8*(1), 83–109.

Salvatore, N. (1982). *Eugene V. Debs: Citizen and socialist*. University of Illinois Press.

Schneirov, R. (n.d.). *The Pullman Strike*. Northern Illinois University Digital Library. Retrieved May 23, 2024, from https://digital.lib.niu.edu/illinois/gildedage/pullman

Sherman Anti-Trust Act (1890). National Archives. https://www.archives.gov/milestone-documents/sherman-anti-trust-act

Smith, C. (2007). *Urban disorder and the shape of belief: The Great Chicago Fire, the Haymarket Bomb, and the Model Town of Pullman*, Second Edition. University of Chicago Press.

Whitten, D. O. (2001). *The Depression of 1893*. EH.Net Encyclopedia. https://eh.net/encyclopedia/the-depression-of-1893/

World History Project. (n.d.). *Causation—Alphonse the Camel*. Retrieved May 23, 2024, from https://www.oerproject.com/OER-Materials/OER-Media/PDFs/Origins/Era1/Causation-Alphonse-the-Camel

Appendix

Lesson Plan

1. Lesson Plan Title: Exploring the Complexity of the Pullman Strike Through Causal Mapping
2. Theme: This lesson plan fits with the NCSS theme of "Time, Continuity, and Change." In particular, it relates to the statement that "Knowledge and understanding of the past enable us to analyze the causes and consequences of events and developments, and to place these in the context of the institutions, values and beliefs of the periods in which they took place ... " (NCSS, n.d., para. 6). By studying the actions, intentions, and outcomes of the Pullman Strike within the political, social, and economic structures of the Gilded Age, students will develop a richer understanding of this time period and an ability to reason critically about historical causation
3. Grade Level: 10th and above
4. Course: United States History
5. Time Required: 90 minutes
6. Essential and Supporting Questions:
   a. EQ: What makes a labor leader or labor action successful?
   b. EQ: How do broader social, political, and economic forces enable or constrain the ability of labor leaders and organizations to make meaningful changes?
   c. SQ: What were the causes and consequences of the Pullman Strike? How are those causes and consequences connected to each other? What underlying conditions influenced the nature, outcome, and significance of the Pullman Strike? (D2.His.1.9-12; D2.His.14.9-12.; D2.His.15.9-12).
   d. SQ: What can current labor organizers learn from the Pullman Strike? (extension activity) (D4.7.9-12).

7. Objectives:
   a. Students will be able to differentiate and explain the relationship between agentic actions and structural conditions relevant to the Pullman Strike (D2.His.1.9-12; D2.His.14.9-12).
   b. Students will be able to differentiate and explain the long-term and short-term causes and consequences of the Pullman Strike. (D2.His.1.9-12.; D2.His.15.9-12.).
   c. Students will be able to apply lessons from the Pullman Strike to individual or collective action in the present (D4.7.9-12) (extension activity).

8. Standards (from the National Council for the Social Studies [NCSS]):
    a. D2.His.1.9-12. Evaluate how historical events and developments were shaped by unique circumstances of time and place as well as broader historical contexts.
    b. D2.His.14.9-12. Analyze multiple and complex causes and effects of events in the past.
    c. D2.His.15.9-12. Distinguish between long-term causes and triggering events in developing a historical argument.
    d. D4.7.9-12. Assess options for individual and collective action to address local, regional, and global problems by engaging in self-reflection, strategy identification, and complex causal reasoning.

9. Classroom Materials:
    a. "Alphonse the Camel" passage and graphic organizer
        - See passage at https://www.oerproject.com/OER-Materials/OER-Media/PDFs/Origins/Era1/Causation-Alphonse-the-Camel.
    b. Secondary narrative text of the Pullman Strike
        - There are many accessible secondary texts about the Pullman Strike online. Teachers may use the narrative passage above or the Schneirov (n.d.) text linked in work cited section.
    c. Paper or digital causal mapping materials.
        - For creating causal maps on paper, teachers will need large chart or graphing paper, sticky notes or index cards, and markers.
        - For digital causal mapping, students can use free software programs like Cmaps (cmap.ihmc.us) or Lucidchart (lucidchart.com).

10. Instructional Plan:
    a. **Entry Task: Causal Analogy Activity** [10 min]—To effectively engage in this lesson, students will need to understand that there are different ways of explaining or classifying causes in history. Teachers can do this by introducing the story of "Alphonse the Camel" (Chapman, 2003; WHP, n.d.) or a similar causal analogy narrative (e.g., Honold & Franchi, 2023). The teacher can hold a discussion where students identify causal factors in the story and classify them as short-term or long-term, agentic or structural, and classify causal roles as enabling, constraining, influencing, or triggering.
    b. **Teacher-Directed Instruction** [15 min]—In transition from the entry activity, the teacher can tell students that they will be learning about a major strike in the 1890s that was triggered by a specific event but that

has many deeper causal factors. The teacher should briefly overview the time period of the strike and the decades that preceded it, including the rapid industrialization and urbanization after the Civil War, the conditions of late 1800s factory work, the development and decline of early labor organizations, and the violent labor clashes at Haymarket and elsewhere. The teacher can then introduce students to the key details of the Pullman Strike, such as who was involved, when it took place, and what were the major issues at stake. This should include instruction on any key individuals or terms that students might not yet be familiar with (e.g., Eugene Debs, Sherman Anti-Trust Act, court injunctions). After, the teacher can gauge students prior knowledge of the strike. If students have no prior knowledge of the strike, the teacher can ask them to make predictions about how they think the strike played out based on what they know about the time period. Finally, the teacher can introduce the essential and supporting questions of the lesson.

c. **Guided & Independent Practice [35 min]—**
Identifying Causes and Effects [10 min]. The teacher will pass out a secondary text reading about the Pullman Strike. The teacher will explain to students that they are looking for and highlighting information about the causes and outcomes of the strike. The teacher can model this practice using a smart board or document camera. Students will continue reading and highlighting the passage on their own. When students are finished, the teacher can do a "whip around" where each students shares a factor they highlighted. The teacher can record students' identified factors on a white board or computer.
Categorizing Causal Factors [10 min]. The teacher will model (i.e., "think-aloud") about how to categorize causal factors as agentic or structural, short-term or long-term, and broad or proximate. The teacher can also model using structural classifications, such as "economic," "political," or "social." Students will then work individually or in small groups to continue categorizing the causal factors they previously identified.
Mapping Causes and Effects [15 min]. The teacher will introduce the causal map, where the X and Y axis represent distance and time from the event. The teacher will model how to plot causal factors and outcomes on the map. They will then model how to draw appropriate connections between causes and outcomes. Working individually or in small groups, students will continue to plot and connect relevant factors.

d. **Discussion** [15 min]
  - **Significance** [5 min]—The teacher will ask students to use their maps to try to determine what causes and consequences they think are the most significant in explaining the Pullman Strike. This can be a whole-class discussion or small-group discussion.
  - **Map Comparison** [5 min]—Students will trade maps with a partner or with another group to compare their maps and discuss similarities and differences.
  - **Reflection** [5 min]—The teacher can ask the following small-group or whole-class discussion questions:
    1. What were some of the major similarities or differences in the maps you compared?
    2. We all read the same secondary text, so why don't our maps look perfectly identical?
    3. How would you go about transforming what you put in your map into your own narrative about the Pullman Strike?

e. **Exit Task** [15 min]—Students will write short answer responses to the following prompt:
  - What were the causes and consequences of the Pullman Strike? And how did political, social, and economic forces shape the strike and its outcome?

11. Assessment: Students will create a causal map of the Pullman Strike and use the map to answer a prompt.
12. Community Engagement: As an extension activity, students could pick a local business and hypothesize or research how factors surrounding the Pullman Strike (e.g., wages, living conditions, economic recession) may or may not be relevant to that business in present times. For instance, students may compare and contrast the situation of Pullman workers to local grocery store clerks. They could also consider how responses from management to workers' demands might be similar or different. As part of this extension activity, students could interview workers or union representatives in their towns.

History and Memory at *Les Lieux de Mémoire*: The Commemoration of the Haymarket Affair

Adam J. Schmitt

On the evening of Tuesday, May 4, 1886, as Chicago police marched on a labor rally where speakers were addressing a crowd of workers from the back of a hay wagon, a bomb arced through the air, fell in the midst of the oncoming police and detonated. The blast, and the ensuing violence, resulted in the death of eight officers and four workers, with several others on both sides of the fray being wounded. The Haymarket Affair,[1] as this event came to be known, is often viewed as an integral moment in American and international labor history as well as jurisprudence related to freedom of speech and belief and has therefore been variously commemorated and remembered in different ways since it happened. As Green (2006) notes:

> The Haymarket case refuses to die because it involves so many troubling questions about the causes of violent conflict and the limits of free speech, about the justice of conspiracy trials and the fairness of the death penalty and about the treatment of immigrants, particularly foreign-born radicals, by the police, the newspapers and the courts. And perhaps most troubling of all, the Haymarket case challenged, like no other episode in the nineteenth century, the image of the United States as a classless society with liberty and justice for all. (p. 12)

The multifaceted nature of the Haymarket Affair, as well as the repercussions it had on the labor movement and political radicalism in the United States and abroad, has resulted in contested meanings and a struggle to grapple with how to remember an event that is so complex.

The space where the Haymarket Affair took place has been variously marked since the time of the event, with each commemorative iteration relating to who had the power to officially determine the meaning of the event and site. The first memorial[2] to the Haymarket Affair was erected in 1889 on the site of the altercation and was dedicated to the memory of the police officers who were killed by the bomb. After a long history of being vandalized, the Police Monument was permanently moved from the site in 1972, gradually finding a home outside of Chicago Police Headquarters on the city's south side. After the relocation of the Police Monument, the former site of the Haymarket was devoid of a marker until the dedication of a new memorial in 2004.

There have been several studies about the Haymarket Affair that attend to the shifting political atmosphere that has led to its various commemorations and have addressed the different audiences who have a stake in how the event is remembered (e.g., Barrett, 2012; Kelland, 2005; Shackel, 2011). In this paper, I take that work and situate the site of the Haymarket Affair as a *lieu de memoiré*, or site of social memory and consider the impact such a distinction has on how the space, and its various memorials, has functioned pedagogically over time.

My goal in thinking about the memorial and pedagogical elements of the Haymarket Affair commemorations is to consider how collective memory and history intersect and interact in the process of commemoration and the mediating role both play in how the space is experienced and pedagogically made sense of by those who encounter the memorial. I then use the commemoration of the Haymarket Affair to consider larger questions inherent in what happens in the history classroom, specifically in how elements of one's identity (Epstein, 1998, 2010; Peck, 2010), internal processes (Farley, 2007; Garrett, 2017), and the constructed nature of history (Segall, 1999, 2006, 2013) play a role in how history is understood and remembered.

Theoretical Framework

Conceptually, this piece draws upon the field of public pedagogy, which "focus[es] on various forms, processes, and sites of education and learning occurring beyond formal schooling" (Sandlin, O'Malley, & Burdick, 2011, pp. 338–9). Sandlin, O'Malley, and Burdick outline four main strands of pubic pedagogy research, two of which are important here. The first, public intellectualism and performative social action, mostly focuses on the role that public intellectuals play in society but also attends to grass-roots movements and activist work. I consider the labor movement as a form of activist public pedagogy. On one level, the labor movement's use of collective action, songs, and the sanctification of the movement's martyrs is meant to educate workers about the limits and/or evils of capitalism and the importance of a united working class that is able to work together towards common, mutually beneficial goals. On another level, though, organized labor activities, such as picketing, are meant to educate the general public about the same issues. As any commemoration of the Haymarket Affair intrinsically makes a statement about the labor movement as it relates to this specific event, it is important to consider what ideas about the labor movement are presented as well as the degree to which a social activist stance is present or encouraged.

Sandlin, O'Malley, and Burdick (2011) also identify a strand of public pedagogy research dedicated to informal institutions and public sites, such as memorials. This strand views informal institutions and public sites as having been "consciously created with pedagogical ends in mind" (p. 348). The work of Ellsworth (2005) has been especially salient in this field, in terms of reconsidering how pedagogy functions, not through engagement with settled knowledge but through the "embodied experiences that pedagogy elicits" in the encounter with a space and one's own self (p. 2).

In order to explore how the Haymarket Affair is made sense of and pedagogically engaged with, I draw upon Nora's (1989) concept of *les lieux de mémoire*. Nora establishes a distinction between *milieu de memoiré* (real environments of memory) and *les lieux de mémoire* (sites of memory), where the former is an actual site where the memory of the past is visibly present, and the latter which only bears a trace of the past, but is imbued with meaning meant to serve the purposes of a larger group, often the nation (den Boer, 2010). In the specific example of the Haymarket Affair, the *milieu de memoiré* would be the Haymarket itself, a site which no longer exists, beyond a small remnant of a cobblestone alley. The *lieu des memoiré* of the Haymarket Affair is comprised of the monuments that have marked the space, as well as the meaning that has been attached to it. Nora's work is founded upon the idea that *milieu de memoiré* no longer exist, so I take up the mantle of *les lieux de mémoire* in order to uncover how the meaning of the Haymarket Affair is constructed in the present through a memory-based understanding of the past.

Through the framework of *les lieux de mémoire*, Nora establishes a distinction between memory and history, which can help establish how meaning is attached to the space and commemoration of the Haymarket Affair. To Nora, memory and history are "in fundamental opposition" (p. 8). Collective memory is concerned with affect, is malleable, particular to the group it helps constitute, and "takes root in the concrete, in spaces, gestures, images, and objects" (p. 9). History, on the other hand, is a "reconstruction, always problematic and incomplete, of what is no longer" and "belongs to everyone and to no one, hence its claim to universal authority" (pp. 8–9). Whereas collective memory is rooted in and seen as foundational for the experiences of a specific group of people, history seeks to establish what happened in the past in order to create a more universal understanding of an event. In this paper, I use Nora's model of the relationship between history and memory, as well as draw upon Ellsworth (2005), to explore the meaning of the Haymarket, as represented by its historical representation, and the pedagogy of commemoration as it relates to the memories that are preserved and operationalized as one encounters the memorial vis-à-vis their own understanding of the events.

In the rest of the paper, I will provide some historical background about the Haymarket Affair, followed by brief descriptions of each of the monuments related to the event's commemoration. I will then move towards explicating what the commemoration of the Haymarket demonstrates about the relationship between memory and history and how people make sense of the event, as well as connections to similar processes found in history education.

Historical Background

In early May 1886, strikes were taking place across the city of Chicago in support of an eight-hour workday. While the work stoppages were not violent, violence did break out on May 3 at the McCormick Reaper Works. In the course of a clash between striking workers, strikebreakers and police, two workers were killed by police. As a result, anarchists called for a meeting at the city's Haymarket Square in order to discuss the eight-hour movement and the events at McCormick.

The next evening, Tuesday, May 4, a rally was held at the Haymarket, located on Desplaines Street between Randolph Street and Lake Street. While the number of workers present at the rally is unknown, most estimates place the number of attendees at 3,000 (Green, 2006). Despite Chicago mayor Carter Harrison attending part of the rally and explicitly telling police there was no need to intervene in the peaceful gathering, fears that the rally had been called to instigate a riot permeated the business community as well as the police force. As a result, police marched on the Haymarket towards the rally's conclusion. As they approached, an unknown person threw a home-made bomb at the advancing column of police, ultimately killing eight officers. The police opened fire and, in the resulting chaos, at least four workers were killed and several police officers and workers were wounded (Green, 2006). The bomb thrower was never identified.

In the aftermath of the Haymarket affair, eight men were put on trial. Four of the men (August Spies, Adolph Fischer, Oscar Neebe, and Michael Schwab) were known for their work with the *Arbeiter-Zeitung*, a radical working-class newspaper that had publicized the May 4 meeting. The others charged were activists Albert Parsons and Samuel Fielden, as well as known anarchists George Engel and Louis Lingg (Green, 2006). Of those charged, only two were present at the Haymarket at the time of the bombing, while two others were nearby, having spoken earlier, and four were not present at all that day. The resulting trial was marked by the assumption that all of the accused were guilty due to their anarchist political identities with little attention paid to the evidence. In the end, seven of the eight men were sentenced to death, with the eighth being sentenced to fifteen years in prison. Fielden and Schwab would go on to have their sentences commuted and Lingg committed suicide the day before his scheduled execution (Green, 2006). On November 11, 1887, Engel, Fischer, Parsons, and Spies were hanged (Green, 2006).

The Haymarket Monuments

In this section I will briefly describe the three main memorials to the events of the Haymarket Affair. Arranged chronologically, I will briefly outline what each memorial entails, a brief history of how each came to be, and its current relationship to the physical site of the Haymarket Affair.

The Police Monument

The Police Monument (Figure 2.1), originally dedicated in 1889, is currently located outside the west entrance of the Chicago Police headquarters at Michigan Avenue and E. 35th Street. The statue depicts a police officer, standing with legs shoulder length apart and right arm outstretched, palm facing outward. The 11-foot-high pedestal the statue stands on includes eight columns, each representing one of the police officers who died, and is meant to represent the people's support of the police (Chicago Police Headquarters, 2017). A plaque affixed to the front of the memorial's base reads *In the name of the people of Illinois I command peace*, the words spoken by Captain William Ward moments before the bomb exploded. A plaque affixed to the back of the pedestal list the names of the officers who were killed, while one on the side details information about the statue's rededication in 2007, noting that the statue is a

> testament to the bravery of the eight Chicago police officers who died as a result of the Haymarket Conflict of May 4, 1886, and to all police officers who have sacrificed their lives to serve and protect the citizens of this great city.

The Police Monument, funded by businessmen with the support of the Chicago Tribune, was the first official commemoration of the Haymarket and has had a tumultuous history, due to its location in a working-class neighborhood largely sympathetic to the labor movement and critical of the use of police power on the night of the bombing. The memorial, placed at the site of the bombing in Haymarket and meant to preserve and perpetuate the police narrative of the Haymarket events, has been vandalized several times during its history. In 1903, the crest of the city and the state was stripped off the statue (Kelland, 2005; Foote, 1997). On the anniversary of the Haymarket Affair in 1927, a streetcar

Figure 2.1: Haymarket Memorial Statue (The Police Monument), Chicago, IL (own photo).

driver intentionally jumped the tracks and hit the statue, knocking it from its pedestal (Foote, 1997). After being moved to Union Park and being vandalized there, the statue was once again relocated a platform that was built overlooking the Kennedy Expressway, near the original site of the Haymarket. There it was bombed twice, in 1968 and 1969 (Kelland, 2005; Foote 1997). In 1972 it was moved to the courtyard of the police training academy, and in 2007, it was relocated to its current location at Chicago Police headquarters.

Today the Police Monument's representation of the Haymarket has been somewhat reconfigured. For many years, the police, especially those involved with the bombing and riot, would hold annual anniversary gatherings. One such event in 1907 involved 50 officers who gathered in the same room where they had been given the instructions to march on the demonstration 21 years earlier, with the reporter noting that weeping was prevalent (Chicago Daily Tribune, 1907). Beginning in 1950, after the death of the last Haymarket "veteran," police commemorations held on the Haymarket anniversary became more broadly focused on the loss of police officers in the line of duty throughout Chicago's history (Chicago Daily Tribune, 1950). Once the memorial was ensconced in an interior courtyard, the public demonstrations came to an end. Today, the Police Monument, while once again located outside, continues to serve this broader narrative. Stationed outside the west entrance to Chicago Police headquarters, it serves as a memorial to police loss, spatially connected to the hallway that one encounters upon entering the building, which prominently features the badge of every police officer who died in the line of duty.

The Martyrs' Monument

Although the Haymarket Martyrs' Monument (Figure 2.2) is located outside of Chicago's city limits in nearby Forest Park and is thus separate from the commemoration at the Haymarket site itself, it is still beneficial to briefly describe it as it relates to criticisms about how the Haymarket is currently memorialized. Whereas the police memorial represents the police narrative about the Haymarket, the Martyrs' Monument is the site dedicated to preserving the workers' point of view. The monument, located in Waldheim Cemetery, is the burial site for the eight men convicted in the aftermath of the Haymarket Affair and depicts a hooded female figure standing before a worker in repose. She is holding a laurel over his head, but looking out and away from the man, as if both protecting him and looking towards the future. Below the woman is the date 1887, when Spies, Fischer, Parsons, and Engel were hanged. At the base of the monument are the words spoken by Albert Parsons before he was executed: "The day will come when our silence will be more powerful than the voices you are throttling

Figure 2.2: The Haymarket Martyrs' Monument, Forest Park, IL (own photo).

today." On the rear of the monument is an excerpt of Governor John Altgeld's pardon of the other three anarchists, Neebe, Schwab, and Fielden. In addition, the names of the five men who died in prison (the above, plus Lingg) are etched into the monument, and the names and dates of death of the other three men (Neebe, Schwab, and Fielden) are included on a plaque.

The Martyrs' Monument was funded by the Pioneer and Aid Society, an organization founded by Albert Parsons' wife, Lucy, for the purpose of raising money for the families of the Haymarket defendants (Pendarvis, 2016). Waldheim Cemetery was chosen as the burial space as the men were not allowed to be buried within the city of Chicago. The monument was unveiled in 1893, with the dedication ceremony attracting thousands of onlookers (Barrett, 2012) and served as a counterpoint to the official police narrative that occupied the physical space of the altercation.

Whereas the Police Monument uses a more literal depiction of a police officer in the act of doing his job, the Martyrs' Monument employs a more figurative and ideological form to deliver its message. Here, the hooded female figure could be construed as representing justice, especially as she is protecting a fallen worker while looking out to the horizon, gazing toward a more equitable future. The overall pedagogical address of the monument relates back to the concept of justice, especially due to the choice of quote, which speaks to the continuing impact of the Haymarket martyrs' sacrifice, and the inclusion of a portion of Altgeld's pardon, outlining the miscarriage of justice that resulted in the men's conviction. In short, the Haymarket Martyrs' Monument encapsulates the radical laborers' point of view, all the more bolstered by the cemetery becoming a place where several anarchist and socialist leaders, such as Lucy Parsons and Emma Goldman, are buried.

The Haymarket Memorial

After the removal of the Police Monument in 1972, the Haymarket site carried no commemorative trace for over 30 years. In 2004, a statue, created by Mary Brogger and supported by the Illinois Labor Historical Society, the Federation of Labor, the Fraternal Order of Police and Mayor Richard M. Daly was unveiled on the site of where the speaker's wagon stood, on Des Plaines Street between Lake Street and Randolph Street. The area bears little resemblance to what it once was. Most of the Haymarket was removed to make way for the Dan Ryan Expressway, a portion of Interstate 90 and Interstate 94. The rest has been converted into a trendy, gentrified neighborhood, with a Fiat dealership, condo buildings and a high concentration of some of Chicago's most notable restaurants.

The Haymarket Memorial, situated along the sidewalk on the east side of Des Plaines Street, depicts twelve human figures, with no discernible facial features, in the act of either constructing or deconstructing a wagon (the platform from

Figure 2.3: The Haymarket Memorial, Chicago, IL (own photo).

which the speakers delivered their remarks). Two figures, who stand on top of the highest board of the wagon, supported by the arms of another figure, are positioned in the act of addressing the imagined assembled crowd. A plaque, facing the sidewalk, contains information about the event, noting that the wagon stands on the "precise location where the wagon stood" and that the site has:

> Become a powerful symbol for a diverse cross-section of people, ideals, and movements. Its significance touches on the issues of free speech, the right of public assembly, organized labor, the fight for the eight-hour workday, law enforcement, justice, anarchy, and the right of every human being to pursue an equitable and prosperous life. For all, it is a poignant lesson in the rewards and consequences inherent in such human pursuits.

Other information on the monument pertains to establishing what happened on the night of May 4, 1886. There is also space for plaques from international labor groups to be mounted, as a nod to the Haymarket Affair's international significance to the labor movement. Several such plaques have been installed in countries such as Sweden, Germany, New Zealand, Japan, and Iraq.

Unlike the Police Monument and the Haymarket Martyrs' Memorial, the Haymarket Memorial seeks to cater to all interpretations of the event, most evident from the exclusion of the names of the fallen police officers or the labor leaders who were sentenced to death in the aftermath. Therefore, the ambiguity and the absence of violence are purposeful as Brogger argued "the violence didn't seem important because this event was made up of much bigger ideas than one particular incident" and wanted to "suggest the complexity of truth" and "people's responsibility for their actions and for the effects of their actions" (as cited by Kinzer, 2004). As a result, the Haymarket Memorial overlooks the more radical aspects of the event, its aftermath and the salience of social class, in favor of a historical narrative that fits into the story of American progress and the expansion of rights. Brogger even made sure to use easy to clean materials, lest her sculpture be vandalized, like the Police Monument before it (Kinzer, 2004).

Discussion

As stated in the introduction to this chapter, the commemoration of the Haymarket Affair affords an opportunity to explore the intersection of collective memory and history and to think about the possible connection these concepts have to how the commemoration of the event acts pedagogically. In order to explore this connection, I want to first establish the Haymarket as a *lieu de memoiré*, or site of social memory (Nora, 1989) and then discuss how the political control of the narrative of the Haymarket space aids in thinking about the capacity the site holds for pedagogical engagement or disengagement.

The Haymarket as a *Lieu de Memoiré*

The site of the Haymarket Affair has long served as an important site for labor groups, particularly radical ones. The events there, especially in the aftermath of men being put on trial for their political ideology as opposed to their actions, have strongly tied radical groups' collective memories to the site and helped foster their own group identities. Even though the radical interpretation of the Haymarket is well ensconced at Waldheim Cemetery, that monument's position outside of the Chicago city limits hampers the radical claim to the Haymarket site itself. Labor radicals have wanted to control that space, especially in getting recognition for the Haymarket martyrs at the site, as a means to support their own political agenda (Mitchell, 2008). Politically, radical labor's attempt to control the Haymarket space has been limited by widespread American fear of labor radicalism (an ironic outgrowth fostered by radicalism's role in the Haymarket Affair) and the Chicago business community's initial desire to place the police at the center of the event's narrative and, later inability to see the value in commemorating an act of radical labor violence (Barrett, 2012).

Despite radical labor never taking full control of the meaning of the Haymarket space, there has still been an active presence related to their interpretation of events. As mentioned above, the Police Monument was consistently, and often violently, vandalized regardless of its location in proximity to the site of the Haymarket Affair (Foote, 1997; Kelland, 2005). In addition, the site has a long history as a site for labor tourism both from domestic and international visitors, including during the time period when there was no commemoration (Barrett, 2012), as well as continued labor activism at events like annual May Day rallies. There are also smaller acts of protest and commemoration, such as anarchists tagging the monument with the circle-A, or visitors leaving behind flowers (both reactions to the monument I've seen on different visits).

In addition, the Haymarket Memorial was recently temporarily relocated to nearby Union Park. While the memorial's temporary home was in a much more working-class neighborhood, situated near several union offices, such as the IBEW, Fraternal Order of Police, and Chicago Pipefitters, the temporary location did not hold the same meaning that the Haymarket site does, despite being somewhat more appropriate as a space to learn about labor history. These actions point to Haymarket's status as a *lieu de memoiré*. Nora (1989) defines *lieux de memoiré* as sites where "memory crystallizes and secretes itself" and where "a sense of historical continuity exist(s)" (p. 7). The radical labor depiction of the site as one of loss that bolsters the need for action has been a constant of the space, regardless of the politics that have affected how the Haymarket has been officially remembered.

While the Haymarket Martyrs' Memorial in Forest Park serves a similar purpose, and represents a radical remembrance of the Haymarket Affair, there is a desire for the legitimacy that the actual space where the event happened confers. Therefore, part of the continued radical activism around the Haymarket space seems caught up in Nora's (1989) fundamental purpose of *lieux de memoiré*: "to stop time, to block the work of forgetting, to establish the state of things, to immortalize death, to materialize the immaterial" (p. 19). One of the ironies of *lieux de memoiré*, though, is the fact that they memorialize an event or concept that does not truly exist. In this case, the radical labor ideology that groups wish to bring to the fore no longer exists in the same form that it did in 1886 and in 1886, radical ideology proved to be a major setback to the labor movement in the aftermath of the bombing. In fact, while radicalism is lightly acknowledged at the Haymarket Memorial, the focus seems to partially be on labor's contribution towards the attainment of freedom of speech (ironic given the events and aftermath of the Haymarket largely being related to the violation of that right) and the ever broadening umbrella of who is included in the labor movement, despite the continuing decline of union membership in the country (Bureau of Labor Statistics, 2017). Despite the competing memories that still attach to the site, though, the Haymarket Affair has been seen as fundamental to the history of the labor movement, especially in relation to the forging of a radical labor identity.

The Relationship of Memory, History, and the Individual

Due to the still competing nature of how the Haymarket Affair is remembered, what can be said about how it engages the relationship between memory and history and how meaning is made by the individual who encounters the space of the Haymarket Affair? Situating the site as a *lieu de memoiré* points to the way that memory is actively at play at the site, as regardless of what is enshrined on the physical landscape, the site has been imbued with a variety of meanings based on the way it connects to one's affective reaction and group identity. History is also present, though. Regardless of the sources I explored, the main facts remain the same: a peaceful protest was interrupted by the police, a bomb went off, and in the aftermath police and workers were killed and radical labor organizers were sentenced to death for their beliefs. Therefore, one level of the site's commemoration is the establishment of those facts and the statue itself. The current commemoration of the sites further situates those facts into a broader theme, as one event in a larger history of securing freedom of speech and assembly, a narrative that, under the view now represented at the site, can be seen as largely complete.

Using a simplistic and problematically dichotomous understanding of the relationship between curriculum and pedagogy, one could think of the history presented through the Haymarket Memorial as the intended curriculum of the commemoration. Ellsworth (2005) argues that dominant educational discourses "take knowledge to be a thing already made and learning to be an experience already known" (p. 5). In this view, the pedagogy of a public space is determined by what is on display. If one were to visit the Haymarket in the early 1900s, the police narrative is what would be learned. If one were to visit the Haymarket today, one would learn about the importance of free speech and the consequences of one's actions.

Drawing on Ellsworth (2005), though, I argue that it is important to view the curriculum of the space as inherently intertwined with its pedagogy, as the relationship among curriculum, pedagogy, and learning is not that simple. I mentioned earlier the labor movement acts as a form of activist public pedagogy. It is through the experiences of picketing, going on strike, singing songs and taking part in other forms of labor solidarity that help those involved, directly or indirectly, make sense of the pedagogy that is being put forward. Similarly, it is through the pedagogy of those types of actions (visiting Haymarket, using it as a site for political demonstrations, investing it with meaning regardless of physical representation) that their curriculum is able to take on meaning. In other words, just as history and memory are intertwined with one another, so are curriculum and pedagogy.

Ellsworth (2005) argues that pedagogy can encompass curriculum and that pedagogy is to some degree "a learning self in the making" (p. 5). Therefore, if we wish to understand how the Haymarket functions pedagogically we also have to take into account the fact that visitors bring different identities and memories to their encounter. An anarchist might walk by the Haymarket Memorial and see a lost opportunity to engage the "real" meaning of the event—the importance of anarchist ideology in confronting capitalist institutions. Likewise, a school group may visit the site and come away with the story the memorial portrays—one of the sanctity of the freedoms of speech and assembly. Just as likely, people may walk by and not "see" anything, completely unaware of what took place at the site and the competing interpretations that vie for dominance. What makes the Haymarket pedagogical, then, is not the site and/or the memorial in and of themselves, but rather the interaction between the self and the site which creates a pedagogical encounter.

Implications, Importance, and Pedagogical Strategies

I have used the commemoration of the Haymarket Affair to elucidate the interconnected nature of memory and history and how such a relationship, in concert with one's own identity, plays a role in how one makes sense of representations of the past. Beyond being a seminal moment in American labor history, the Haymarket Affair provides an opportunity to understand how different conceptions of a historical event are constructed, perpetuated and used. As seen in the lesson plan (see Appendix), analyzing the Haymarket monuments provides a material way for engaging how history functions publicly and how narratives of an event can continuously be rewritten as our understanding shifts.

The former site of the Chicago Haymarket is not the only place where this understanding can be developed. The ongoing debate about whether or not to remove Confederate memorials indicates that the issues outlined in this chapter are prevalent and will not be going away any time soon. Part of the argument against Confederate memorial removal is that the absence of a marker on the landscape will somehow lead to an absence of knowledge, where history is erased. At the same time, there is an assumption that just because there is a memorial presence, a certain, privileged understanding of the past will most likely be taken up by those who interact with the space. The case of the Haymarket shows us that while the nature of a commemoration, and its attendant curriculum, can have impact, there are also ways in which certain understandings persist regardless of what interpretation of the past is on display. Thinking about the implications for labor history education, there is a need to further explore how the relationship between history and memory in the construction of the past can be engaged in the classroom, especially as narratives about the nature of unions and their declining membership obscure the importance of their history and continued presence.

Notes

1 This event is known by a few different names including the Haymarket Massacre and the Haymarket Riot. I chose to refer to it as the Haymarket Affair as it does not convey an overt bias towards either the workers or police involved.

2 Since all of the memorials have very similar names, I will refer to them, in the rest of the chapter, as the Police Monument, the Martyrs' Monument, and the Haymarket Memorial.

References

Barrett, J. R. (2012). The heritage of social class and class conflict on Chicago's South Side. In *On Location* (pp. 15–35). Springer New York.

Bureau of Labor Statistics (2017).

Burdick, J., Sandlin, J. A., & O'Malley, M. P. (2014). Breaking without fixing: Inhabiting aporia. In J. Burdick, J. A. Sandlin, & M. P. O'Malley (Eds.), *Problematizing public pedagogy*. (1–11). New York, NY: Routledge.

City of Chicago (2017). Chicago Public Art Program: Chicago Police Department Headquarters. Retrieved from: https://www.cityofchicago.org/city/en/depts/dca/supp_info/chicago_s_publicartchicagopolicedepartmentheadquarters.html

Chicago Daily Tribune. (1907, May 5). Tell of Haymarket Riot: Police veterans hold memorial to dead comrades. *Chicago Daily Tribune.*

Chicago Daily Tribune. (1950, May 8). Service honors police killed while on duty: Combined with memorial for Haymarket dead. *Chicago Daily Tribune.*

den Boer. P. (2010). Loci-memoriae—lieux de memoiré. In A. Erll & A. Nünning (Eds.) *A Companion to Cultural Memory Studies* (19-25). Berlin, Germany: De Gruyter.

Ellsworth, E. (2005). *Places of learning: Media, architecture, pedagogy*. New York, NY: Routledge.

Epstein, T. (1998). Deconstructing differences in African-American and European-American adolescents' perspectives on US history. *Curriculum inquiry*, *28*(4), 397–423.

Epstein, T. (2010). *Interpreting national history: Race, identity, and pedagogy in classrooms and communities*. New York, NY: Routledge.

Farley, L. (2007). The "shadowy underside" of learning history. *The Review of Education, Pedagogy, and Cultural Studies*, *29*(5), 423–40.

Foote, K. E. (1997). *Shadowed ground: America's landscapes of violence and tragedy*. Austin, TX: University of Texas Press.

Garrett, H.J. (2017). *Learning to be in the world with others: Difficult knowledge & social studies education*. New York, NY: Peter Lang.

Green, J. (2006). *Death in the Haymarket: A story of Chicago, the first labor movement and the bombing that divided gilded age America*. New York, NY: Anchor Books.

Hague, E. (2008). Remembering Haymarket. *ACME: An International Journal for Critical Geographies*, 7(1), 88-97.

Kelland, L. (2005). Putting Haymarket to Rest?. *Labor*, *2*(2), 31–8.

Kinzer, S. (2004, September 15). In Chicago, an ambiguous memorial to the Haymarket Attack. *The New York Times.* Retrieved from: www.nytimes.com

Mitchell, D. (2008). Which side are you on? From Haymarket to now. *ACME: An International Journal for Critical Geographies*, 7(1), 59–68.

Nora, P. (1989). Between memory and history: Les lieux de mémoire. *Representations*, *26*, 7–24.

Peck, C. L. (2010). "It's not like [I'm] Chinese and Canadian. I am in between": Ethnicity and students' conceptions of historical significance. *Theory & Research in Social Education*, *38*(4), 574–617.

Pendarvis, P. (2016). A Tale of Two Cemeteries: The Paris Commune, the Haymarket Affair, and the Politics of Memorialization.

Sandlin, J. A., O'Malley, M. P., & Burdick, J. (2011). Mapping the complexity of public pedagogy scholarship: 1894–2010. *Review of Educational Research*, *81*(3), 338–75.

Segall, A. (1999). Critical history: Implications for history/social studies education. *Theory & Research in Social Education*, *27*(3), 358–74.

Segall, A. (2006). What's the purpose of teaching the disciplines, anyway? The case of history. In A. Segall, E. E. Heilman, & C. H. Cherryholmes (Eds.), *Social studies—the next generation: Re-searching in the postmodern* (125–39). New York: Peter Lang.

Segall, A. (2013). Revitalizing critical discourses in social education: Opportunities for a more complexified (un) knowing. *Theory & Research in Social Education*, *41*(4), 476–93.

Shackel, P. A. (2011). Remembering Haymarket and the control for public memory. *Heritage, Labour, and the Working Classes*, 34.

Appendix

Lesson Plan

1. Lesson Plan Title: Commemorating the Haymarket Affair
2. Theme: In this lesson, students explore the various commemorations of the Haymarket Affair to first understand which version of the event the memorial is commemorating, and then to have a larger conversation about how we should decide whose version of events to remember.
3. Grade Level: 6–12
4. Course: U.S. History
5. Time Required: Two to three 50-minute class periods
6. Essential and Supporting Questions:
   a. How should we commemorate the past?
   b. How do we decide whose interpretation of the past should be remembered?
   c. How has the Haymarket Affair been commemorated?
7. Objectives:
   a. Students will be able to identify and describe the various perspectives inscribed in public memorials to the Haymarket Affair.
   b. Students will be able to design and justify their own concept for a Haymarket Affair memorial.
8. Standards (from the National Council for the Social Studies [NCSS]):
   a. D2.His.6.9-12. Analyze the ways in which the perspectives of those writing history shaped the history they produced.
   b. D2.His.7.9-12. Explain how the perspectives of people in the present shape interpretations of the past
9. Classroom Materials:
   a. LCD projector
   b. Individual or group access to images of the Police Monument, the Martyrs' Monument, and the Haymarket Memorial. Images can be taken from the preceding chapter.
   c. Paper
   d. Art supplies
10. Instructional Plan:
    a. Entry Task to Establish Context [est. 10 minutes—Class 1]
       i. The teacher should begin class by projecting an artistic rendering of the Haymarket Affair on the board (available via: https://www.illinoislaborhistory.org/the-haymarket-affair)
       ii. The teacher should then use the Visual Thinking Strategy to engage students in making sense of the painting. The teacher should pose

the following three questions, focusing first on surface-level details and then moving deeper into analysis:

1. What is going on in this picture?
2. What do you see that makes you say that?
3. What more can we find?

b. Teacher-Directed Instruction [est. 15 minutes—Class 1]

i. The teacher should then build off the entry task/image analysis, by providing the historical context (available in the attached chapter) of the Haymarket Affair to students. Students should have a basic grasp of what happened at the Chicago Haymarket and how it relates to the labor movement.

c. Student-Centered/Engaged Learning (Student Inquiry Activity/Activities) [est. 25 minutes—Class 1, up to 25 minutes—Class 2]

i. Students should be divided into groups of three and given a picture of each of the Haymarket Memorials. Using the images and brief contextual information, students should tease out what narrative is being presented in each. Students can use the Visual Thinking Strategy questions from the entry task to stimulate conversation. They can also be given more information, such as what the plaques say and the geographic location of each monument (information found in chapter).

ii. Students should record notes about the perceptions of each memorial:

1. Who/what does the memorial depict?
2. Whose perspective is being shown in this memorial?
3. Whose perspective missing from the memorial?
4. Who do you think supported (supports) this version of events?

iii. Once students have completed their answers to the above question, the teacher can pull students back together, solicit their answers, and provide further context (such as when the monuments were created, who funded them, etc.), as needed.

iv. The teacher should then hold a class discussion centered on the following questions:

1. Which depiction of the Haymarket Affair do you think best represents what happened at the event? Why?
2. How do these memorials help us understand the role of perspective in history?

d. Exit Task for Summarizing Answer(s) to Essential and Supporting Questions [25 minutes or a third class period as needed]. Students should complete the assessment detailed below.

11. Assessment: Based on their findings and the class discussion, students should get in groups of three and collaboratively design a memorial for the Haymarket Affair. They should annotate or provide a written justification of the choices they made, including whose perspective they are highlighting and why.
12. Community Engagement: Students can extend their learning by seeking out and analyzing monuments/memorials in their local communities. Whose perspectives are being shown, why do those perspectives exist, and how are those perspectives thought about today?

Monument 1

Name: *Haymarket Memorial Statue*

Date: 1889

Original Location: Haymarket Square, Chicago, IL

Current Location: 3510 S. Michigan Ave, Chicago, IL (Chicago Police Department Headquarters)

Monument 2

Name: *Haymarket Martyrs' Monument*

Date: 1893

Location: Forest Home Cemetery, Forest Park, IL

Monument 3

Name: *The Haymarket Memorial*

Date: 2004

Location: 175 Des Plaine St., Chicago, IL

Labor During the "Roaring 1920s": Mary Barker, the American Federation of Teachers, and Local #89

JoAnn Wood and Chara Haeussler Bohan

Introduction and Historical Context

At the very same moment when many unions were hemorrhaging members and shrinking their programming, the Atlanta teacher union during the 1920s was strong and becoming stronger. By examining membership records, the expanding list of benefits achieved, the admiration that the local garnered, and its involvement with the American Federation of Teachers during this time, a different story from that of mainstream unionism may be discerned. Teacher unionism has always been an anomaly within the larger union movement, because teaching by its very nature is different from industrial labor. A few factors contribute to this difference: a large percentage of teachers are women, and teaching and schools are publicly funded. These attributes mean that the contours of general labor history and those of teacher unions are often out of synch. If teacher unions appear at all in general labor histories, their early histories are ignored while most historians highlight the 1960s and the clash of the union with community members in New York City. Overlooking the history of teacher unions like the Atlanta Public School Teachers Association (APSTA) yields an incomplete labor history and invites us to remedy that oversight.

For a time in the late nineteenth and early twentieth centuries, teachers organized, initially joining organizations such as the American Federation of Teachers (AFT), and the National Education Association (NEA). The NEA was the older organization formed initially in 1857 by and for school leaders, and only recognized classroom teachers in 1912. The NEA began actively recruiting teachers as members in 1916. The AFT, in contrast, formed in 1916 as an organization of rank-and-file teachers and described themselves as a union from the start (Murphy, 1990, p. 4). Against the backdrop of the broader union movement, the story of the schoolteachers of Atlanta, why they organized, and how successful they were in meeting their goals is a little known but fascinating story. The story of how and why Atlanta teachers organized contrasts with the larger industrial union history in several important ways (Newman, 1978). The general image of union laborers and the groups they joined, taking radical actions—picketing, striking, and staging slowdowns to force management to negotiate better working conditions—–undergoes some shape-shifting when the workers are women and the work they do is educating the nation's children. The APSTA, and particularly one of its leaders, Mary Barker, provides a story of teacher unionism different from that of locals elsewhere (Murphy, 1990; Rousmaniere, 2002; Blount, 2002). Within her own local, Barker herself was an anomaly. She seized issues that put her at odds with her colleagues, extended her work beyond the mainstream in fascinating ways, and even critiqued both the local and the AFT generally.

Teachers during this period of rapid growth and change occupy the crossroads of women studies, labor studies, and southern history studies and that intersection provides new layers of complexity and dimension to the conversation. The life and activism of one union activist, Mary Barker, and the APSTA, Local #89, allows us to look at union history from the margins. What might radical resistance look like at that intersection and in those margins?

This chapter relies on narrative historical methods, and archival work was essential to its completion. Both primary and secondary sources helped to reconstruct Barker's story. Her papers at Emory University provide a fascinating record of a tireless crusader. This archival research is also enhanced by examination of presidential addresses, AFT journals, conference records, publications, and correspondence from these years.

General labor histories for the first half of the twentieth century generally omit early teacher unionism from analysis. When teacher unions are discussed, they usually are those of the 1960s and beyond. The secondary literature for the early years of teacher unions is somewhat dated but remains indispensable for insights and analysis (Murphy, 1990; Urban, 1982). These works from the 1970s and 1980s only reinforce the need for more up-to-date studies of these early teacher unions. Joseph Newman's 1978 dissertation devoted more time to Barker than any of the larger teacher union studies, but Barker and her work was not his focus, and she has largely slipped into the margins of teacher union history (Newman, 1978). Recovering her thinking and her work is another way in which education history may be repaired and remedied.

This chapter nestles largely within the roaring twenties as Barker became a union leader during this time. During the decade, labor languished but American business prospered. Presidents Warren Harding, Calvin Coolidge, and Herbert Hoover enjoyed an enlightened capitalist perspective and led pro-business administrations. In fact, the United States, with the highest standard of living at the time, had become the world's first mass-consumption society (Dubofsky & McCartin, 2017). Moreover, the working class gained greater access to credit, and allegedly drove "Fords and "Chevvies," watched the same movies, listened to the same radio programs, wore look-alike factory-made clothing, and danced the Charleston" (Dubofsky & McCartin, 2017).

Yet, the prosperity driven by big business was not enjoyed by all Americans. In Jim Crow Atlanta, Black teachers' experiences provide graphic evidence of racist policies and practices. Within the Atlanta School System, segregated by law and practice, Black and white teachers taught in separate schools and formed distinct teacher unions by race. Barker pointed out that the Board of Education (BOE) strategy of discriminatory pay served to keep teachers disunited and fighting one another rather than seeking equal and adequate salaries for all. Her attempts to open membership in the APSTA to the city's Black teachers were met with virulent and vocal racist resistance by APSTA members and led to Barker's marginalization within her own union. Ultimately campaigns for improved salaries were pursued through different and distinct strategies. The Black teacher group, known as the Gate City Teachers Association, worked with Black community leaders, churches, and other organizations to pursue better school buildings, conditions, and salaries, ultimately employing legal challenges to force the BOE to equalize salaries by race in the 1940s (Newman, 1978).

Within the broader union movement, the momentum slowed in the 1920s as the Supreme Court outlawed picketing and local unions began losing members even while they continued to press for child labor legislation and for minimum wages for women workers. Unionism became linked in the minds of conservatives to radicalism, subversive political activity, and specifically to communism. The fight to remove "reds" within unions presented a real crisis and plagued unions and caused internal dissension that left permanent scars within locals and their national counterparts. Barker played an active role in this controversy at both local and national levels. David Montgomery in *The Fall of the House of Labor* called the decade after 1923 a "remarkable hiatus in the evolution of the labor movement itself" as strike activity fell to an all-time low and "corporate mastery of American life seemed secure" (Montgomery, 1987, p. 7). How did Atlanta teachers, and Mary Barker in particular, fare in navigating this larger reality?

Mary Barker and the APSTA

Barker is briefly mentioned in several teacher union histories, and within a dissertation about her local, the Atlanta Public School Teachers Association, yet she remains largely unknown. For a time, Barker was a driving force within Atlanta's teacher union and led the American Federation of Teachers (AFT) as well. What were some of the issues and conditions fueling her activism?

Mary Barker was born in 1879 in Atlanta, began her schooling in Polk County, Georgia, and later attended Agnes Scott College, completing the normal program in 1900. She started teaching elementary school upon graduation and became a third-grade teacher in Atlanta Public Schools (APS) in 1904. APS was a segregated school system at this time with white and Black schools carefully delineated and a teaching corps also divided by race. As a white teacher and a native Georgian, Barker would have grown up in this segregated world, and yet developed ideas that bridged this divide. This parallel and divided system worked with internal tensions which increased over time, as racial inequities became more blatant and more pressing. In the meantime, Barker quickly rose to a principalship, although at this time principals were also teachers who did the administrative work on top of their teaching load. At about the same time that her work responsibilities were increasing, she became more active within the local teacher organization (Newman, 1978).

The APSTA was organized in 1905; Barker joined from the start, but her engagement increased when the local began considering affiliation with the larger labor movement in the city and the American Federation of Labor. Barker was appointed as a member of the three-person committee to research union affiliation and report back to the membership. Newman wrote in his dissertation on the APSTA that the committee was made up of three members: one of whom (Julia Riordan) was pro-union, one who was neutral on the issue, and the third (Barker) who was not in favor of affiliation. She then met and talked with Atlanta labor leaders, including Ed L. Sutton, head of the Typesetter's union and Jerome Jones, the "Samuel Gompers of the South," who gave her a crash course in union history and principles. From there, she became a committed unionist for the rest of her life. The committee reported back to the membership with a unanimous recommendation to affiliate and the membership voted overwhelmingly in favor of that plan. The APSTA became Local #89 in the American Federation of Teachers in 1919 (Barker, 1950).

Barker's work on the committee and her abilities as a speaker, writer, and advocate quickly gained her a following, so much so that she was elected president of the APSTA and served from 1921 to 1923. Her local grew and represented nearly all of the white teachers of Atlanta, which helped her gain a national following and led eventually to her election as AFT president from 1925 to 1931. In these roles, she took on many critically important issues, both those considered professional and those labeled "bread and butter." Naturally she received the most support from her members in the pursuit of equal and adequate salaries, teacher tenure, a credit union, pension benefits, sick leave, and other benefits today's teachers often take for granted. She had less support when it came to professional issues such as professional development to promote intellectual growth, formal participation in school and district governance, and solutions to wider social problems of inequity and poverty. Some of these issues involved crossing the racial divide while others challenged religious, class, gender, and regional strictures and led her members to regard her as too radical for them (Murphy, 1990; Newman, 1978; Urban, 1982).

The campaign for teacher tenure had its roots in an ugly episode of religious bigotry. Another APSTA leader, Julia Riordan, was an outspoken union advocate and the communications chair for the local. She also happened to be Roman Catholic. In this highly protestant city, there were some APS board members elected who were active members of the Ku Klux Klan and determined to purge the schools of the Pope's influence. They voted not to retain nine longtime employees, including Julia Riordan, claiming that they were promulgating their religious beliefs in their classrooms and schools. All of them appealed and were reinstated in their jobs, all except Julia Riordan. The situation rapidly deteriorated, with Riordan airing her grievances publicly, even as the APSTA worked feverishly behind the scenes to have her at least given a due rights process of appeal. Barker, head of the committee assigned the Riordan defense, sought support from their Atlanta local labor council, but they were not successful. In Barker's committee report on the Riordan case, she chided the Atlanta Federation of Trades for their lack of support as she noted, "The sentiment in [the federation] in favor of Labor principles was outweighed, it appeared, by the sentiment of religious intolerance and fear of the political power of that intolerance" (Newman, 1978, p. 88; Barker, 1920–21). This episode ended with a furious Julia Riordan, a smug board of education charged with religious bigotry, and Mary Barker determined to put into place a teacher tenure policy that would prevent such arbitrary and discriminatory firings in the future. In short order such a policy was enacted (Barker papers, 1950).

Gender also played a pivotal role in a few of Barker's major campaigns. The first was Barker and the APSTA's push for equal salaries for male and female teachers, which took place over many years. The salary schedule in place in Atlanta Public Schools in the 1920s was very complex, with different steps and salaries by race, by gender, and by level of teaching (grammar and high school at this time). One of the earliest initiatives was to equalize salaries within levels so that male and female teachers were paid the same within the high school level and within the grammar school level, although high school teachers still had higher salaries. One might speculate that the Board of Education members deliberately made the salary schedule complex so that only they would be able to understand its permutations, making it more difficult to challenge. Some of the arguments used by Barker and other union leaders against the gender discrimination were that female teachers were expected to set an example and be a model of middle-class respectability for their students and they could not do that on their inadequate and unequal salaries. They also pointed out that the vast majority of teachers were grammar school teachers who were women and argued that attracting the best people for the important job of teaching the city's children required better and equal salaries (Carter, 2002).

Besides gendered salary inequities, there were also salary issues that were tied to the larger economic conditions within which the school systems operated. During economic downturns teachers might receive cuts in pay or might be paid in scrip, and large numbers of teachers lost their jobs outright. Another mechanism by which the Atlanta school board discriminated against female teachers was the sporadic "marriage bars"—policies which prohibited the hiring of married women teachers. The rationale behind such bars, which were used throughout the country when times were lean, was that if budgets only permitted a limited number of jobs and paychecks, they should go to the males, who were assumed to be heads of households and earning a "family wage." Female teachers might be supporting just as many or more dependents as their male counterparts, and many might not have husbands who could or would contribute to the support of the household, so such marriage bars created a double barrier. Some married women teachers who lost their jobs found that their seniority also disappeared, so that when economics were rosier and jobs were available, they found themselves back at the first step of the pay scale and starting all over (Carter, 2002, Kessler-Harris, 1982 & 1990; Murphy, 1990).

Gender was not the only dynamic affecting salaries, nor was it the most explosive. Race was very much at the heart of every salary dispute and was used very effectively by the Board to divide teachers and pit them against one another. The Board would hold a bond issue to raise salaries, buildings, and improve conditions on the promise that salary increases would be granted to both Black and white teachers, although they frequently reneged on their promises. Any money the board set aside for salaries was allocated in a racially discriminatory way, and white teachers—who already made higher salaries than their Black counterparts in every job category–repeatedly received higher wage increases than their Black colleagues. In time, Black teachers worked with the larger Black community to oppose the bond issues since they argued that they would see no benefits that improved conditions for Black teachers or students (Newman, 1978).

Barker persistently argued with her APSTA members about how the Board was driving teachers apart by race to keep from paying all of them adequately. She tried to merge the Black and white teacher groups so that they would be a more powerful lobby against Board practices, but her members' racism and the Jim Crow realities of the time prevented anything that hinted at integration. When her local refused to merge, she encouraged the Gate City teacher group to affiliate separately with organized labor and they became a separate AFT local. The APSTA membership resisted integration with all their might from the 1920s to the 1940s, thus forcing the Black local to work with the larger Black community and the NAACP to pursue legal action to compel integration within Atlanta Public Schools (Newman, 1978).

What made the APSTA different from other teacher unions around the country at this time? One obvious difference was the attempt by some of their leaders, including Mary Barker, to advocate for both tangible bread and butter benefits and professional growth opportunities and governance responsibilities. Another sharply different element in their story is the central role that race played in the union's local political dynamics. The Atlanta Board of Education worked to drive a wedge between Black and white teachers by establishing and reinforcing racially inequitable salary schedules throughout the first half of the twentieth century. The BOE promised higher salary increases to Black teachers, at the bottom of the scale by every measure, and then when funds fell short, as they inevitably did, they would break those same promises. Using their votes as a weapon, Black teachers, who were encouraged to support school bond measures by these broken promises, began working with their own Black communities to educate and defeat the bond measures. Mary Barker and a few other leaders of APSTA pointed out that uniting the demands of ALL the teachers and working to address inequities would benefit everyone, but few stepped across that color line with her. In the end, she worked through a variety of interracial civic groups to try to lay the groundwork for integration and moved around her own union's racism. Here then is evidence of Barker's radicalism on the issue of race (Du Bois, 1903; Newman, 1978).

Barker also worked with the Phillis Wheatley Y.W.C.A. and the Gate City Teachers Association on a variety of initiatives to improve teaching and living conditions. After she became president of the AFT in 1925, she argued in vain with APSTA leaders about the counter-productiveness of segregated unions, as the AFT moved closer to policies which would eventually demand integrated locals. It was not until the 1940s that the APSTA was finally expelled from the AFT for its refusal to integrate, and then the local instead chose to become an affiliate of the NEA. By the 1960s both the AFT and NEA were fully integrated and the separate white union withered away (Barker papers; Newman, 1978).

The Atlanta teacher unions were different in other ways from those in New York City and Chicago, which are often held up as the template for teacher union development against which others were measured (Murphy, 1990; Rousmaniere, 2002; Urban, 1982). One difference was in the mingling of both teachers and administrators (school and district level) within the union. Although there were ways in which this collaboration strengthened the union, especially in the early years, it became a problem later and one that Barker criticized harshly. What she observed was a tendency of some principals to browbeat their teacher employees to join the union in name only but then squelch any vocal opposition on the part of teachers on union matters. She also warned that some administrators were using their union leadership role as a steppingstone to the superintendency or other district-level position, and pointed out that teachers and administrators sometimes had conflicting interests. She suggested that too much power in the hands of some union leaders was leading to a decrease in democratic involvement in union affairs and an increase in autocracy among the leaders rising throughout the 1930s and 1940s. Barker's internal critique of her own local is yet another way in which she might be considered radical (Barker papers, 1950).

Tracing Barker's ideas about race involves digesting the materials in her correspondence and organizational files. One of the pivotal events that influenced her thoughts about racial segregation was the 1906 Atlanta Race Massacre. This uprising took place in the downtown area from September 24 to 26, and was marked by white mobs who killed several dozen Black Atlantans, wounded many more, and damaged or destroyed a number of Black businesses. In the aftermath of the massacre some leaders from both the Black and white communities worked together to restore order and create some lines of communication designed to prevent further such events. The Neighborhood Union was one of those interracial organizations, and one in which Barker was active. Later, a young African American communist named Angelo Herndon was arrested and convicted of "attempting to incite insurrection" in 1932. Barker followed this case closely, wrote letters in Herndon's support, and the case seemed to crystallize her thoughts about communism, segregation, and racism in ways that further distanced her from many in her union. After five years of appeals, Herndon was eventually freed in 1937 after the United States Supreme Court overturned his sentence (Barker papers; Hatfield, 2020).

Economic benefits for teachers were also part of Barker and the local's broader campaign. Among them were economic supports such as credit unions and pensions. By the 1920s many longtime teachers who had devoted themselves to teaching careers realized that they had no means in place for support beyond retirement. They learned from colleagues in other cities and states of a variety of plans that might be beneficial. The salary schedule continued to be a challenge and making a solid plan that was logical and transparent for all was quite difficult.

From the 1920s through the 1970s, salaries and a rational salary schedule were often on the union agenda (Newman, 1978).

Barker, unlike most of her APSTA colleagues, envisioned a union that focused both on what has been called "bread and butter" issues and "professional" issues. Barker was convinced that if teachers were going to be agents of democracy and model full citizenship, they needed to enhance their own skills and abilities, both in teaching their students and in influencing governance of the schools. She wanted to see teachers in leadership roles who helped to form policy, because she believed that teachers knew best what the actual work of teaching and learning was and therefore should have more defined roles in policy making. Some of the schemes she devised included regular lectures on topics designed to "professionally develop" her peers, a shared governance structure to establish a precedent for teacher influence on policy development, and involvement with other labor councils as well as affiliated bodies within the AFT. Her efforts at building professionalism met with mixed success (Newman, 1978).

The American Federation of Teachers, 1925–1931

Marjorie Murphy, in her book on teacher union history, stated that unions developed as cities grew and school systems were centralized. Three main obstacles to organization were teachers own resistance to considering their own well-being as a professional concern, a red-baiting atmosphere that generated fear, and the chronic fiscal crisis that has always surrounded public education. Because school districts were locally funded that meant that the tax system remained fiscally conservative and that national solutions could not be enacted. Murphy focused largely on the AFT since it is a history that emphasized locals, with the national and state organizational levels being less powerful. Chicago was the most powerful union until WWII, then prominence later shifted to New York City. Atlanta was a leading local until 1957 before the big rupture over race (Blunt, 2002; Murphy, 1990, p. 3).

In 1925, Mary Barker was elected president of the American Federation of Teachers. There were several reasons for her success: the APSTA was one of the largest locals in the AFT and the local had successfully run an ambitious and multi-faceted program for improvements in teaching and learning. Barker was seen as a smart and strategic leader at a time when the national was fighting an anti-union backlash. She had helped to build the growth of AFT in Georgia and was seen as someone who took on tough issues and was devoted to the union cause. Her success within AFT would also be a source of contention between her and most of her APSTA colleagues, who believed that she was becoming too liberal for their tastes and would not "stay between the lines" which segregated life dictated (Murphy, 1990, p. 118–23).

Barker had already answered for herself the question of why teachers should unionize back when her local was deliberating about AFT affiliation in 1919. She also followed John Dewey closely and he voiced his own support for teacher unions. In a 1927 essay entitled, "Why I Am a Member of the Teachers Union," Dewey articulated his rationale of union membership as he spoke to a Membership Meeting of the Teachers Union of the City of New York. He believed that the members of the union exhibited "the spirit of courage, of straightforwardness, of energy, of practical idealism, a sense of justice for all who are in any way wronged or in danger of being wronged" and was proud to be among such people (Dewey, 1928). He spoke to the objections that some people had to teachers being in the labor movement because it brought teaching down the level of work, and argued that this sort of class snobbery about the work of teaching is neither sound nor effective in uplifting the profession. Beyond the need to discuss academic questions and subject matter and methodology, Dewey stated, there was also a need for an organization representing

> the interests that teachers have in common, and which, in representing them, represents also the protection of the children, and the youth in the schools against all of the outside interests, economic and political and others that would exploit the schools for their own ends, and in doing so, reduce the teaching body to a condition of intellectual vassalage. (Dewey, 1928, p. 4)

He went on to list the many causes which the union had advocated and posed the question of what life for working people would be like if there were no unions (Dewey, 1928, p. 4).

He addressed the fact that some were critical of the teachers union as "unprofessional" for focusing on the economics of teaching as a job. He remarked that teachers, including himself, had to buy groceries and house rent like everyone else, and so he made "no apology for saying that one reason for being a member of the Teachers Union is the fact that it does emphasize the economic aspect of the teaching profession" (Dewey, 1928, p. 4). He added that it was not the Teachers Union that placed the schools under the control of the "largest taxpayers and tax dodgers" and then attempted "to keep the teachers" mouths shut on all questions that were of economic interest to all excepting a numerically small group of big business concerns" (Dewey, 1928, p. 4–5). He went on to talk about other ways in which the union served a role unlike other organizations—in working to limit the influence and control by those who would use the schools for their own purposes: to institute military training and recruitment into the schoolhouse, to "inculcate a warlike spirit, a kind of wild, red-eyed patriotism" (Dewey, 1928, p. 5). These same forces were using their power over schools to brand individuals as radical and dangerous for opposing war, people like Jane Addams, for example. He pointed out that the enemies of unions claimed unions were controlled by Moscow for opposing the Lusk Laws. Dewey raised the matter of child labor, as many of these union opponents tried to keep children working, which prevented young people from obtaining an education. If teachers could not speak their minds on child labor, what subjects were considered appropriate for them to address? Dewey went on to articulate that anti-unionist arguments are weakened because of artificial distinctions between head and hand, work and books, and action and ideas and criticized education for being too academic and too pedantic and not tied to actual problems of life. Those who have read Dewey will know that these ideas are at the very heart of his philosophy of education. The time will come, Dewey declared, when rather than being asked why one should join the teachers union, they will instead ask why should not everyone do so?

> The time will come when the principle of organization and cooperation and the recognition of common interests of all of those who work in any way, whether mostly with their head or with their hands, or mostly with their voice, will be so clear that the explanations and the apologies and arguments will have to come from those who are not members of the Teachers Union. (Dewey, 1928, p. 6)

One of Dewey's most enduring mantras was adopted by the AFT as its slogan, "Democracy in Education, Education for Democracy," and it is one to which Barker was devoted her entire professional life. She saw it as equally important that teachers live and work as active citizens of a democratic society and workplace, and urged teachers to show by example to their young charges how to act in the world. Not only was it important for her that teachers have a say in their working lives and be able to live with dignity and some level of comfort, but it was also equally if not more important that students have opportunities to engage in the actual problems of society and to think about how they could best serve their communities and the nation. In her presidential addresses to the AFT between 1925 and 1931, she spoke often of her beliefs about democracy. Her 1929 address stated that: "... the American Federation of Teachers is demanding the necessary freedom for teachers and pupils to develop the qualities of citizenship that are most desirable in a democracy" (Barker papers, 1929, p. 1). She detailed AFT demands for safe and sound school buildings, reasonable class sizes, manageable hours of work, "just compensation" and "opportunity for every child to receive adequate educational advantages" (Barker papers, 1929, p. 1). She indicated that opposition to these conditions comes from those who fail to understand the true costs of education or who are preoccupied with their own self-interest.

The only way to eliminate these barriers, she declared, was through collective action of those who envision better schools and teaching, and she found that action via the AFT. Pursuing this agenda, Barker argued, required funds for organizing and building the locals. It required aligning with other groups that shared AFT's interests, groups such as the League of Women Voters, the National Women's Trade Union League, and the National Council for the Prevention of War. As to the relationship of the AFT with organized labor, Barker stated that,

> the principles of Organized Labor are sound, that organization of workers into unions is a necessary part of the human machinery that has been set up in the world to promote human progress … we know that the labor movement is not just a selfish demand on the part of a particular group for something that it does not have but wants to possess. It is a humanitarian movement whose watchword could be stated thus: Help yourself to attain the conditions necessary for you to function as a human being, as a worthy member of your community. Help others to help themselves. Overcome the obstacles to your aspirations by cooperating with your fellow workers to get the necessary power to bring about desirable conditions. (Barker, 1929, p. 3)

In this same address, she related the many times that teachers were told to mind their own business, when in fact the issues at hand were their business. She discussed how teachers' citizenship is often truncated when they are told they cannot address controversy, when all of real life is about those essential controversies. Rather than repressing and controlling ideas it would be better, she argued, to encourage the dynamic interchange of ideas, as long as those interests are not self-seeking and do not exploit others (Barker, 1929, pp. 2–6).

Barker did not spare her own union from her critique. Writing a history of her local in 1950, she fiercely condemned some within the APSTA for failing to live up to union ideals. One of the mistakes she thought the local made was to allow both teachers and administrators within the local, since some administrators coerced and exerted undue influence over members of their teaching staff within the union. She indicated that the twisting of administrative and teaching roles within the union was a "major disaster" and served as a fatal flaw within the union in its waning years (Barker, 1950, pp. 2–8).

"Reds" in the Union

Throughout the history of the APSTA both the local and the national teachers union grappled with charges of radicalism, which might mean anything from being pacifist in wartime to being too politically active, to being involved in communist and socialist groups. For most of the leaders within AFT, who generally held liberal or progressive beliefs, the charges of radicalism were a time-consuming and member-draining distraction they could not afford to ignore. During the 1920s and 1930s the AFT dealt with unruly locals, some of which were charged with being overtaken by communists while others were intent on purging the union rolls of radicals. These tensions and attempts to reconcile the purge with their general support of academic freedom resulted in countless meetings, charges and counter-charges, and eventually led to the AFT expelling three locals in 1941 (AFT, 1941).

The issues around "reds in the union" were complex and became knotty for the AFT during this period. On the one hand, the union supported academic freedom and the civil rights of teachers and bore the costs of defending teachers under attack. On the other hand, being identified as "red" or a haven for "reds" was anathema for the union, threatening their very existence. For the social liberals and progressives who led the AFT, like Mary Barker, they were placed in an untenable position. Throughout the 1920s and Barker's tenure as president, the union wrestled internally with the limits of tolerance for radical ideas within their ranks. Every convention document and issue of the union journal featured articles and updates on this tug-of-war between the principles of academic freedom and the realities of life in the country at this fractious time. And, as if this situation was not enough of a conundrum, race and radicalism became entangled and forced the union to take stances that at times seem contrary to their ideals. The story of how AFT dealt with "reds" in the union is complex and was an omnipresent issue throughout the 1920s and persisted into the 1960s. Barker was involved with the early part of this story and John Dewey and George S. Counts, her allies, remained active on this issue for longer than Barker (Murphy, 1990).

Briefly, the 1930s and the early 1940s were increasingly tense for the AFT, as dissension threatened to tear it apart. Eventually after several procedural and policy moves, the union expelled three locals for their radical actions and then focused on repairing their organization. Barker, by this time, was less directly involved with the national but remained aware of events and continued to communicate with leaders grappling with the tensions. During this time, Barker shifted her attention to establishing and working with the Summer School for Women Workers, her own form of radical activism. Convinced that workers in a democracy needed unions to be able to express their common concerns and balance out the power of management to control their lives, she helped to found and played key roles in the Southern School for Women Workers. From 1927 to 1951 she poured her energies into fundraising, writing curriculum, and helping to manage the school which trained women workers from industrial settings, both Black and white, at different summer "schools" in the southeastern mountains. Because of their "race mixing" they had to move locations frequently and were constantly seeking out funding from the General Education Board, the Rosenwald Fund, and other philanthropic sources. The curriculum addressed both academic skills and explicitly taught union strategies and leadership skills (Barker, 1927–51).

Loyalty Oaths

Examining Barker's concerns as she took national office in the 1920s offers evidence of the persistence and intransigence of many of the tensions embedded in schooling in America. Her leadership provides a model of resistance over time. Two issues of interest Barker had during her AFT presidency were those of academic freedom and loyalty oaths. Both concerns endure in American education, albeit in different guises at different times, and are part of the larger story of teacher unions.

Barker's ideas about democracy and her priorities for the AFT may be gleaned from her presidential addresses and from other AFT publications. During this period of retrenchment and attack by anti-union forces, the union faced challenges with recruitment and with defending teachers in their ranks. Loyalty oaths and attacks on academic freedom were two issues, among many, that concerned Mary Barker (Murphy, 1990). Examining how Barker combatted these anti-democratic measures and grounding her arguments in historical context may prove illuminating to today's educators, who face similar restraints.

Concerns about academic freedom and loyalty oaths are centered on the tensions inherent in democracies—how do we ensure individuals the greatest possible degree of freedom while preserving democracy that may be threatened by extremist thought? How does this question resonate within schools? How do teachers navigate the politics of deciding the ideas teachers may hold and those they may teach? Some of the difficulties with academic freedom and loyalty oaths centered on how to defend teachers' rights to choose their own political beliefs even if those beliefs are challenged by those in power at times of heightened political polarization. These issues arose during World War I and have persisted off and on to the present. Many women teachers during World War I opposed the war, having either pacifist or socialist views. The country roiled with competing ideas about how governments should work while ideas about anarchy, socialism, and communism intensified across the social spectrum.

In response, some school districts began requiring teachers to pledge loyalty oaths that they would support the war, which violated their rights to support pacifist ideas. Then, as now, anti-immigration sentiments were stirred as some groups blamed immigrants for bringing in radical ideas and attempted to keep both people and ideas out. The fight for loyalty oaths squared off against freedom of speech and expression and the AFT was embroiled in this controversy from the start (Barker papers, 1929–1943; Cain, 2009; Guerry, 1937; Howlett & Howlett, 2008; Howlett & Howlett, 2019; Murphy, 1990, pp. 95–8).

Dewey, too, weighed in on the issue of academic freedom, especially in reference to the Lusk Laws (Dewey, 1928, p. 5–6). The Lusk laws in New York developed from a legislative committee in 1919 led by Clayton R. Lusk to investigate what were termed "alien enemies." The group gathered information by raiding offices, seizing documents they considered seditious, and subpoenaing witnesses to testify before the committee. The committee especially targeted left-wing socialists and the Industrial Workers of the World, and was particularly critical of socialist efforts to organize American Negroes. The committee issued its report in 1920 and it spawned a number of mandates affecting teachers. One was the limitation of educational institutions to those who could be controlled by the legislature, and another was the requirement that teachers take loyalty oaths. The legislation was vetoed by New York's governor, Al Smith, who said that some lawmakers were "mainly interested in the control of liberal thought" (Lusk Committee, 2020). The laws, while contested and short-lived, nonetheless generated publicity and resulted in widespread fears among teachers that they would be labeled "red" or "radical" and lose their jobs. Loyalty oaths were not confined to New York, as they spread from state to state and school district to school district across the country. The issue of loyalty oaths and academic freedom also influenced teachers' decision of which national education organization they would join.

Murphy's analysis of teacher union history concerned the contest between the AFT brand against that of the National Education Association (NEA) and sought to distinguish the two organizations in tone, intent, and rhetoric, especially during the period of 1917–20. Barker vehemently opposed loyalty oaths imposed on teachers, both because of their repressive anti-democratic roots and the ways they were used to further entrench segregation in the Jim Crow South. Although loyalty oaths were not simply a southern phenomenon, the version of loyalty oaths imposed in the South was distinctly abhorrent to her. During the years that she campaigned against these in her various union roles, the Georgia Constitution mandated segregated schools and the oath specifically required teachers to sign that they would support the state's constitution, which meant supporting segregation in education (Murphy, 1990, pp. 98–124).

The AFT leadership during this period was outspoken in its defense of academic freedom, not only teachers' freedom of speech but their freedom to associate with other like-minded citizens. They allied with the American Civil Liberties Union to fight for these rights. Teachers were castigated for not supporting the war, not buying war bonds, and for not signing loyalty oaths. The NEA, by contrast, was closely associated with the American Legion, an instigator of the loyalty oath requirements, and were situated on the opposite side of this issue. The NEA gained membership during this time, while the "radical" AFT's membership dwindled. Conservative and radical factions within AFT caused the issue of academic freedom to be among the most explosive. The seeds of dissension over academic freedom issues were sown during this period and proved to be remarkably resilient through the coming decades. The AFT also struggled with their sometime ally, the American Federation of Labor. Led by Samuel Gompers in this time period, the AFL was unenthusiastic about its teacher members and, fearing the "red menace," withdrew organizing support from the AFT just when the organization was at its neediest. Nonetheless, the AFT survived and even rebounded under the leadership of Mary Barker in the 1920s. Murphy noted that struggles with the AFL, conservative/radical bickering, and the generational split that widened between younger teachers and their older colleagues hampered the union's growth (Murphy, 1990; Webb, 2016).

As the 1920s ended and the stock market crash catapulted the nation into the Great Depression, school funding became the subject of much criticism. Teachers were said to be too well paid and schools too lavish and the curriculum irrelevant, while the reality was that pay cuts were endemic, some teachers were paid in scrip, cheaper unqualified teachers were hired for classrooms, and budgets were severely cut while class sizes rose. The American Legion and other right-wing organizations, assisted by the Hearst newspapers coverage, continued to insist that teachers be required to take loyalty oaths. Loyalty oaths were particularly aimed at AFT members, targeting progressive teachers who criticized the American economic system (Murphy, 1990, pp. 131–7).

Parallels between the 1920s and 2020s with respect to teacher unions are evident. And, similar forces constricted teachers' academic freedom while consequences for pushing at those boundaries persisted. One great echo is that of the politicization of schools. Recent curbs on curriculum and expression in the classroom to remove "divisive concepts" in the name of ridding the schools of politics have only revealed more blatantly the explicitly political agenda being enacted. Then as now, certain voices have had more influence and control and then as now teachers must be organized and strategic in combating forces that would take away their academic freedom. During both eras opponents of the over commercialization in schools and white supremacist curricular materials were labeled "socialist" and are, when possible, squeezed out of teaching. Thus, it matters when individual educators band together and push back against these forces. Perhaps Mary Barker and the APSTA may serve as a guide in how to persevere in polarized times.

Pedagogical Strategies

The lesson plan addresses three objectives aligned with the historical content knowledge established with this chapter. Students will be able to identify reasons why teachers chose to affiliate with organized labor in the 1920s. Students will be able to identify and critically evaluate various arguments used in support of teacher unions voiced by Mary Barker and John Dewey, in order to make and support claims about which arguments were the most effective. Students will be able to identify some of Mary Barker's leadership qualities and which of her beliefs may have challenged her colleagues within her local and her national union. These objectives are achieved through teacher-directed student engagement with the materials, and student-centered process (see Appendix).

Archival Resources

AFT 1941 Convention Transcript, American Federation of Teachers Historical Collection, Walter F. Reuther Library, Wayne State University. http://projects.lib.wayne.edu/aft/ Series XIII, Box 15, folders 9–11 and Box 16, folders 1–3.

American Federation of Teachers Collection, Walter P. Reuther Library Archives of Labor and Urban Affairs, Wayne State University Archives.

Atlanta Public School Teachers Association Records and Atlanta Education Association Records, 1905–1971, Southern Labor Archive, Georgia State University Special Collections and Archives.

Barker, M. C. papers, 1902–1971, Stuart A. Rose Manuscript, Archives, and Rare Book Library, Emory University.

Box 3, Folder 9—"Miss Mary Barker's History of the Atlanta Public School Teacher's Association, Local 89, written 1950."

"The Riordan Case Statement Prepared by Mary C. Barker, Chairman Special Committee," Barker Papers, Box 3, folder 10 "Atlanta Public School Teachers" Association Records, 1920-1921."

Mary Barker, President's Address to the Thirteenth Convention of the American Federation of Teachers, July 1–6, 1929, Box 1, Folder 7.

Civil liberties Issues and Cases, 1929–1943 (including material on cases of Angelo Herndon, Scottsboro Boys), Box 8, Folder 2.

Southern Summer School for Women Workers In Industry, Boxes 5-6. Mary Cornelia Barker papers, Stuart A. Rose Manuscript, Archives, and Rare Book Library, Emory University.

The American Teacher (American Federation of Teachers), 1930–1952, Box: 16, April 1941 issue. Southern Labor Archives periodicals collection, L-Periodicals. Special Collections, Georgia State University Library.

References

Blount, J.M. (2002) "Ella Flagg Young and the Chicago Schools," in *Founding Mothers and Others: Women Educational Leaders during the Progressive Era*, Eds. Sadovnik, A. and Semel, S. Palgrave.

Cain, T. R. (2009). "The NEA's Early Conflict Over Educational Freedom," *American Educational History Journal*, Vol 36, no. 2, p. 361–75.

Carter, P. A. (2002). *Everybody's Paid But the Teacher: The Teaching Profession and the Women's Movement.* Teachers College Press.

Dewey, J. (1928) "Why I Am a Member of the Teachers Union," *American Teacher*, January, p. 3–6.

Dubofsky, M., & McCartin, J. A. (2017). *Labor in America: A History, 9th edition*, Wiley Blackwell.

Du Bois, W. E. B. (1903). *The Souls of Black Folk.* New American Library.

"Georgia Teachers Win a Point," *The Christian Century*, April 14, 1954.

Guerry, A. (1937). "Teachers' Loyalty Oaths," *Bulletin of the American Association of University Professors (1915–1955)*, Vol. 23, No. 3: 229–33. https://www.jstor.org/stable/40219854

Hatfield, E. "Angelo Herndon Case." New Georgia Encyclopedia, last modified Aug 3, 2020. https://www.georgiaencyclopedia.org/articles/history-archaeology/angelo-herndon-case/

Howlett, C. F. and Howlett, P. (2019) "Undemocratic, Barbaric, and Scholastically Wholly Unwise:" Conscientious Educators Under Fire From the Great War Through the Present," *Peace and Change*, Vol. 44, No. 2, 169–206.

Howlett, P. and Howlett, C. F. (2008) "A Silent Witness for Peace: The Case of Schoolteacher Mary Stone McDowell and America at War," *History of Education Quarterly* 40: 3, History of Education Society, p. 371–96. https://doi.org/10.1111/j.1748-5959.2008.00156

Kessler-Harris, A. (1982) *Out to Work: A History of Wage-Earning Women in the United States.* Oxford University Press.

Kessler-Harris, A. (1990) *A Woman's Wage: Historical Meanings and Social Consequences.* The University Press of Kentucky.

Lusk Committee webpage—https://www.archives.nysed.gov/sites/archives/files/res_topics_bus_lusk.pdf

Montgomery, D. (1987) *The Fall of the House of Labor: The Workplace, the State, and American Labor Unionism, 1865-1925*, Oxford University Press, p. 7.

Murphy, M. (1990) *Blackboard Unions: The AFT and the NEA, 1900–1980.* Cornell University Press.

Newman, J. W. (1978) *A History of the Atlanta Public School Teachers Association, Local 89 of the American Federation of Teachers, 1919-1956*. Georgia State University ProQuest Doctoral Dissertation, 1978, 7900116.

Rousmaniere, K. (2002) *Citizen Teacher: The Life and Leadership of Margaret Haley.* State University of New York Press.

Urban, W. (1982) *Why Teachers Organized*. Wayne State University Press.

Webb, R. K. (2016) *Red, White, and Black: The Meaning of Loyalty in Georgia Education*. [Ph.D. diss., Georgia State University]. https://doi.org/10.57709/8575442.

Appendix A: Lesson Plan

1. Lesson Plan Title: "Labor During the Roaring 1920s": Mary Barker, The American Federation of Teachers, and Local #89"
2. Theme: Although American unions generally weakened during the decade of the 1920s, teacher unions in several locations flourished and chose to affiliate with the American Federation of Teachers at this time. One of those areas of union growth was in Atlanta, where the Atlanta Public School Teachers Association affiliated with the AFT in 1919. For the next several decades, led by able leaders such as Mary Barker, teachers in Atlanta were able to make gains in obtaining benefits and job security they had long desired.
3. Grade Level: Grades 9–12
4. Course: U.S. History, American Labor History
5. Time Required: 1–2 class periods
6. Essential and Supporting Questions:
    a. Who is an educational reformer? Why did some teachers organize during the early twentieth century?
    b. Why did teachers in Atlanta choose to affiliate with organized labor?
    c. What were some gains and challenges for teacher unions in the 1920s?
7. Objectives:
    a. Students will be able to identify reasons why teachers chose to affiliate with organized labor in the 1920s.
    b. Students will be able to identify and critically evaluate various arguments used in support of teacher unions voiced by Mary Barker and John Dewey, in order to make and support claims about which arguments were the most effective.
    c. Students will be able to identify some of Mary Barker's leadership qualities and which of her beliefs may have challenged her colleagues within her local and her national union.
8. Standards (from the National Council for the Social Studies [NCSS]):
    a. **D2.His.9-12** Evaluate how historical events and developments were shaped by unique circumstances of time and place as well as broader historical contexts.
    b. **D2.His.9-12** Analyze how historical contexts shaped and continue to shape people's perspectives.
9. Classroom Materials: excerpt of three primary sources (see the following plan)
10. Instructional Plan:
    a. Entry Task to Establish Context (5 min)—read through and discuss the three objectives for the lesson to set a purpose for reading and discussion of the lesson text.

b. Teacher-Directed Instruction (15–20 min)—Assign students to read or listen to the chapter text independently or in pairs or small groups, depending on needs of students. Remind them to take bullet point notes on the readings that are relevant to the lesson objectives.
c. Student-Centered/Engaged Learning (30 or more minutes, depending on schedule; this may require additional class meetings)—Divide the class into four large groups (call these 1, 2, 3, and 4 corresponding to the source analyzed), and assign each group one of the primary sources to analyze. Primary Sources are located at the end of this lesson plan. Each group can use the primary source analysis tool they are familiar with, including the National Archives document analysis guide, or the Library of Congress document analysis guide, or the Say-Mean-Matter strategy. The last strategy involves students jotting down their thoughts about a piece of written text in a 3 column format. Column 1 is *Say*—what does the text actually say. This is the place to analyze words, look up unfamiliar concepts, and try to paraphrase what the author is saying. Column 2 is *Mean*—what does the text actually mean. This is the explanation that goes beyond the literal text to include inferences, questions, and reflections on the text. Column 3 is *Matter*—why does the text matter? What is the big So What, the significance, the Aha or implications behind the text? The second step of this Jigsaw strategy takes place after each group member becomes "expert" on the source assigned to them. Now reorganize students into new groups of four, with each group consisting of one member from each of the original groups. The "expert" teaches the other three members of their group what they learned from the primary source and how that helped address the student objectives. Experts share until all four sources have been discussed.
d. Exit Task for Summarizing Answer(s) to Essential and Supporting Questions—After completing the group primary source analysis activity, assign an exit ticket that has students respond to the essential and supporting questions. Use student responses to formatively assess and adjust future instruction.

11. Assessment: See exit task earlier.
12. Community Engagement: One way to extend this lesson into the community might be to ask students to survey members of their families or communities about the role of unions and why unions were formed in the United States. Having students report back on their survey results could provide material for further discussion and analysis.

Note: NCSS National Curriculum Standards: https://www.socialstudies.org/standards/national-curriculum-standards-social-studies-introduction

Primary Source 1: a photograph with an essay by Mary Barker, written in 1930 (Mary Cornelia Barker papers, Stuart A. Rose Manuscript, Archives, and Rare Book Library, Emory University, Box 2, folder 3)

The Public-School Teacher Awakes

By MISS MARY C. BARKER
President The American Federation of Teachers

PRIOR to April, 1916, there were about a dozen local unions of teachers scattered over the country. These groups were affiliated, each and severally, to the American Federation of Labor. Being chartered directly and individually by the A. F. of L., they had no relation to each other.

Without knowledge in many cases as to what causes brought about these unions of teachers in scattered localities it is safe to say that in every case the Union was the manifestation of a desire to improve the status of the teacher and the status of teaching in that community; for in all too many communities and for all too long a time teachers in public schools had been looked upon as respectable but impotent persons of migratory tendency who ever and anon sought the bounty of charitably inclined school trustees, offering to "teach school," and expecting to receive in return such remuneration as obviously, to the trustee, was sufficient to enable such persons to eat food and wear clothes in keeping with the status of such persons in the community.

This low estate of the teachers, we must recognize, should not be charged up wholly to the community exclusive of the teachers. These people who were called teachers, or who undertook to teach, and who in many cases did teach, some remarkably well, were just as much to blame for their unseemly status as were all other people of the community. If

A "Radical"?

MISS MARY C. BARKER
Atlanta, Georgia

eration; to obtain for them all the rights to which they are entitled; to raise the standard of the teaching profession by se-

servient silence in school and educational affairs, from his (her) traditional position of fear and cowering docility in relations with school administrations, the American Federation of Teachers planned to organize classroom teachers outside of administration influence. This was getting at the root of the matter, therefore radical! Happily so.

The spirit of those who organized the American Federation of Teachers fifteen years ago, their social vision, and their conception of their responsibility in education was well set forth in the preamble to the Constitution:

"We believe in democracy, and in the schools as the chief agency of democracy.

"We believe that the schools have failed of their fullest attainment because of undemocratic administration, adherence to tradition, and lack of responsiveness to the needs of the community; and that the teachers must find the remedy, if it is to be found.

"We believe that servility breeds servility, and that if the schools are to produce free, unafraid men and women American citizens of the highest type, the teachers must live and work in an atmosphere of freedom and self-respect.

"We believe that the teacher is one of the most highly productive of workers and that the best interests of the schools and of the people demand an intimate contact and an effective co-operation between the teachers and the other work

Excerpts from essay:

"There were bad conditions in the schools, in the school system. These had grown up because of bad practices, and the only way to correct the conditions was to work on the bad practices, the roots out of which the conditions had grown.

To get the classroom teacher away from his (her) traditional habit of subservient silence in school and educational affairs, from his (her) traditional position of fear and cowering docility in relations with school administrations, the American Federation of Teachers planned to organize classroom teachers outside of administration influence. This was getting at the root of the matter, therefore radical! Happily so."

She continued, quoting from the preamble of the AFT Constitution:

"We believe in democracy, and in the schools as the chief agency of democracy.

"We believe that the schools have failed of their fullest attainment because of undemocratic administration, adherence to tradition, and lack of responsive. ness to the needs of the community; and that the teachers must find the remedy, if it is to be found.

> "We believe that servility breeds servility, and that if the schools are to produce free, unafraid men and women, American citizens of the highest type, the teachers must live and work in an atmosphere of freedom and self-respect.
>
> "We believe that the teacher is one of the most highly productive of workers, and that the best interests of the schools and of the people demand an intimate contact and an effective co-operation between the teachers and the other workers of the community--upon whom the future of democracy must depend."

Primary Source 2—excerpts from an essay by John Dewey, "Why I am a Member of the Teachers Union," delivered at a Membership Meeting of the Teachers Union of the City of New York, November 18, 1927. Originally published in *American Teacher* 12 (1928): 3–6.

> Now, as to why I am a member of the Teachers Union, the query that comes naturally to mind is why should I not be? … I have found that the spirit of courage, of straightforwardness, of energy, of practical idealism, a sense of justice for all who are in any way wronged or in danger of being wronged … is the animating spirit of the Union … there is need for a working, aggressive organization that represents all of the interests that teachers have in common, and which, in representing them, represents also the protection of the children, and the youth in the schools against all of the outside interests, economic and political and others that would exploit the schools for their own ends, and in doing so, reduce the teaching body to a condition of intellectual vassalage.
>
> It is said that the Teachers Union as distinct from the more academic organizations over-emphasizes the economic aspect of teaching. Well, I never had that contempt for the economic aspect of teaching, especially not on the first of the month when I get my salary check… I find that the respect in which they individually and collectively are held in the community is closely associated with the degree of economic independence which they enjoy.

Primary Source 3—Excerpts from Mary Barker, "President's address to the Thirteenth Convention of the American Federation of Teachers. July 1–6, 1929" p. 1. Mary Cornelia Barker papers, Stuart A. Rose Manuscript, Archives, and Rare Book Library, Emory University, Box 1, folder 7.

> In the first place the program of the American Federation of Teachers is a teacher's program and it has to do with the spirit of education. We lay a most particular emphasis upon the conditions under which teachers and pupils work, and upon the objectives in the processes and practices of education as a social function. We recognize the fact that the fact that the two principals to the process of education, the teacher and the pupil, have not had a square deal as it were. We believe that it is the business of teachers to

exert themselves to promote the development of just and favorable conditions under which to carry on the mutual activities of pupils and teachers. It follows that we believe the teachers of America should organize to accomplish this purpose. Hence our major and immediate concern is to organize the teachers in local communities to work for desirable local conditions and to cooperate thru [sic] the national organization for the development of desirable conditions everywhere.

From the foregoing viewpoint, the American Federation of Teachers is demanding the necessary freedom for teachers and pupils to develop those qualities of citizenship that are most desirable in a democracy. …

We are insisting upon housing conditions that are physically safe and that may be expected to produce socially sound reactions in the young people who inhabit our school buildings. We are opposing the practice of overcrowded classes, overworked teachers and factory standards of production for the school. We are insisting upon just compensation for teachers and upon opportunity for every child to receive adequate educational advantages. We are placing emphasis upon social values in education.

Primary Source 4—Excerpts from Bessie S. Stafford, "Educational Ideas and Ideals are Discussed by Miss Barker," *The Atlanta Constitution*, August 8, 1926.

"The changes that educational ideas and ideals are undergoing only serve to emphasize anew the importance of the child's teacher in the scheme of things," says Miss Mary Barker, of Atlanta, the first southerner to be elected president of the American Federation of Teachers, and who was reelected for a second term at the annual convention in New York last month.

"Out of the schools must come in increasingly larger measure the stock ideas of the future citizens, for the changing conditions of life are forcing the child into other hands than his parents' for training and orientation in the world about him."

"The schools, too," continued Miss Barker, "must furnish to a greater extent the social experiences in which children are to acquire fitness for responsible citizenship; for the increasing complexities of living are depriving the home of adequate opportunity for directing such activities. In short, the teaching profession must be prepared to assume responsibility for the training of the citizen who is to make or unmake the civilization of tomorrow. In this development the importance of the personality and equipment of the teacher grows apace."

"If we are to prepare youth for a social environment in which we expect him to succeed we need to have a first-hand knowledge of that environment ourselves. Unless we have such knowledge of the community life, its industries, its government, its social activities, its educational outlook, its history, its people, unless we know what it means to participate in that life, we shall not be able to get over to pupils that which they most need to appreciate," she concluded.

CHECK ONE and return completed worksheet to your acquiring editor. We must have this on file before your book can be released to the printer.

__X__ I certify that no permissions are necessary.

_____ I certify that I have sought and secured all permissions needed for the worldwide distribution of my publication in print and e-book format.

Author/Editor: JoAnn Wood & Chara Haeussler Bohan. **Date:** 9-29-24

Title: Labor During the "Roaring 1920s": Mary Barker, the American Federation of Teachers, and Atlanta Local #89

PERMISSION TRACK LIST

You can use this checklist to help you keep track of permissions required for your text. You can alter this table in whatever way works best for you.

Material for which permission is needed	Institution/ Person Permission Requested from	Date of Request			Rights Received *(follow-up on any partial rights as the permission is otherwise not complete)*			Credit Line	Fee/ Date paid	No. of Gratis Copies Requested
		First	Second	Third	Print	E-book	Territory Covered			
photograph with an essay by Mary Barker, written in 1930 (Mary Cornelia Barker papers, Stuart A. Rose Manuscript, Archives, and Rare Book Library, Emory University, Box 2, folder 3).	NA, document is more than 70 years old and no one holds copyright on these archives							Mary Cornelia Barker papers, Stuart A. Rose Manuscript, Archives, and Rare Book Library, Emory University, Box 2, folder 3	NA	
excerpts from an essay by John Dewey, “Why I am a Member of the Teachers Union,” delivered at a Membership Meeting of the Teachers Union of the City of New York, November 18, 1927. Originally published in *American Teacher* 12 (1928): 3–6.	NA, document is more than 70 years old							*American Teacher* 12 (1928): 3–6	NA	

Material for which permission is needed	Institution/ Person Permission Requested from	Date of Request			Rights Received *(follow-up on any partial rights as the permission is otherwise not complete)*			Credit Line	Fee/ Date paid	No. of Gratis Copies Requested
		First	**Second**	**Third**	**Print**	**E-book**	**Territory Covered**			
Excerpts from Mary Barker, "President's address to the Thirteenth Convention of the American Federation of Teachers. July 1–6, 1929" p. 1. Mary Cornelia Barker papers, Stuart A. Rose Manuscript, Archives, and Rare Book Library, Emory University, Box 1, folder 7.	NA, document is more than 70 years old and no one holds copyright on these archives							Mary Cornelia Barker papers, Stuart A. Rose Manuscript, Archives, and Rare Book Library, Emory University, Box 1, folder 7.	NA	
Excerpts from Bessie S. Stafford, "Educational Ideas and Ideals are Discussed by Miss Barker," *The Atlanta Constitution*, August 8, 1926.	NA, document is more than 70 years old							Excerpts from Bessie S. Stafford, "Educational Ideas and Ideals are Discussed by Miss Barker," *The Atlanta Constitution*, August 8, 1926.	NA	

The Women's Bureau: Advancing Women's Labor Rights in the 1920s

Adam I. Attwood

Introduction

This chapter focuses on the advancement of women in the U.S. workforce during the 1920s. This period is crucial as it marks the establishment of the federal office in 1917 that would be known as the Women's Bureau in 1920 onward. Originally founded in 1917 as the Women in Industry Service, the office was renamed the Women's Bureau in 1920 and played a pivotal role in promoting women's economic advancement throughout the 1920s. The chapter concludes in 1930, coinciding with the onset of the Great Depression, which marked a significant turning point in the Bureau's influence, as evaluated by Mastracci (2004), who assessed its role after 1930 but not during its formative decade. There remains a gap in the scholarly literature regarding the Bureau's early history and its impact on policy changes related to women's labor rights. This chapter offers an original historical analysis, drawing on both primary and secondary sources, to address this gap. The aim is to identify the Women's Bureau's contributions to labor policies affecting American women, including immigrant women, from 1917 to 1930, enriching the understanding of shifts in labor policy toward women from both social and economic perspectives.

Historical Background

The Women's Bureau, established in 1920 within the U.S. Department of Labor, played a critical role in addressing the challenges faced by women workers in the early twentieth century. Its founding was the culmination of efforts to advocate for women's rights in the workforce, which had gained momentum during World War I as more women entered industries traditionally dominated by men. The Bureau's mandate was to promote the welfare of wage-earning women, improve their working conditions, and increase their efficiency. It was the first federal agency dedicated to the needs of working women, marking an important step toward institutional support for women's labor rights.

Throughout the 1920s, the Women's Bureau focused on researching and documenting the conditions of women in various industries, producing reports that shed light on issues such as long working hours, low wages, and unsafe working environments. Its work was instrumental in advocating for protective labor legislation, particularly for women in factories and other hazardous occupations. The Bureau's efforts contributed to reforms like minimum wage laws and regulations limiting the number of hours women could work in certain industries, helping to elevate women's labor issues in public and governmental discourse.

By 1930, the Women's Bureau had established itself as a key player in the broader labor movement, advocating not only for improved working conditions but also for equal treatment of women in the workforce. It collaborated with labor unions, women's organizations, and reformers to push for policies that would benefit both women workers and their families. Although it operated within the framework of protective legislation that often assumed women's physical limitations, the Bureau's work laid the groundwork for future advancements in women's labor rights and equality, making it a crucial institution in the history of labor reform in the United States.

In 1918, Josephine Schain observed that "a tremendous obligation rests upon the coming generation of women, those who inherit these new opportunities" (p. 120). Just two years later, those opportunities culminated in one of the most significant victories for women's rights in American history: the ratification of the Nineteenth Amendment. This momentous event, which occurred on August 18, 1920, granted women the right to vote nationwide (Ayers et al., 2012). However, another pivotal victory for women occurred just a few months earlier on June 5, 1920, with the passing of House Resolution 13229, officially establishing the Women's Bureau within the Department of Labor (U.S. House of Representatives, 1920). This was a critical milestone in the evolution of the women's rights movement, signaling the beginning of an institutional framework for addressing women's labor issues throughout the 1920s.

The foundation of the Women's Bureau had its roots in 1917, when Congress authorized the formation of the Women in Industry Service in response to "the present emergency" created by the labor shortages during World War I (Weber, 1923, p. 1). This unit, which became operational in 1918, was transformed into the Women's Bureau in June 1920, granting it full bureau status within the Department of Labor. Women had stepped in to fill the labor gaps left by men fighting in the war, setting the precedent for the establishment of the Bureau. Advocacy from women's organizations helped solidify this achievement, as they successfully lobbied Congress to make the Bureau permanent (Weber, 1923). Congressman P. P. Campbell endorsed House Resolution 13229, asserting that it was both "wise" and "humane" for women to oversee their own working conditions (Women's Bureau, n.d.; Weber, 1923, p. 1).

The early contributions of the Women's Bureau were especially impactful regarding its work from 1920 to 1930 on highlighting and advocating on issues of immigrant and native-born women's labor. One such perspective is found in the writings of Italian immigrant George La Piana, who examined the challenges faced by immigrant women entering the American workforce in comparison to their native-born counterparts. While most scholarship has focused on the Bureau's activities after World War II (see Mastracci, 2004), this analysis emphasizes the Bureau's foundational years, during which its annual reports centered on "wage-earning women" and European immigrants amid the broader movement of "Americanization." The Bureau's studies from the 1920s reveal a focus on upward mobility and increasing opportunities for women, analyzing both the bureaucratic and personal dimensions of immigrant women's labor integration (U.S. Department of Labor, 1930; U.S. Department of Labor, 1921, p. 3; Manning, 1930; Gullett, 1995; Olneck, 1989; La Piana, n.d., 1916a, 1916b).

Women's Labor Rights and the Women's Bureau

La Piana, as a Roman Catholic priest and a member of the Harvard faculty, played a role in documenting immigrant women's experiences between the late 1910s and 1930. His perspective on immigration aligns with the concept of "Americanization," a term that can be traced to at least 1930 in the context of women's immigration, as highlighted in Caroline Manning's (1930) annual report for the Women's Bureau. Both La Piana's letters and the reports from the Women's Bureau suggest that the issues of Americanization and economic advancement were closely linked, not so much in direct comparison but rather as parallel developments from personal and bureaucratic viewpoints.

La Piana, originally from Piana degli Albanesi in the Palermo Province of Sicily, emigrated to the United States in 1913, and by 1915, he had joined the faculty at Harvard Divinity School. He made Boston his home, gaining civic prominence through social work, particularly in the city's North End, where he became an officer of the Family Service League. By 1932, La Piana had reached the pinnacle of his career, becoming the John H. Morison Professor of Church History. His writings reflected both his personal and professional experience with immigrant life, particularly the aspirations of immigrant Catholics. As immigrants from western and central Europe, many were Catholic or familiar with Catholic practices, blending old traditions with inevitable changes as they interacted with native-born Americans and other immigrant groups (La Piana, n.d., 1916a, 1916b, "George La Piana, 1978–1972").

Prior to the ratification of the Nineteenth Amendment and the creation of the Women's Bureau as a model for women's government programs, there was significant debate over the direction of the women's movement and immigrant integration. The Daughters of the American Revolution advocated for the "immediate acculturation" of immigrants through "Americaniz[ation]" that was marked by "'an imperious … conformity'" (Gullett, 1995, p. 77). In contrast, more progressive voices like Jane Addams (1923) and Josephine Schain (1918) emphasized a broader vision of equality. This debate unfolded against the backdrop of the "Red Scare of 1919–20," which intensified the political climate (Dumenil, 1998, p. 82). Addams described exploitative working conditions for young girls, which led to poor pay and brutal environments, views that found resonance in the advocacy efforts of the Women's Bureau under Mary Anderson's leadership. Schain's (1918) position ultimately prevailed, as both men and women increasingly embraced gender equality as crucial for social and economic progress.

The ratification of the 19th Amendment in 1920 came down to a dramatic tie-breaking vote. Harry Burn, a 26-year-old junior senator from Tennessee, cast the decisive vote in favor of women's suffrage after receiving a compelling letter from his mother, Febb King Ensminger Burn, who urged him to "vote for suffrage!" (Burn, 1920, as quoted in Grunwald and Adler, 2005). While the 19th Amendment is often celebrated as the defining victory for women's rights in the early twentieth century, the creation of the Women's Bureau in 1918 was another pivotal, though largely forgotten, achievement of the women's movement. Initially established as a temporary "war agency" under the Department of Labor with the name "Women in Industry Service," the Bureau was charged with "developing standards and policies to ensure the effective employment of women while conserving their health and welfare" (Weber, 1923, pp. 1–2). It was renamed the Women's Bureau following the passage of H. R. 13229 on June 5, 1920.

The Bureau's mandate was expanded to include "formulat[ing] standards and policies which shall promote the welfare of wage-earning women, improve their working conditions, increase their efficiency, and advance their opportunities for profitable employment" (U.S. Department of Labor, Women's Bureau, 1920). Key phrases like "increase their efficiency" and "profitable" likely appealed to the U.S. Department of Labor, reflecting a shift toward viewing women's participation in the labor force through an economic lens. This marked a significant moment in history when feminism began to influence government policy directly. Unlike factionalized women's clubs of the time, the Women's Bureau operated as a unified, hierarchical entity, shaping labor policies at a national level (see Gullett, 1995; Haarsager, 1997; Mastracci, 2004).

The Bureau was particularly focused on how economic empowerment could drive gender equality, advocating that "authentic data on women workers" was essential for progress. Women's increasing entry into the workforce during the

1920s significantly contributed to national growth (U.S. Department of Labor, Women's Bureau, 1930, p. 6). Under the leadership of Mary van Kleeck, initially appointed director of the Women in Industry Service, and Mary Anderson, who succeeded her as director of the permanent Women's Bureau, the organization took a proactive stance in shaping labor standards for women. By 1931, the Bureau had a staff of 50, all but the director having passed the Civil Service Examination. Among its most significant achievements was the establishment of formal standards governing women's employment, an effort lauded as the Bureau's crowning contribution to labor reform (U.S. Department of Labor, Women's Bureau, 1930, pp. 2, 4). Anderson, retained by President Warren Harding, guided the Bureau into a permanent fixture in U.S. labor policy (U.S. Department of Labor, Women's Bureau, "Fact Finding," 1930).

While the professional sector represented the most prestigious gain in women's employment during the early twentieth century, significant numbers of women also entered the industrial workforce. The largest concentrations of female employment were in manufacturing, particularly in the automobile and electrical supply industries. By the mid-1920s, over half of the women employed were working in the industrial sector (see Dempsey, 1922; U.S. Department of Labor, Bureau of Labor Statistics, 1927). In 1927, the Women's Bureau conducted a case study using Ohio's manufacturing employment records from 1914 to 1924. Ohio, which held the third-largest employment figure in the manufacturing industry nationwide, provided key insights into women's industrial labor (see U.S. Department of Labor, Women's Bureau, 1927). The study revealed that "women fared better, proportionally, than did men between 1919 and 1924," particularly during the economic downturns of 1920–1921 and 1924. Unlike men, who faced higher rates of job loss, women maintained their employment at a higher rate. In fact, by 1924, women constituted 16.8 percent of all wage earners, up from 15.8 percent in 1919. This marked a significant shift in the workforce, with one manufacturer commenting in 1921 that factory and milling work had become "'as much a woman's job as a man's'" (van Kleeck, 1921, p. 3).

Mary van Kleeck, who served as the "head of the department of industrial studies of the Russell Sage Foundation," played a prominent role in advocating for women in industrial labor. Mary Anderson, whose career began as a labor leader in Chicago, also made significant contributions. Before her appointment as assistant director of Women in Industry Service, Anderson was a leader of the Boot and Shoe Workers' Union, Local 94, and served on the Executive Board of the Women's Trade Union League of Chicago. In 1910, she supported a strike organized by the United Garment Workers of America (Walkowitz, 1990; Women's Trade Union League of Chicago, 1910).

Anderson (1926) also authorized several Women's Bureau reports on various industries, including agriculture. One such report, prefaced by a "Letter of Transmittal" in Autumn 1923, focused on a "survey of women employed in seasonal industries in the State of Washington" (Anderson, 1926, p. ix). This case study explored the conditions faced by women in agro-industrial labor. Anderson's letter officially sanctioned the report, which highlighted "problems" related to the treatment of agricultural female workers, particularly in relation to their work hours and overall welfare. The Bureau emphasized the importance of accommodating personal and family responsibilities within work schedules, without penalizing women by threatening their employment—a stance that aligned with its broader efforts to improve working conditions for women (U.S. Department of Labor, Women's Bureau, 1925).

Historical Implications for Labor Rights

The Civil Service Examination

The question of women's eligibility for the Civil Service Examination was of particular significance in advancing their access to federal employment. According to Mastracci (2004), Mary van Kleeck did not advocate for Women in Industry Service to function as an enforcement agency. However, Mary Anderson (1926) embraced a more enforcement-oriented approach. Anderson recognized that systemic discrimination against women in the Civil Service Examination process was a barrier keeping many from entering federal bureaucratic roles. This issue marked the first instance where Anderson redirected the Women's Bureau toward an enforcement strategy. Conservative factions within the government had frequently barred women from taking the examination, but the Women's Bureau argued that the few women allowed to take it had consistently performed well (see U.S. Department of Labor, Women's Bureau, 1920).

Anderson highlighted the importance of the Civil Service Examination in her "Letter of Transmittal," which introduced the Bureau's report *Women in the Government Service*. Through this report, Anderson exercised the Bureau's mandate for policy-making (see Nienburg, 1920; Anderson, 1926), prioritizing legislative efforts to open the Civil Service Examination to all qualified women. She viewed this as critical for amplifying women's voices on broader employment policies that affected them.

The Women's Bureau formally presented its case in the *Women in the Government Service* report, submitted on November 5, 1919, to the Civil Service Commission. Remarkably, only "10 days after receiving the report, the Civil Service Commission passed a ruling opening all examinations to both women and men" (Nienburg,

1920, p. 7). This early policy victory was a landmark achievement for the newly established Women's Bureau and a significant political milestone for women in government. Anderson's decision to pursue a more aggressive stance than her predecessor was soon validated when the federal government was declared to be "the greatest employer of women in the country" (U.S. Department of Labor, Women's Bureau, 1920, pp. 3–4). Women not only proved they were qualified to take the examination but also demonstrated their capacity to perform as well as men. This policy success substantially increased women's representation in federal employment, particularly in the professional career category.

The Labor Leadership of the Women's Bureau

The prestige of the Women's Bureau had increased substantially as it gained power. The U.S. Department of Labor appropriated $40,000 to the Women's Bureau for its first year of operation. The next year, director Mary Anderson and staff secured a near doubling of its annual appropriation to $75,000 (U.S. Department of Labor, Women's Bureau, 1921). This was a prodigious increase in funding for such a young bureau, especially when considering that there was a national recession during 1920 and 1921 (U.S. Department of Labor, Women's Bureau, 1929). The U.S. Department of Labor was impressed by the fiscal situation. By 1925 it was written "that the volume of work the [B]ureau is called upon to perform increases with each year of its existence" (U.S. Department of Labor, Women's Bureau, 1925, p. 1). Evidently the Department tended to agree early in the Bureau's history when considering its fiscal appropriations.

Under Anderson's leadership, the Women's Bureau was secure in probing the federal labor laws and pushing Congress toward policy reform to promote women's employment (U.S. Department of Labor, Women's Bureau, 1924). The conclusion of the Bureau's investigations in 1927 was upbeat. It had been of "genuine assistance" in getting standards agreed upon within the federal government to have female workers placed under labor contracts that could improve their efficiency. These contracts included the Bureau's recommended standards on hours, wages, and working conditions (U.S. Department of Labor, Women's Bureau, 1927, p. 4). This labor law review process began during the war years and continued during the 1920s to include an eight- or nine-hour workday, standard mealtimes, and sanitary working conditions with safety equipment readily available. State industrial commissions also agreed to establish health protection protocols for women doing night work.

Most economically notable was the provision that wages were to be "based on occupation and not on sex nor race" (U.S. Department of Labor, Women's Bureau, 1927, p. 4). In August 1918, the Women's Bureau (then known as Women in Industry Service), succeeded in getting state industrial commissions to agree to women's health protection controls during night work. Summarizing the Bureau's first five years of accomplishments, Weber (1923) noted that he saw the significance of the history of the Bureau as an agency that "cooperated" at the federal, state, and local levels to influence policies and legislation that favored better labor standards for women's job protection. The maintenance of local employment flexibility and the use of statistical analysis to suggest a funneling of female workers to districts that were facing labor shortages augmented the Bureau's substantial analyses.

According to Smith (1925) and Dempsey (1922), both employees of the Women's Bureau, women's employment increased with the help of the Women's Bureau. They claimed that women comprised 21.2 percent of the U.S. workforce in 1920. Although women had been employed in industrial labor jobs, there was a shift of gainfully employed women into professional careers. Of all Americans gainfully employed in 1880, 14.7 percent were women. By 1920 that percentage had risen to 21.1 percent. 43.3 percent of "professional" jobs—as defined by the Women's Bureau—were held by women in 1920. She first noted that the original census data showed a total of 1,693,361 Americans employed in "professional" jobs. Of that number women comprised 43.3 percent. Florence Patteson Smith (1925) arrived at even higher percentage by combining the original census data from the U.S. Bureau of the Census with her own analysis of the "public serv[ice]" positions that women held. Smith's (1925) combination of "extraction of minerals and public serv[ice] jobs" raises the total number of Americans employed in professional jobs to 2,143,889. Of this number, women accounted for 2,186,924, or 47.4 percent. By combing these data, she posited that women may even have comprised an astounding 47.4 percent of the total professional jobs in 1920 (Smith, 1925, p. 6). The largest gainful occupational category for women was the domestic services at 67.1 percent. There was a downturn of professional employment between 1910 and 1920 because of the occupational skewing that the First World War created. The economic depression after the war caused an overall drop of the proportion of women in gainful employment, but the recovery of the 1920s reversed the downward trend, preparing the labor market for an infusion of immigrant women who would work for lower wages for employers more accustomed to wage-earning women of any national origin (see Smith, 1925; Dempsey, 1922).

To be "gainfully occupied" was to be a "wage-earner," or better yet, a salaried employee. Gainful occupations suggested professionalism. In either case, maximum production value was key for employers. And women employees knew that advancement was possible. Mary Veronica Dempsey (1922) drew attention to the census data for proof of this: "every time a woman invaded an occupation hallowed for generations as a pursuit for men only, attention was called to the fact by the woman's coworkers and in some cases by the press" (p. 1). One manufacturer commented in 1921 that factory and milling work was "'as much a woman's job as a man's'" (quoted in van Kleeck, 1921, p. 3). An increase in the number of gainfully employed women necessitated a shift in some of the men's perspectives toward gainfully employed women. Dempsey (1922) noted that the media attention surrounding historically male-dominated occupations created the false impression that "vast numbers of women were taking up gainful employment for the first time" (p. 2). The census statistics, however, showed that "21.3 per cent of all women 16 years of age and over were employed in nonagricultural pursuits in 1920, as compared with 20.7 per cent similarly employed in 1910" (Dempsey, 1922, p. 2). Specific occupational percentages showed that there was a 13.6 percent decrease of women in "domestic and personal service," a 140.4 percent increase of women in "clerical occupations," and a 38.5 percent increase in women employed in "professional service" in 1920 relative to 1910. The study continued by noting that the number of gainful occupations that women were hired for showed little sign of decreasing (Dempsey, 1922, pp. 2–3, 28). Dempsey (1922) suggested that this was an indication that women's office occupations were at least remaining relatively constant with 1920 beginning with 8,549,511 women 10 years of age and over gainfully employed. A twofold change occurred during the Bureau's early years. First, women had indeed been gainfully employed for many years despite the popular misconception and, second, the Women's Bureau's research empowered it to draw upon the factual evidence about women's employment.

The increase in the number of women in professional service occupations showed an overall arc of increase from 1910 to 1930. Professional services included such positions as "bookkeepers and cashiers, teachers, [and] saleswomen" (Dempsey, 1922, p. 3). These jobs were the most prestigious because of the power and salary of this level of work as well as the financial self-sufficiency. They also generally required political connections and advanced education but hard work from entry level can lead to promotions (see Tables 1 and 2). Wages were out of balance, however. The largest employer of women throughout the 1920s for professional services was always the federal government. Mary Anderson was at the front of women's advancement in the government apparatus. As a bureaucrat, her contribution to the women's movement was "an important achievement both in the status of the [B]ureau and in the advancement of the position of women" (U.S. Department of Labor, Women's Bureau, 1931, pp. 3–4).

Women who were in the professional/managerial ranks advanced their pay rate toward that of men by 1925, largely in federal occupations—no small part of which was the Women's Bureau itself. Female representation in the professional careers increased to such an extent that by 1929 the demand for the Bureau's study of female professionals was high and so they were paid according to that market demand (U.S. Department of Labor, Women's Bureau, 1929). Anderson was paid a salary of $5,000 per year and she was also given an assistant who was paid $3,500 per year (see House Resolution 13229 as quoted in U.S. Department of Labor, Women's Bureau, 1922). These salaries placed Anderson and her assistant in the upper economic class. And this was being accomplished despite "the depression of 1920–1921" (U.S. Department of Labor, Women's Bureau, 1929, p. 13). This is another indication that the Women's Bureau had influence within the federal bureaucracy and especially President Warren Harding's administration.

Focusing Labor in New Ways

Examples of the Women's Bureau centering women who were immigrants are examined. George La Piana's papers are analyzed in conjunction with the Bureau's for a case study on the different views of a bureaucracy and an individual on the woman immigrant's employment in American society. The majority of his analysis centers on Italian immigrants, so this is a focal point in which specific mention of Italian and western European immigrants by the Women's Bureau will be compared for analysis.

President Harding addressed the first-ever Women's Industrial Conference in January of 1923 by declaring his personal convictions about gainfully employed women:

> Long before women were called to that broader participation in public affairs which is now both their duty and the public's advantage I was personally strongly convinced of the great benefits which would be derived from a more insistent expression and more general consideration of women's point of view in relation to social and industrial concerns. (Quoted in U.S. Department of Labor, Women's Bureau, 1923, pp. 2–3)

His precedent-setting support for feminist activity suggested that the Women's Bureau and women laborers had reached a new level of public support from the executive branch of the U.S. government. The Conference of 1926 was the second Bureau-sponsored conference of its kind in which the Bureau focused on "the investigation of foreign-born women in industry [which] was begun in December 1924" (U.S. Department of Labor, Women's Bureau, 1926, pp. 2, 10). Considering the influence gained from the success of the first Women's Industrial Conference in 1923, the one in 1926 continued the Bureau's influence beyond the technically narrow economic purpose of the U.S. Department of Labor and into the social aspects of economic change. Having established itself with years of economic analyses of gainfully employed women, the Bureau commented on the socioeconomic of immigrant women.

The *Tenth Annual Report of the Director of the Women's Bureau: Fiscal Year Ended June 30, 1928* unequivocally stated that immigrant women were "of interest and importance and in harmony with the purposes and duties of the Women's Bureau" (U.S. Department of Labor, Women's Bureau, 1928, p. 8). Women entered the professional ranks more than in any other previous era. According to historian Daniel Walkowitz, "the immigrant origins of the [female social worker] staff were highly visible [in New York City]" (Walkowitz, 1990, p. 1056). This immigrant background in large urban areas assisted in professionals' ability to understand the most recent immigrants who often prompted new words for the results of their integration. La Piana specifically notes, for example, that to find work some immigrants paid "a tip to a boss." This was "common among Italian" workers in the United States. The situation was irregular in their native country, however, so immigrants made a new word for their new type of boss in America: "'la bossatura'" (La Piana, 1916a, p. 8). Regardless of the ethical dimension to this fee system, it featured a person—*la bossatura*—who, as an immigrant, sought profit like most of the recent immigrants.

In 1924, the Women's Bureau conducted field research of "foreign-born women in industry" (U.S. Department of Labor, Women's Bureau, 1926, p. 10) by conducting interviews and analyzing the "facts and figures on questions vitally affecting wage-earning [native-born and foreign-born] women, and to formulate practical standards for wage-earning women in industry in each of the 48 States" (U.S. Department of Labor, Women's Bureau, 1924, p. 2). This endeavor was accomplished with the help of "progressive managers," despite popular anti-immigrant sentiments (see Goldberg, 1999, p. 153; Harwood, 1986, p. 202). The Women's Bureau published large portion of the Philadelphia and Lehigh Valley study in 1930, having interviewed 2,146 European immigrant women (see Manning, 1930, p. 3).

A new trend in immigrant women's gainful employment was that they were able to earn high enough wages to be relatively self-supporting. President Harding told the Women's Industrial Conference of 1923:

> The revolutionary change that has taken place in the status of women in the world of business and affairs has not only justified but necessitated that broader and more intimate activity of women in behalf of the particular phases of public and social interests … very definite public benefit. (U.S. Department of Labor, Women's Bureau, 1923, pp. 2–3)

Married women began to be at least co-supporters with their husbands in financial matters. Co-support with the husband went beyond the basic contributions to the family income. Some women became the main source of family income, especially when the husband was unemployed or irregularly employed because of injury or illness. Even when the husband was working regularly as a co-supporter, the women's wage was a significant portion of the family income (Manning, 1930). A certain amount of independence was possible for women with the increasing wage trends of some unskilled and semi-skilled jobs.

Wage increases were quite noticeable for semi-skilled immigrant women (Manning, 1930). Angelina of Italy, for example, began as a laundry worker earning $3.15 per week when she came to America. She had ambition for more than this, however, and sought a career position in a dress shop. She began earning $10 at a dress shop and then $12. She worked very hard, having "not lost a day except for holidays and layoffs of a week or so each summer. She was proud of the money she earned." Three years after advancing to $12 per week she was promoted to forelady at $13 per week. Her fiancé at the time had a wage of $14 per week, and for Angelina, "the girls whispered about it with awe" (quoted in Manning, 1930, p. 15). Angelina was making almost as much as her fiancé and she was sending money back to the old country where she had family depending on her financial support. Five years after her promotion to forelady, her husband could not work because of illness, so she supported her two children on her own wage (see Manning, 1930).

La Piana (1916a, 1916b) contended that emigrants to America came because they had "the knowledge of the existence of the other market in which wages are higher" (1916b, p. 5). This is part of what La Piana contends was a three-step process in why his European contemporaries emigrated to America. The first two steps before "knowledge of the existence of the other market in which wages are higher" were: "existence of two markets in which the wages and means are different" and the two markets have "a system of communication" (La Piana, 1916b, p. 5). So, after realizing that they could make more money in America, they emigrated. La Piana was suggesting that immigrants are basically capitalists—a philosophical fit for the America of the "Roaring Twenties." A shift had taken place in the intervening years between 1916 and Manning's (1930) report. The Italian migrant had become more inclined to acculturate, and successive generations lost their ancestral linguistic dialect. La Piana wrote that America was the "best field" for Europeans to begin anew. Italians were especially "led to come to America" if their lands were not yielding sufficiently (La Piana, 1916b, p. 5).

The Women's Bureau workers who interviewed Italian and other European immigrants found many very receptive to the attention. This is shown in the sheer amount of data procured by Women's Bureau interviewers. Although some of the data indicated depressed immigrant women, there were many who could be seen as happy to have the economic opportunity that was available in the United States. La Piana (1916a, 1916b) remarked on what he saw of the Italian laborer class, and not necessarily on what he personally believed about America. This is relevant because it adds to a portrait of the immigrant experience in gainful employment. In other words, economic realities are linked with social constructs. La Piana found that Sicilians from remote villages were not "enthusiastic for America" because they did "not find this country beautiful, and for him [the Sicilian/Italian immigrant] the most wonderful things of America are the elevated trains, the subway, and the breweries" (La Piana, 1916a, p. 7). Angelina of Italy, for example, suggested this in her career-oriented outlook during her interview with the Women's Bureau employee. Her success outside of the home caused "whispers" among some, but the suggestion from the interview context of the Women's Bureau was that many immigrant women quietly approved (see Manning, 1930, p. 15).

The Bureau's substantial case study of Philadelphia and Lehigh Valley in 1927–1928 was "based on interviews with foreign-born women in and near Philadelphia and in the Lehigh Valley" (U.S. Department of Labor, Women's Bureau, 1927, p. 16). The composite statistics were representative of Ohio largely because this state had 3,321,963 women gainfully employed at the time of the 1920 census. Florence Patteson Smith (1925) concluded that:

> earnings of women interviewed ... were higher in the Lehigh Valley than in Philadelphia; 29 per cent of the women in the Lehigh Valley, in contrast to 17 per cent of those in Philadelphia, earned as much as $20 a week. ... The median of the week's earnings for all women reporting on this was $15.35 in Philadelphia and $16.75 in the Lehigh Valley. (Smith, 1925, p. 10; U.S. Department of Labor, Women's Bureau, 1928, p. 10)

The median weekly income in the Lehigh Valley was $1.40 higher than in Philadelphia. This is significant because immigrant women were not necessarily confined to the urban areas for gainful employment.

About 17 percent of the textile employees in Philadelphia were foreign-born women in 1920 and also in the United States in 1920, "of the 1,930,341 women employed in manufacturing and mechanical industries, more than one in every five was foreign born," according to Caroline Manning (1930, p. 3). The clothing industry was one of the largest of the industrial employers of women. The immigrant women whom the Bureau interviewed frequently worked for wages so that they could feed their families. The stories of these women were "of great courage and enduring patience" according to Manning (1930), the industrial supervisor of the Women's Bureau. One interviewee, named Jeanie, was 21 years old when she came to the United States. She got a job in a textile factory because she was efficient and agreed to the low wage. After she became a mother, she had to quit her job. She eventually found a company that allowed her to work from home making clothes (see Manning, 1930, p. 138). This was a notable change in labor relations because of women's ability to directly exercise some control over their work conditions and home life. As discussed by Walch (1994), home ownership was one of the "dominant values of American society" (p. 68), which in turn was in parallel with immigrants' aspirations.

While the Philadelphia and Lehigh Valley case study revealed a generally promising economic development, the study also inadvertently echoed the issue of what has been called "urban-rural conflict" by some historians (see Eagles, 1989; Brown, 1994/2008, p. 97). There was a disparity in wages between urban Philadelphia and the rural Lehigh Valley. This situation was not uncommon to immigrant women from southern Europe. The issue of rural-urban borders was important to immigrants' social integration because in Sicily and southern Italy "the custom of keeping boarders is unknown" (La Piana, 1916a, p. 13). Immigrant populations began to house individuals together who were not of the same family. Internal immigration from urban to rural districts was not uncommon because of economic incentives (see Eagles, 1989; Brown, 1994/2008).

Americanization has been known as a loosely defined movement that seeks to assimilate immigrants into the English language by eliminating immigrant language and culture. Gayle Gullett, in her article on the role of women's clubs in Americanization campaigns in California, suggests that workplace competition between native-born and immigrants in the 1920s occasionally fueled what had been called an "imperious" phenomenon (Gullett, 1995, p. 77). Goldberg (1999) argued that so-called "old-stock" Americans' fear of immigrant economic competition in the first couple of decades of the twentieth century added to the negative connotations of the term (Goldberg, 1999, p. 153). La Piana (1916a, 1916b), however, did not think of Americanization as a negative phenomenon. He defined Americanization as a "higher standard of living," (La Piana, 1916a, p. 3) because the United States was generally seen as a place with economic opportunity. Olneck (1989) came closest of the secondary sources to paralleling La Piana's (1916a) definition of the phenomenon. Despite the "upsurge of nativist sentiment" in the 1920s, Olneck (1989) contended that Americanization courses were not necessarily a clunky imperialist endeavor, but, rather, a refined attempt to make sure immigrants knew that "self-reliance," among other qualities, was a part of the American character. Therefore, immigrants could see Americanization as a less threatening "symbolic" process of cultural integration rather than assimilation (Olneck, 1989, pp. 399, 408).

Regardless of which side—nativist or immigrant—invoked the term, each had an economic basis for doing so. The motivation for economic empowerment brought immigrants into competition with some native-born citizens because of a *perception* of competition even if actual competition was not necessarily there (Gullett, 1995; Goldberg, 1999). Masao Suzuki (1995) noted that some immigrant groups were highly successful with acculturation, and they "improved their occupational status both in terms of the growing proportion of gainfully employed in 'middle-class' occupations and in terms of a declining proportion of unskilled workers" (pp. 890–1). Expanding fiscal power among immigrant communities was seen by native-born wage earners as a threat to their job security. Polling percentages during the 1920s indicated an anti-immigrant sentiment among urban and rural districts (Eagles, 1989). There was a growing discontent in the U.S. Congress in 1920–1921 that increased isolationist tendencies briefly. Most notable of the anti-immigration legislation was the National Origins Act (1921) and the Johnson-Reed Act (1924). Both temporarily restricted immigration via draconian quotas, nearly barring immigration completely from several countries for a time (see Kyvig, 2004, p. 173).

Immigrant women who did make it into the county before the anti-immigration laws found it difficult, but not impossible, to acculturate in order to abate some of the resentment from native-born workers. The Women's Bureau found in its Philadelphia and Lehigh Valley case study that "[o]nly 60 per cent of the women were able to speak English. ... Less than a third of the women could read English, and one in seven could not read at all" (U.S. Department of Labor, Women's Bureau, 1928, p. 8). This finding was used to support what was ostensibly the attitude of some "[o]rganized women [who] began supporting Americanization efforts" (Gullett, 1995, p. 73), because more women's organizations temporarily became concerned with the notion that some immigrant groups were not seen as fully assimilating into American culture (Ngai, 1999).

The Women's Bureau again addressed the Americanization phenomenon in its reports that were sympathetic to the female immigrant, because immigrant women were part of its mandate (see U.S. Department of Labor, Women's Bureau, 1928, p. 8). The Bureau interviewed immigrant women to get their perspective in their own words. The 1930 report stated that,

> after talking with women who for years have done some of the heaviest and most disagreeable tasks in our factories and mills, but whose hearts and minds still dwell in the Carpathian Mountains, Americanization seems little more than a strange word and a vague ideal as yet far from attainment. (Manning, 1930, pp. 2–3)

George La Piana crystallized the meaning of the term "Americanization" from his Italian immigrant perspective. Writing about how the immigrants he knew thought of Americanization as meaning a "higher standard of living," he continued to say that the term was a "problem" because it seemed "like a body without a soul" (La Piana, 1916b, p. 21). He suggested—much like the quote found in the Women's Bureau's 1930 report (see Manning, 1930)—that some immigrants still had their "soul" set in the Carpathian Mountains. They were still thinking of their ancestral home in Europe. Nevertheless, the domestic tradition of Italian women was surprisingly flexible in its new American surroundings. Despite widespread nostalgia for their country of birth, La Piana (1916b) suggested that immigrant women recognized the economic "environment" of their new country as the pivotal item for immigrants to acculturate into if they were to be accepted and achieve financial security.

The older generation of Italian women thought that once a woman "learned how to prepare the oatmeal she was already Americanized" (La Piana, 1916b, p. 20). The first generation seemed to emphasize assimilation more often than not, at least from La Piana's (1916b) perspective. Even if culinary acculturation seemed cursory, it was noteworthy for its tendency to be an item quickly to be assimilated into the popular culture. Food adoption was a visible sign that the immigrant was integrating into local society. If Italian immigrant women deemed the action of cooking oatmeal as evidence of their successful acculturation, then native-born women's acceptance of Italian food evidenced their acceptance of the newcomers. This diffused some of the tension in urban and rural areas. La Piana went so far as to claim that "many Americans were Italianized because they liked macaroni and spaghetti almost with the same enthusiasm [as] Italians themselves" (La Piana, 1916b, p. 20). Fostering familiarity was seen as a positive for economic advancement and component of acculturation (La Piana, 1916b, p. 1, p. 20).

The threat of "single capital consideration," according to La Piana (1916a, p. 4), was that "to americanize [sic] the Italian immigrants, we have to put them in a favourable [sic] condition" (La Piana, 1916a, p. 4). In other words, the environment had to be favorable economically for acculturation. La Piana (1916a) suggested that equalizing pay would assist immigrants' integration in their new society, though, at first, they would likely work for less. As La Piana (1916a) wrote, they would initially "atone for their coming" (pp. 21, 202). Successfully assimilating immigrants meant different things to different people. Gullett (1995) and Graham and Koed (1993) echoed the same concept in suggesting that champions of Americanization in 1910s and 1920s, including many women's clubs such as those in California, over-emphasized aggressive assimilation.

Olneck (1989) claimed that school coursework successfully "resulted in individual regeneration" and "ultimately in collective transformation" of the immigrant into an American (pp. 409–10). But trying to force assimilation was not nearly so successful, according to La Piana (1916a, 1916b), although he did agree with the women's clubs that declared education to have been the "crucial point" for immigrants' integration and economic advancement (La Piana, 1916a, p. 20). He suggested that the women's clubs and charities were rarely well-situated to address immigrants' situation through their programs. But when they were successful, acculturation took the form of education that benefited immigrant's employment prospects. So "willed learning," as noted by Olneck (1989, p. 409), was successful if immigrants obtained jobs.

With greater work abilities came greater cultural integration, because the immigrants became invested in their new country. The aggressive acculturation campaigns of the Daughters of the American Revolution (DAR) left out the dynamics that different immigrants brought to the United States. Many native-born citizens adopted immigrant foods, for example. America's tradition of individualization historically undermined the very acculturation that the DAR tried to accomplish (see Gullett, 1995, p. 77; Graham & Koed, 1993, pp. 28–9). For some it was through the medium of food and for others it was through leaving the domestic sphere for the workplace.

Examining and Promoting Labor through Data

The Women's Bureau reports used interviews and cliometrics as the main method of investigation. According to Gullett (1995), the Daughters of the American Revolution, the California Federation of Women's Clubs, and the General Federation of Women's Clubs "demanded that the newcomers [female immigrants] learn from them how to become acceptable women citizens" (p. 73). The Women's Bureau, however, decided not to "demand" uncompromising consistency from immigrants. Instead, the Women's Bureau maintained its mandate of "promot[ing]" women who were immigrants with statistically grounded reports (see U.S. Department of Labor, Women's Bureau, 1920, p. 3). In keeping with its mandate, the Women's Bureau espoused flexibility as opposed to the rigid Americanization agenda of several prominent women's clubs of the time (Gullett, 1995, pp. 73, 77; Haarsager, 1997, p. 316).

Caroline Manning (1930) oversaw a report that indicated how female immigrants were integrating into the work force through acceptance of—at first—comparatively low wages that got them hired. This finally gave them the opportunity for advancement once they had established themselves in the workplace. She built further upon Mary Veronica Dempsey's report of 1922.

Dempsey's (1922) study of businesses that employed 1,000 or more women and men in 1910 and 1920 revealed a situation that was unanticipated during its time: "the changes in rate of increase or decrease for the two sexes were entirely disproportionate, and in by far the greater number of cases the women took the lead in the rate of increase" (p. 4). Although men were still numerically higher in number in gainful occupations, women's disproportionate increase in industrial employment indicated the growing opportunities for women in the workforce. Dempsey (1922) deduced that women had "enlarged their field of work by entering in greater numbers occupations in which formerly they had but scant representation" (p. 4). This increase led to friction with some conservative employers, as indicated by one of the Women's Bureau's interviewees. Jeanie, an immigrant woman who was 21 years of age, quickly got a job in a textile factory but was eventually told by her employer that "she was earning too much" (as quoted in Manning, 1930, p. 138). This was an industrialist's admission that there was an economic shift in favor of young immigrant women, as had been indicated in Dempsey's report. That mentality from industrialist would change. Economic advancement continued, and the Women's Bureau continued to study and support women's economic opportunity (U.S. Department of Labor, Women's Bureau, 1923, 1924, 1925, 1926, 1927, 1928, 1929).

An ironically unintended consequence of the anti-immigrant legislation of 1920–1921 was that such legislation benefited some young women who were immigrants already in the United States. Oshima (1984) noted that "the annual average of immigrants fell from 856,000 in 1900–1915 to 356,000 in 1915–1930" (p. 163). This downward trend put pressure on the manufacturers to find "unskilled labor" and spurred the drive for "the substitution of machines for unskilled labor throughout the 1920s" (Oshima, 1984, p. 164). However, employers in the manufacturing sector were not able to adapt to mechanization in a day or a year; therefore, they became eager for the dwindling supply of inexpensive unskilled labor caused by the anti-immigration laws, hence immigrant women were suddenly becoming more employable (Oshima, 1984). This phenomenon was being uncovered at the time by labor advocates such as Mary van Kleeck—first director of what became the Women's Bureau—in her book *Women and Machines* (van Kleeck, 1921). She wrote that there was a "drift of women ... to novel adventures in mechanics" (p. 4). Van Kleeck was referring to the growing number of women employed in manufacturing industries throughout the 1910s into 1920. The types of jobs available to women increased proportionally to the point where employability considerations were nearly "sexless." And even when gender was considered, "the fact is impressive that of the firms questioned in 1919 who had recruited women for [industrial] job[s] during the war, more than half were retaining them" (van Kleeck, 1921, pp. 5–6). This upward employability change was to prove lasting even for immigrant women.

The Women's Bureau had "Unpublished data [that] show[ed] that nearly four-fifths of [immigrant women] were under 25 years of age when they arrived" and "indeed, they lost little time in finding a job" (Manning, 1930, p. 135). This trend was evidence that many of those immigrants who did succeed in getting admitted into the United States were female (Oshima, 1984). They were able to take advantage of the legislated immigration squeeze of 1921–1924 that tended to exclude as many men as women from entering the United States. The prevention of further immigration increased the demand for inexpensive unskilled labor—primarily those immigrants who had made it into the country. Consequently, the mechanizing manufacturers hired those who fit their criteria of a large pool of labor who could be paid low wages. This workforce model increasingly trended toward young female immigrants (Oshima, 1984; Manning, 1930). In 1920 there were "1,930,341 women employed in manufacturing and mechanical industries" out of a total of 8.5 million employed women. 21.1 percent of the American workforce was women in 1920 (Manning, 1930, p. 3). Although this percentage was down from 1910, the proportion of downturn was less than that of men—2.3 percent as opposed to 3.1 percent, according to Smith (1925, p. 5). By 1930, 10 million women were employed in America, according to Women's Bureau report "Fact Finding with the Women's Bureau" (U.S. Department of Labor, Women's Bureau, 1930a, 1930b). This large proportional statistic suggested that those groups previously frowned upon for arbitrary reasons or archaic social conventions were especially prime labor markets, because they were eager for gainful employment. Initially, employers were more likely to lay off men than women because of the economic priority of cutting costs.

Conclusion

Immigrants came to America primarily for economic advancement. La Piana's discussion of acculturation in the late 1910s showed immigrants were not always afraid of the acculturation, but rather welcoming it if acculturation promoted their own economic advancement. Some immigrant women's native-born peers rose in the ranks of gainful employment along with them. La Piana (1916a) summarized the situation during the interwar years: "[immigrants, both men and women] are here to make money" (p. 7). Those women who were immigrants interviewed by the Women's Bureau in the 1910s and 1920s seemed to want to start a new life in which women could and would enforce their rights to earn money and advance in the workforce. The U.S. Women's Bureau was a precedent-setting unit within the U.S. Department of Labor that promoted and accelerated the advancement of women's rights by researching the issues under its mandate, interviewing people affected by policy, and promoting legislative action.

Pedagogical Strategies

A high school U.S. history lesson plan centered on this chapter's exploration of immigration, acculturation, and women's workforce participation during the early twentieth century can effectively contextualize these themes within broader historical narratives. By integrating primary sources like reports from the Women's Bureau and studies by scholars such as La Piana, educators can illustrate the intersection of economic pressure, legislative changes, and cultural adaptation in shaping immigrant experiences. As seen in the lesson plan for this chapter, activities can be designed that engage students with statistical data from the Women's Bureau to analyze workforce trends, while fostering discussions on how immigration policies influenced demographic shifts and labor demands. Furthermore, students can examine the role of organizations like the Daughters of the American Revolution and the Women's Bureau to understand contrasting approaches to acculturation and advocacy during this era. Such interdisciplinary approaches would not only highlight the challenges faced by immigrant women in the workforce but also connect these historical developments to broader debates on gender, labor, and identity, fostering empathy and critical thinking skills in high school students.

References

Addams, J. (1923). *A new conscience and an ancient evil*. Macmillan. Open Collections Program, Widener Library, Collections Development Department, Harvard University. http://nrs.harvard.edu/urn-3:FHCL:436848

Anderson, M. (1926). [Letter of Transmittal]. *Women in the fruit-growing and canning industries in the State of Washington*. United States Department of Labor, Women's Bureau. Washington, DC: Government Printing Office. Immigration to the United States, 1789–1930, Open Collections Program, Baker Library, Harvard University. http://ocp.hul.harvard.edu

Ayers, E. L., Gould, L. L., Oshinsky, D. M., & Soderlund, J. R. (2012). *American passages: A history of the United States* (Brief 4th ed.). Wadsworth Cengage.

Brown, M. E. (1994/2008). Parents and children fundamental questions about immigrant family life. In T. Walch (Ed.), *Immigrant America: European ethnicity in the United States* (pp. 89–102). Routledge.

Burn, F. K. E. (1920/2005). 1920: August, Febb Burn to Harry Burn. In L. Grunwald & S. J. Adler (Eds.), *Women's letters: America from the Revolutionary War to the present* (p. 489). The Dial Press.

Dempsey, M. V. (1922). *The occupational progress of women: An interpretation of census statistics of women in gainful occupations* (Bulletin of the Women's Bureau, no. 27). United States Department of Labor, Women's Bureau. Government Printing Office. http://nrs.harvard.edu/urn-3:HBS.BAKER:123561

Dumenil, L. (1998). Re-shifting perspectives on the 1920s: Recent trends in social and cultural history. In J. E. Haynes (Ed.), *Calvin Coolidge and the Coolidge Era* (pp. 63–96). Library of Congress.

Eagles, C. W. (1989). Congressional voting in the 1920s: A test of urban-rural conflict. *Journal of American History, 76*(2), 528–34. https://doi.org/10.2307/1907989

George La Piana, 1878–1972. [Immigration to the United States, 1789–1930]. Open Collections Program, Harvard University. http://ocp.hul.harvard.edu/immigration/people_lapiana.html

Goldberg, D. J. (1999). *Discontented America: The United States in the 1920s*. The Johns Hopkins University Press.

Graham, O. L., Jr., & Koed, E. (1993). Americanizing the immigrant, past and future: History and implications of a social movement. *Public Historian, 15*(4), 24–49. https://doi.org/10.2307/3378635

Gullett, G. (1995). Women progressives and the politics of Americanization in California, 1915–1920. *Pacific Historical Review, 64*(1), 71–94. https://doi.org/10.2307/3640335

Haarsager, S. (1997). *Organized womanhood: Cultural politics in the Pacific Northwest, 1840–1920*. University of Oklahoma Press.

Harwood, E. (1986). American public opinion and U.S. immigration policy. *The Annals of the American Academy of Political and Social Science, 487*(1), 201–12. https://doi.org/10.1177/0002716286487001013

Kyvig, D. E. (2004). *Daily life in the United States 1920–1940: How America lived through the 'Roaring Twenties' and the Great Depression*. Ivan R. Dee.

La Piana, G. (n.d.). [Italian Woman at home]. Andover-Harvard Theological Library, Harvard Divinity School, Cambridge (Papers, 1878–1972 inclusive, Manuscripts MS 104/11, folders 5–18, mass. sequence 75–89). Open Collections Program, Baker Library, Harvard University. http://nrs.harvard.edu/urn-3:DIV.LIB:828929

La Piana, G. (1916a, January 17). [Social Work Among Italian Immigrants]. Andover-Harvard Theological Library, Harvard Divinity School,

Cambridge (Papers, 1878–1972 inclusive, Manuscripts MS 104/11, folders 5–18, mass. sequence 54–74). Open Collections Program, Baker Library, Harvard University. http://nrs.harvard.edu/urn-3:DIV.LIB:828929

La Piana, G. (1916b, October). [Italians in America]. Andover-Harvard Theological Library, Harvard Divinity School, Cambridge (Papers, 1878–1972 inclusive, Manuscripts bMS 104/11, Folders 5–18, mass. sequence 32 of 325). Open Collections Program, Baker Library, Harvard University. http://nrs.harvard.edu/urn-3:DIV.LIB:828929

Manning, C. (1930). *The immigrant woman and her job* (Bulletin of the Women's Bureau, no. 74). United States Department of Labor, Women's Bureau. Washington, DC: Government Printing Office. Open Collections Program, Baker Library, Harvard University. http://nrs.harvard.edu/urn-3:HBS.BAKER:452545

Matthews, J. V. (2003). *The rise of the new woman: The women's movement in America, 1875-1930.* Ivan R. Dee.

Mastracci, S. H. (2004). Backstage and spotlight activism: One survival strategy of the Women's Bureau and its price. *Labor History, 45*(1), 85–99. https://doi.org/10.1080/0023656042000202990

Ngai, M. M. (1999). The architecture of race in American immigration law: A reexamination of the Immigration Act of 1924. *Journal of American History, 86*(1), 67–92. https://doi.org/10.2307/2567407

Nienburg, B. M. (1920). *Women in government service* (Bulletin of the Women's Bureau, no. 8). United States Department of Labor, Women's Bureau. Washington, DC: Government Printing Office. Open Collections Program. Baker Library, Harvard University. http://nrs.harvard.edu/urn-3:HBS.BAKER:136884

Olneck, M. R. (1989). Americanization and the education of immigrants, 1900-1925: An analysis of symbolic action. *American Journal of Education, 97*(4), 398–423. https://doi.org/10.1086/443935

Oshima, H. T. (1984). The growth of U.S. factor productivity: The significance of new technologies in the early decades of the twentieth century. *Journal of Economic History, 44*(1), 161–70. https://doi.org/10.1017/S0022050700031429

Schain, J. (1918). *Women and the franchise*. Chicago: A.C. McClurge & Company. Open Collections Program, Harvard University, Schlesinger Library on the History of Women in America. http://nrs.harvard.edu/urn-3:RAD.SCHL:134371

Smith, F. P. (1925). *Facts about working women: A graphic presentation based on census statistics and studies of the Women's Bureau* (Bulletin of the Women's

Bureau, no. 46). Washington, D.C.: Government Printing Office. Open Collections Program. Baker Library, Harvard University. http://nrs.harvard.edu/urn-3:HBS.BAKER:477001

Suzuki, M. (1995). Success story? Japanese immigrant economic achievement and return migration, 1920-1930. *Journal of Economic History, 55*(4), 889–901. https://doi.org/10.1017/S0022050700042200

United States Department of Labor. Bureau of Labor Statistics. (1927). *Handbook of Labor Statistics, 1924-1926*, 439. Government Printing Office. http://ocp.hul.harvard.edu/ww/

United States Department of Labor, Women's Bureau. (1920). *Second Annual Report of the Director of the Women's Bureau for the Fiscal Year Ended June 30, 1920*. Washington, DC: Government Printing Office. Open Collections Program, Baker Library, Harvard University. http://nrs.harvard.edu/urn-3:HBS.BAKER:508406

United States Department of Labor, Women's Bureau. (1921). *Third Annual Report of the Director of the Women's Bureau for the Fiscal Year Ended June 30, 1921*. Washington, DC: Government Printing Office. Open Collections Program, Baker Library, Harvard University. http://nrs.harvard.edu/urn-3:HBS.BAKER:508406

United States Department of Labor, Women's Bureau. (1922). *Fourth Annual Report of the Director of the Women's Bureau for the Fiscal Year Ended June 30, 1922*. Washington, DC: Government Printing Office. Open Collections Program, Baker Library, Harvard University. http://nrs.harvard.edu/urn-3:HBS.BAKER:508406

United States Department of Labor, Women's Bureau. (1923). *Fifth Annual Report of the Director of the Women's Bureau for the Fiscal Year Ended June 30, 1923*. Washington, DC: Government Printing Office. Open Collections Program. Baker Library, Harvard University. http://nrs.harvard.edu/urn-3:HBS.BAKER:508406

United States Department of Labor, Women's Bureau. (1924). *Sixth Annual Report of the Director of the Women's Bureau: Fiscal Year Ended June 30, 1924*. Washington, DC: Government Printing Office. Open Collections Program. Baker Library, Harvard University. http://nrs.harvard.edu/urn-3:HBS.BAKER:508406

United States Department of Labor, Women's Bureau. (1925). *Seventh Annual Report of the Director of the Women's Bureau: Fiscal Year Ended June 30, 1925*. Washington, DC: Government Printing Office. Open Collections Program. Baker Library, Harvard University. http://nrs.harvard.edu/urn-3:HBS.BAKER:508406

United States Department of Labor, Women's Bureau. (1926). *Eighth Annual Report of the Director of the Women's Bureau: Fiscal Year Ended June 30, 1926*. Government Printing Office. Open Collections Program. Baker Library, Harvard University. http://nrs.harvard.edu/urn-3:HBS.BAKER:508406

United States Department of Labor, Women's Bureau. (1927). *Ninth Annual Report of the Director of the Women's Bureau: Fiscal Year Ended June 30, 1927*. Government Printing Office. In *Women Working, 1800-1930*. Open Collections Program. Baker Library, Harvard University. http://nrs.harvard.edu/urn-3:HBS.BAKER:508406

United States Department of Labor, Women's Bureau. (1928). *Tenth Annual Report of the Director of the Women's Bureau: Fiscal Year Ended June 30, 1928*. Government Printing Office. In *Women Working, 1800-1930*. Open Collections Program. Baker Library, Harvard University. http://nrs.harvard.edu/urn-3:HBS.BAKER:508406

United States Department of Labor, Women's Bureau. (1929). *Eleventh Annual Report of the Director of the Women's Bureau: Fiscal Year Ended June 30, 1929*. Government Printing Office. In *Women Working, 1800-1930*. Open Collections Program. Baker Library, Harvard University. http://nrs.harvard.edu/urn-3:HBS.BAKER:508406

United States Department of Labor, Women's Bureau (1930a, December 9). *Fact Finding with the Women's Bureau* (Women's Bureau Bulletin, no. 84). St. Louis Federal Reserve, Discovery Economic Center. https://fraser.stlouisfed.org/title/5392

United States Department of Labor, Women's Bureau. (1930b). *Twelfth Annual Report of the Director of the Women's Bureau: Fiscal Year Ended June 30, 1930*. Government Printing Office. In *Women Working, 1800-1930*. Open Collections Program. Baker Library, Harvard University. http://nrs.harvard.edu/urn-3:HBS.BAKER:508406

United States Department of Labor, Women's Bureau. (1931). *Activities of the Women's Bureau of the United States* (Bulletin of the Women's Bureau, no. 86). St. Louis Federal Reserve, Discovery Economic Center. https://fraser.stlouisfed.org/files/docs/publications/women/b0086_dolwb_1931.pdf

United States House of Representatives. (1920). *41 Stat. L., 987—An Act to Establish in the Department of Labor a Bureau to be known as the Women's Bureau*. https://uscode.house.gov/statviewer.htm?volume=41&page=987

van Kleeck, M. (1921). *Women and machines*. The Consumer's League of the City of New York. Open Collections Program. Baker Library, Harvard University. http://nrs.harvard.edu/urn-3:HBS.BAKER:500055

Walch, T. (Ed.). (1994). *Immigrant America: European ethnicity in the United States*. Garland Publishing.

Walkowitz, D. J. (1990). The making of a feminine professional identity: Social workers in the 1920s." *American Historical Review, 95*(4), 1051–75. https://doi.org/10.2307/2163478

Weber, G. A. (1923). *The Women's Bureau: Its history, activities, and organization*. Baltimore, MD: The Johns Hopkins Press. Open Collections Program, Widener Library, Harvard University. http://nrs.harvard.edu/urn-3:FHCL:123612

Women's Bureau. (n.d.). In *Women Working, 1800-1930.* Open Collections Program, Harvard University. http://ocp.hul.harvard.edu/ww/

Women's Trade Union League of Chicago (1910, October 29). *Official report of the Strike Committee: Chicago Garment Workers' Strike*. Women's Trade Union League of Chicago. Open Collections Program, Widener Library, Harvard University. http://nrs.harvard.edu/urn-3:FHCL:458789

Acknowledgment

This chapter is adapted from Adam I. Attwood's previously published open access (CC BY licensed) research paper on the Women's Bureau. The CC BY license allows for republishing. This chapter is modified from that version and is in compliance with the CC BY license ("Share—copy and redistribute the material in any medium or format for any purpose, even commercially. Adapt—remix, transform, and build upon the material for any purpose, even commercially"). Attribution to original version: Attwood, A. I. (2021), "A history of the United States Women's Bureau 1917–1930: Economic opportunity and immigration," in S. Dixit & S. Moid (Eds.), *Women Empowerment and Well-being for Inclusive Economic Growth* (pp. 139–57, IGI Global, https://doi.org/10.4018/978-1-7998-3737-4.ch010).

Lesson Plan

Lesson Plan Title
The Women's Bureau: Advocacy for Women Workers in the 1920s

Theme
Exploring the role of the Women's Bureau in the U.S. labor movement, highlighting the progress and challenges faced by women workers in the 1920s.

Grade Level
11th Grade

Course
U.S. History

Time Required
55 minutes

Essential and Supporting Questions
Essential Question: How did the Women's Bureau contribute to improving working conditions for women in the 1920s?

Supporting Questions:
- What were the key issues faced by women workers in the 1920s?
- What strategies did the Women's Bureau use to advocate for women?
- How did gender roles and societal expectations influence the work of the Women's Bureau?
- In what ways did the Women's Bureau help shape future labor legislation?

Objectives:
By the end of this lesson, students will be able to:
1. Identify the key objectives of the Women's Bureau during the 1920s.
2. Analyze the impact of the Bureau's work on labor conditions for women.
3. Explain the societal context that shaped the Bureau's efforts and limitations.
4. Evaluate the legacy of the Women's Bureau in the broader context of U.S. labor reform.

Standards (from the National Council for the Social Studies [NCSS]):
1. D2.His.9-12 Evaluate how historical events and developments were shaped by unique circumstances of time and place as well as broader historical contexts.

2. D2.His.9-12 Analyze how historical contexts shaped and continue to shape people's perspectives.

Classroom Materials:

- Primary source: excerpts from the Women's Bureau reports (printed or digital).
- PowerPoint presentation on the history and activities of the Women's Bureau.
- Whiteboard or smartboard for group discussions.
- Handout: timeline of labor legislation affecting women workers (provided in class or accessible digitally).

Instructional Plan:

1. Introduction (10 minutes):
   - Begin with a brief overview of the U.S. labor movement during the early twentieth century.
   - Introduce the Women's Bureau, discussing its establishment in 1920. Use a PowerPoint slide to highlight key figures and the Bureau's mission.
   - Pose the essential question: How did the Women's Bureau contribute to improving working conditions for women in the 1920s?

2. Primary Source Analysis (15 minutes):
   - Distribute excerpts from the Women's Bureau reports, detailing conditions for women workers in industries such as textiles and manufacturing.
   - In small groups, have students analyze the excerpts and discuss:
   - What were the major issues reported?
   - How did the Bureau propose addressing these issues?
   - Have each group share their findings with the class, writing key points on the board.

3. Discussion and Lecture (15 minutes):
   - Lead a class discussion on the role of gender expectations in shaping the Bureau's advocacy, including both its strengths and limitations.
   - Highlight the impact of the Bureau on labor legislation in the 1920s, such as minimum wage laws and hour limitations for women.
   - Discuss the long-term legacy of the Women's Bureau, tying it to modern labor movements and gender equality efforts.

4. Conclusion and Reflection (10 minutes):
   - Have students individually write a short response (3–5 sentences) to the essential question, using evidence from the lesson.

- End with a whole-class reflection: How does the work of the Women's Bureau relate to current discussions about gender and work?

Assessment:

- Participation in group analysis of primary sources.
- Completion of short written reflection responding to the essential question.
- Informal assessment through class discussion contributions.

Community Engagement:
Encourage students to interview family members or community elders who have experience with labor movements or gender equality in the workplace. Students should write a summary or present their findings to the class, linking their conversations to the history of the Women's Bureau and labor advocacy.

From the Washerwomen of Jackson to Chris Smalls: Countering Labor History as a white Man's History

Meghan Moore-Hubbard and Brandon Beck

Introduction

Former attorney and American Federation of Labor (AFL) leader Richard Trumka once noted that "Racism is part of our inheritance as Americans. Every city, every state and every region of this country has its own deep history with racism. And so does the labor movement" (Trumka, 2014, para.12). The history of labor in the United States is often reduced to a sequence of racial and gender binaries that situate the power and control of the American Labor movement in the hands of the heterosexual white male (Phillips-Cunningham, 2021). While labor historians argue for and against this notion, this chapter aims to highlight the labor history of historically marginalized groups including but not limited to white women, BIPOC men and women, and queer folks of all gender identities (Kelly & Nelson, 2023; Hill, 1996).

Black scholars, including Du Bois (1880), Baldwin (1984) and Wells-Barnett (2012, 2015), have long noted the role that "whiteness" holds in the social context. And recently more scholars have begun to critically examine the role whiteness plays in our society, their examination has been extended to field of history as many historians have begun to critically examine the role whiteness has played in the American labor system (Carstairs, 2001; Roediger, 1991/2007). Thus, we have begun to see labor historians argue that the American Labor system has been designed to perpetuate and advance whiteness (Carstairs, 2001). A notable instance of this is the systematic use of slavery as an organized labor source before 1865, rather than a random and disorganized practice. Consequently, another example highlights the continued extortion of immigrant labor in order to advance the capitalistic ideals of the dominant social group. Yet, the traditional historical record has often ignored the role gender and intersectionality have played in the promotion of American capitalism and in turn white supremacy. Furthermore, there have only recently been attempts to address the ways in which the corporations and the labor movement have engaged in racism, nativism, and sexism to perpetuate a dominant narrative of white male labor (Frank, 2014; Kelly, 2022).

In order to highlight the labor history of historically marginalized groups we must first define labor and examine what groups have traditionally had control of the American labor system. Merriam Webster (2024) defines labor as services performed by workers for wages distinguished from those rendered by entrepreneurs for profits. This definition is simplistic in its attempt to show the basic structure behind the labor system in the United States—by limiting the definition of labor to paid work this definition ignores the unpaid labor of enslaved peoples without whom the wealth of the United States would not have been possible and also ignores the unpaid labor of women who have often been the ones required to complete domestic work. Moreover, this definition positions the concept of labor and therefore the history of labor as one with rudimentary beginnings. Lost, in this definition and within the large context of U.S. labor history, are the stories of the marginalized worker. While history notes the labor or services performed by the marginalized worker, it often fails to include much of the history behind the contributions of these groups to the U.S. labor system and the ways in which marginalized groups were forced to organize outside of traditional unions due to their exclusion and, at times hostility from white male-dominated labor unions.

While this chapter looks to highlight the labor history of various marginalized groups, we are not able to include the histories of every group. Thus, our journey into highlighting these often-overlooked labor histories starts in the southern plantation system of the American South. It is no secret that the rise of American capitalism and the wealth accrued thereunder from the system of chattel slavery in the United States (Phillips-Cunningham, 2021; Robinson, 2000). There remains an absence in the historical record about the contributions, history and narratives of the Black enslaved worker and the countless ways enslaved folks organized themselves to disrupt the system of forced labor they were required to endure (Davis, 1981; Hartman, 2016). Black folks who were enslaved held multiple jobs and skill sets for which they were never paid and for which their descendants have never been compensated. Their roles as cooks, nannies, maids, carpenters, brick-masons and field hands were essential to building the wealth of white American capitalists. Spillers (1987) and Truth (1851) note that on the southern plantation enslaved Black women were expected to toil as hard as men, thus in many contexts the enslaved Black person was ungendered. Further, Hartman (2016) notes that the role that sex and gender have played in the constitution of labor remains complex and ambiguous. In addition, the role that slavery has played on labor fails to account for slavery as a mode of power, domination, and production.

Value was often placed on the production of the enslaved Black body based on its ability for physical production (Phillips-Cunningham, 2021; Robinson,

2000). In turn, the value of the enslaved Black woman is often understated. Due to the legal doctrine of partus sequitur ventrem, which codified that children's status was to follow that of the mother whether enslaved of free, "the belly [was] made a factory of production" (Hartman, 2016, p. 169). When enslavers raped Black women whom they had enslaved it was often to re-exert some control over Black women who dared challenge or question their exploitation, sexual assault was one way in which enslavers were "striving to destroy her proclivities towards resistance" (Davis, 1981, p. 13). While emancipation removed the physical shackles of chattel slavery, formerly enslaved Black men and women remained slaves of the American labor system through the sharecropping and working as domestic servants (Hartman, 2016; Phillips-Cunningham, 2021).

Theoretical Framework

The framework for this paper is informed by Du Bois' (1935) chapter on the white worker in his foundational work, *Black Reconstruction.* His chapter describes the creation of the white worker in the white imagination, especially as it sought to contrast itself to Black enslaved labor. Du Bois (1935) states that although white laborers "received a low wage [they] were compensated in part by a sort of public and psychological wage" (p. 700). Roediger's (2007) text *Wages of Whiteness* expands upon Du Bois' notion of a "psychological wage." He notes, "working class formation and the systematic development of a sense of whiteness went hand in hand for the U.S. white working class" (2007, p. 8). In other words, to some extent white workers' class identities were also racial ones because they were encouraged to and did position themselves as "not Black" and "not slave" (Roediger, 2007).

Additionally, this paper uses the theory of Black Marxism to highlight but also trouble the often generalized class distinctions present in the presence of all labor movements, historical and contemporary, under capitalism. One of the critiques of labor history and labor organizing has been the focus of class discrimination while underpinning or outright ignoring racial discrimination. For this reason, we also use Robinson's (1983) Black Marxist theory to highlight how capitalism has sought to divide the working class. Kelly (2020) asserts that Robinson explains this division as:

> … the dialectic of proletarianization disciplined the working classes to the importance of distinctions: between ethnics and nationalities; between skilled and unskilled workers; and as we shall see later in even more dramatic terms between races. The persistence and creation of such oppositions within the working classes were a critical aspect of the triumph of capitalism in the nineteenth century. (p.xv)

Additionally, we give special attention to Robinson's description of women as "geniuses of resistance" and taking things, one step further notes that, "all resistance, in effect manifests in gender, manifests as gender. Gender is indeed both a language of oppression [and] a language of resistance" (Robinson, 2000, as cited in, Quan, 2005, p. 47). Not only do we apply this understanding to women's labor in this chapter but also to queer, trans, and gender nonconforming folks as well.

Racial capitalism is a tenet of Black Marxism which originated in South Africa noting that "dismantling apartheid without overthrowing capitalism would leave in place structures that reproduce racial and gender inequality and the exploitation of all workers" (Legassick & Hemson, 1976, as cited in Kelley, 2020, p. xiv). Further, this group argued that "racism like heteropatriarchy, operates alongside capitalism as an added irritant that looks to suppress particular subgroups of people based on race and gender while also dividing the working class" (Legassick & Hemson, 1976, as cited in Kelley, 2020, p. xiv). Thus, labor history often fails to highlight the plight and commonalities of the working class due to its focus on class structure and its lack of focus on division within the class structure.

The pairing of these two frameworks highlights the commonality of experience and shared struggle of laboring folks across gender, race, and ethnic lines even as corporations and unions run by white men sought to divide and exclude along those same lines. Our work uses Black Marxism, racial capitalism, and the white worker to build on and address the ways in which white workers have continually failed to recognize and embrace Black, Brown, Asian, Immigrant and Indigenous working people as part of their class. However, our work is not limited to divisions along racial and ethnic lines and also seeks to include the plight of women of all races as well as folks in the LGBTQIA community as will be highlighted throughout this chapter.

Findings

Throughout hundreds of years of labor history in the United States, laborers have organized behind labor leaders and on their own seeking fair pay, safer working conditions, an end of discriminatory practices and countless other rights for workers. While the history of American labor often brings to mind muckraking journalism and white, male union organizing, labor history in the United States is much more diverse than we have been led to believe. From the stories of the washerwomen of Jackson, Mary Harris "Mother Jones," Katsu Goto, Dorothy Lee Bolden, Rose Flores, Chris Small, and other individuals whose work organizing has often been overlooked, our findings highlight folks and who labored in various fields and their connections to, exclusion from, or redefining of traditional labor movements and unions. For extended periods of U.S. history unions were exclusionary based on race, ethnicity, and gender. However, this did not stop BIPOC men, women, and queer folks from organizing their labor.

Attempting to tell often untold histories of labor is difficult because one runs the risk of equating experiences which are inherently incomparable. When white women laborers in Lowell, Massachusetts went on strike in 1836 singing, "Oh, I cannot be a slave; I will not be a slave. For I'm so fond of liberty That I cannot be a slave" while more than two million Black folks were held in bondage throughout the United States there is no comparison to be made. However, white laborers have continuously used analogies of enslavement to attempt to describe their labor conditions (Roediger, 1991). Furthermore, some labor historians have attempted to minimize race as a factor in labor organizing, in his critique of Herbert Gutman's history of the United Mine Workers of America (UMWA), Hill (1988) writes "rather than confronting the complexities of race in labor history he adopted and disseminated a romanticized vision of the working class" (p. 134). Indeed when, in 1877 amidst the Great Railroad Uprising the newspaper *The Labor Standard* stated, "White and black workmen stood together in … struggle. Labor recognizes neither color, creed, nor nationality" (Roediger, 1991, p. 167). But as Roediger (1991) notes, press reports from the city tell a different story, one of racial slurs and a desire among white strike leaders to frame this uprising as associated with white labor. The basis of much of labor history not centered on white men must begin with the exclusion of marginalized groups from traditional labor organizing in major trade unions.

Union Exclusion

In order to adequately reframe labor history as one that belongs to not only white hetero men, we must attend to the ways that whiteness has been used to divide the working class. Much like the rest of U.S. history, labor unions in the United States have not always been kind to BIPOC folks, LGBTQ+ folks, or white women. Unions including but not limited to those industries which employed cigarmakers, railway carmen, wire weavers, firemen, trainmen, locomotive engineers, iron molders, and machinists had explicitly stated policies which barred Black laborers from joining. For example, the Masters, Mates, and Pilots union required that members be a "white person of good moral character …" (Hill, 1988, p. 136). So, this labor history as white man's history did not come about by accident but through strategic policies which systematically excluded a large portion of the labor force. Frances Beale (1970) notes the double burden of race and gender, stating:

> The entire labor movement in the United States has suffered as a result of the superexploitation of [B]lack workers and women. The unions have historically been racist and chauvinistic. They have upheld racism in this country and have failed to fight the white skin privileges of white workers. (p. 150)

Not only did unions initially exclude many groups based on race, ethnicity, and gender identity they were, at times, instrumental in pushing for legislation that was xenophobic.

Samuel Gompers, seen by many as a major architect of the U.S. labor movement, rose to power touting Anglo-Saxon superiority and bowing to Southerners by accepted Black members on a segregated basis only (Mann, 1953). And this was in stark contrast to the policies of other major union organization of the time, the Knights of Labor, which made no distinction of skilled/unskilled labor or of Black/white in its This decision, by the leader of the American Federation of Labor (AFL) set a precedent for the AFL to think in racial terms for years to come (Mann, 1953).

The leadership of multiple union organizations, including the California Workingmen's Party, was opposed to immigration in the late 1800s and they presented particularly harsh stereotypes and lobbied for legislation like that of the Chinese Exclusion Act (Kelly, 2022; Lee, 2019; Mann, 1953). As Samuel Gompers stated in 1907, "There cannot be any honest division of opinion on Chinese exclusion" (Mann, 1953, p. 208). Unfortunately, this was not unique to the early years of labor organizing. Anti-Asian sentiment reared its head in union circles again in the 1970s and 1980s when thousands of autoworkers were laid off in Detroit, many of them blaming the increased accessibility of foreign cars many of which were built in Japan. While members of the United Autoworkers (UAW) held protests destroying Japanese-made vehicles. These images circulated widely and incited fear in Detroit's Asian American community so when Vincent Chin, a Chinese-American man was beaten to death with a baseball bat by a former autoworker while his stepson shouted, "It's because of you little motherfuckers that we're out of work!" those fears were realized (Yoo, 2021, p. 10).

Even when marginalized groups were allowed to join unions, it did not mean that all things were equal or welcoming. In 1900, once Black workers were admitted into some American Federation of Labor (AFL) unions, they were forced to enter into segregated chapters (Hill, 1988). Additionally, some unions maintain the name "brotherhoods" as part of their organization title, like the United Brotherhood of Carpenters and Joiners and the International Brotherhood of Electrical Workers, are still known today and can feel exclusive to women and gender nonconforming folks. Furthermore, ensuring that queer couples' partners could receive the promised healthcare, life insurance, and disability benefits be extended to their "spouse equivalents" was one such issue which has been addressed in some unions in recent years (Frank, 2014). With a legacy of admitting mostly white men, there was much work to be done to ensure that labor unions were also willing to fight for protections workers based on their race, ethnicity, gender, sexual orientation, (dis)ability, as well as the intersections of each of those identities.

Mining, "Rise up and strike!"

The United Mineworkers of America (UMWA) was one such union that had a sordid history in the limitations of their membership. At the time of its inception in 1890, the UMWA allowed membership of anyone who worked "in and around the mines" regardless of race or nationality (Northrup, 1943). This policy, while loosely defined, has lent itself to many labor historians overemphasizing the progressive stance of the UMWA on the issue of race discrimination within mining and the union itself. And although Black workers were able to find an unsegregated home with the UMWA, union leadership and many members held both racist and prejudice ideals which greatly impacted Black miners (Hill, 1988; Kelly, 2022; Northrup, 1943). In his 1943 report titled *The Negro and the United Mine Workers of America*, Herbert Northrup stated that despite equalitarian policies he found an "uneven distribution of jobs" wherein Black miners were more likely to be employed in jobs which were "especially vulnerable to technological displacement" (p. 317). Additionally, the union's policy of non-discrimination remained vague (Hill, 1988).

Black miners made up between 16 and 30 percent of the mining workforce in the Appalachian coalfields between 1890 and 1940 (Northrup, 1943). However, UMWA leadership tended to be lily white. In 1891, after reviewing the list of names for union leadership where no Black man's name appeared, Richard L. Davis, a Black miner, wrote in the UMWA journal, "take the Negro out of the organization and you have a vast army against you, one that is strong enough to be felt and feared" (Hill, 1988, pp. 147–8). Davis' subsequent years in leadership in the UMWA were spent organizing and attempting to convince both UMWA members and leadership that Black miners should be treated equal to their white counterparts. Despite his efforts and legacy, UMWA leadership did not entrust him with much power over ... roles and worse yet, failed to support him despite his pleas for assistance as he died a senselessly early death at the age of 36 (Hill, 1988).

One of the complications of racist practices both in the UMWA and among coal operators was the use of Black miners as strikebreakers by coal companies.

Coal companies recruited Black laborers from the south, companies would promise work and lodging, often not mentioning that they would be replacing union miners who had gone on strike (Foner, 1983; Keiser, 1972). The Virden Massacre provides one example of the complexities of coal companies using Black laborers as strikebreakers, often without their knowledge, and furthermore how the UMWA responded. In 1898 the Chicago-Virden Company recruited Black laborers from Alabama to break a strike at a mine in Illinois. However, upon arriving the Black miners "complained that they had been deceived by the operators and most of them refused to work" (Foner, 1983, p. 156). Unfortunately, this did not stop white miners from opening fire on the train carrying Black workers and the guards hired to protect them. At other times, coal companies spread rumors throughout West Virginia and Alabama, where the UMWA had been attempting to organize, that Black miners would lose their jobs if the union was successful. This was further complicated by the use of Black workers brought to West Virginia to break strikes and increase racial tensions among striking miners (Foner, 1983; Northrup, 1943).

One of the most notable labor organizers in the coalfields was an elder Irish immigrant named Mary Harris "Mother" Jones. Known as "the miner's angel" the Irishwoman was in her 50s when she began her labor organizing work traveling the country. She was a gifted orator who received countless requests from labor organizers across the country to come and speak to their workers. One UMWA journal correspondent wrote, "Mother Jones is worth one hundred agitators in the West Virginia field" (Foner, 1983, p. 49). While most of her work centered around miners' rights in the west and Appalachia, she was involved in organizing labor throughout the United States; Mother Jones also encouraged women to join the fight telling the wives of streetcar workers in New York they "ought to be out raising hell" (Foner, 1983, p. 427). Despite being imprisoned, investigated, and countless threats of violence Mother Jones maintained, "I don't know of a more joyous death than in fighting the battles of you laboring men" (Foner, 1983, p. 419). Although Mother Jones was a staunch supporter of both Black and white workers' rights she was silent when it came to the labor movement's exclusion of and hostility toward Asian workers (Kelly, 2022).

Despite a relatively low percentage of Chinese miners who worked in mines in the western United States, the UMWA leadership was outspoken in their support for U.S. legislation against Chinese immigration (Hill, 1988). However, Chinese miners were often zealous in their labor organizing. As Bill Haywood wrote of striking miners in Hanna, Wyoming "The Chinese took the lead and when the white men were weakening after a long time on strike the Chinese went around to them and offered to double their relief if they would stand firm to win the strike" (Haywood, 1929, p. 136). Unfortunately, the UMWA spouted harmful and divisive ideals about Japanese miners as well suggesting that Japanese employment would result in unemployment for white workers (Hill, 1988). Furthermore, the union's racist views could not be swayed even when their own journal reported that Japanese workers were as "eager and willing to improve their conditions as any of the Europeans" (Hill, 1988, p. 176).

The 1964 Civil Rights Act meant that employers could no longer discriminate on the basis of race, color, religion, national origin, or gender. And for women in the Appalachian coalfields this meant they could now be employed in mines. Diana Baldwin and Anita Cherry were the first women to join the UMWA as underground miners when they were hired at Beth-Elkhorn Coal Corporation in Jenkins, Kentucky in 1973 (Kelly, 2022). However, this did not mean that all coal companies were suddenly willing to hire women so they began organizing. In 1978, lawyer Betty Jean Hall filed alleged hiring discrimination against women by 153 of the nation's largest coal companies forcing coal bosses to pay thousands of dollars of backpay to women who had been denied mining jobs (Kelly, 2022). Like most fields of employment, it is important to note enslaved Black women had been forced to mine coal as early as 1760 in the Appalachian region (Kelly, 2022) so although the fight for women's equal employment is an important one the story did not begin with these two women.

Farm Labor, "Si, Se Puede"

As previously mentioned, one cannot discuss agricultural labor without first acknowledging generations of unpaid labor by Black folks who were enslaved on fields and farms who were the first example of farm labor organizers who resisted in ways large and small against their enslavers. Following emancipation, a system of sharecropping was utilized by former enslavers to continue to bind Black workers to the land. Beginning in 1918, the Progressive Farmers and Household Union of America (PFHUA) recruited hundreds of sharecroppers in Arkansas. In her essay on the ensuing violence, Ida B. Wells-Barnett called this attempt to unionize a "declaration of economic independence, and the first united blow for economic liberty struck by the Negroes of the South!" (Kelly, 2022, p. 158). However, the response from white folks was swift and violent. At a PFHUA chapter meeting inside a local church, white supremacists opened fire into the church and the ensuing onslaught lasted multiple days resulting in the deaths of hundreds with 285 Black folks initially taken into custody and over 100 more in the days to come. All due to an attempt to organize their labor seeking what was owed them from their share of that year's crop (Kelly, 2022).

Indigenous folks have engaged in agricultural practices in North America since time immemorial. At some point, though unclear exactly when, the Lhaq'temish, or Lummi tribe, adopted potatoes as a major source of their agricultural production, as one agent noted, "they raise a goodly number of potatoes" (Friday, 2012, p. 88). In 1887, for 300 people, the Lummi harvested 273 tons of potatoes in addition to hundreds of bushels of other vegetables and tons of hay to feed livestock. The Lummi's ability to grow and barter in ways that provided them an abundance of crops represents important aspect of labor organizing (Friday, 2012). Despite the Lummi's lands having been colonized, the people having been forced onto reservations and colonialist forces that would later result in the further masculinization and colonization of agriculture practices, "Up to the mid-twentieth century women maintained their roles as subsistence agriculturalists for family, clan, and community" which is an important goal of any labor movement, especially those attempting to subvert colonial powers who are attempting to force them to dependency (Ford, 2012, p. 99).

The farmworker movement has long been led by immigrant labor. In the late 1800s and early 1900s workers experienced harsh labor practices on Hawaiian islands' sugar plantations (Lee, 2019). Immigrant workers were often forced to work under multi-year labor contracts and plantation owners intentionally recruited immigrants from a variety of countries to prevent the risk of strike. Their goal was to employ "different nationalities, and thus prevent any concerted action in case of strikes, for there are few, if any, cases of [Japanese], Chinese and Portuguese entering into a strike as a unit" (Kelly, 2022, p. 107). One Japanese farmer was Katsu Goto who had completed his three-year labor contract and became a shopkeeper. Goto often served as a mediator and translator for Japanese workers and he was suspected by local plantation owners has having pro-union sympathies and being capable of inciting unrest among workers (Martinez, 2016). On October 28, 1880, Katsu Goto was lynched. In the years that followed, laborers on Hawaii's plantations organized major strikes and in 1920 formed the Hawaii Laborers' Association made up of laborers from Japan, the Philippines, China, Spain and Portugal (Library of Congress).

In 1942, in the midst of WWII and fears that agricultural industry would suffer with many U.S. laborers gone to serve in the war, the U.S. and Mexican governments agreed to enact the Bracero Program which allowed seasonal workers from Mexico to work in the United States bypassing the restrictive immigration laws of the time (Kelly, 2022). Samuel Gompers, still head of the AFL, was staunchly opposed—just as he had been previously to desegregation of the AFL and in his opposition to Chinese labor. Again, the ramifications of Gompers' xenophobia lasted well beyond his tenure as the AFL refused to organize Latino workers for decades to come (Kelly, 2022).

One of the more widely known figures in organizing farmworkers is Cesar Chavez who founded the National Farm Workers Association. But his fight was not a new one, farmworkers in California had been facing discrimination and low wages for many years. In the midst of the Dust Bowl in 1941 Jose Flores, a Mexican American farmworker, was interviewed about migrant workers who had been evicted from company-owned camps. He stated

> they'd like to go back to the camps but they refuse to go back unless they go back as a union or as a group. They don't want to go back as individuals because they know very well that three weeks or a month after they go back they'll get fired and as a group they won't be able to fire them all. (1941, p. 179)

The power of solidarity was necessary and widespread among farm laborers. In 1965, Larry Dulay Itliong the founder of multiple unions in both factories and farming, was the leader of the Agricultural Workers Organizing Committee (AWOC). He called for a five-year strike for better wages and the right to form a union among Filipino grape farmers. Cesar Chavez, leader of the National Farmworkers Association, at the time, brought this call to his members as well. Following this meeting, 2,000 Filipino workers walked off the job followed two weeks later by 1,200 Latino farmworkers. The Filipino Community Hall where Itliong had initially called for the strike became a gathering place and strike kitchen where Filipino and Mexican workers cooked for one another and built an incredibly powerful cross-cultural coalition which ultimately succeeded in wins for farmworkers. Additionally, the two labor organizations merged into what would become today's United Farm Workers (Kelly, 2022).

Today there are over 2.4 million farmworkers in the United States the majority of whom are foreign-born and 36 percent of whom lack legal work status and 34 percent of whom are women (Farmworker Justice). However, only a small percentage of those farmworkers are able to organize due to so-called right-to-work laws in 27 states, mostly in the southern and midwestern United States (Kelly, 2022).

Factory Labor, "Viva la huelga!"

In 1903, Mother Jones redirected her efforts from organizing from miners to Philadelphia mill workers with particular emphasis on the 16,000 children who were striking for a 55-hour work week (Foner, 1983). Over three weeks, Mother Jones marched alongside three hundred striking men, women, and children from Philadelphia to New York City to march to highlight the labor issue to President Roosevelt. Despite local changes in some factories, the working conditions, wages, hours, and general treatment of workers in factories continue to be a focus of labor organizing.

If history classes discuss labor conditions at all, it is often through the example of the horrors of the Triangle Shirtwaist Factory fire in 1911. The fire resulted in 145 workers, mostly young immigrant women and girls being burned alive or jumping to their death (New York Times, 1911). This devastating event shed a light on the unsafe working conditions of many factories but, unfortunately this attention did not result in safer labor conditions in all or even many factories.

According to the white women striking in East Tennessee in 1929, the owners of the rayon factory where they were employed were lured to their town by "town fathers" promising cheap and unorganized labor (Dowd Hall, 1986). The women working at the American Glanzstoff plant were not part of a union but were instead "girls in their teens [who] decided not to put up with the present conditions any longer" (Dowd Hall, 1986, p. 365). The women walked out on March 12, 1929 protesting low wages, petty rules, and disrespect from bosses. After walking out the striking workers received a charter from the United Textile Workers (UTW) but the union did not have the resources to sustain the strike and workers received no changes to wages, hours, or working conditions, only a promise to not discriminate against union members. Despite what was a disappointing end to worker demands, the sense of solidarity, not only among workers but also among the local farming community from which many of the women had come, helped to sustain the strike and empower workers (Dowd Hall, 1986).

In 1970, 85 percent of the employees at the Farah Manufacturing Company in San Antonio, Texas were Chicana (Kelly, 2022). Rosa Flores became the face of the Farah strike when, in front of news cameras she raised her fist and declared, "Viva la huelga!"—"Long live the strike!" As the workforce organized their union they sought to fight against racism, sexual harassment, low wages, poor working conditions, and lack of job security. However, unionizing was not always guaranteed to represent the intersectional interests of the workers (Kelly, 2022). At the same time, in New York City, many Black and Puerto Rican women working in the garment industry had joined the International Ladies Garment Workers Union (ILGWU). However, as Beale (1970) points out the union leadership of that organization was not representative of its members and was nearly all white and male.

In the midst of the COVID-19 pandemic in 2020, workers at Amazon factories began raising concerns about their health and safety at work. Chris Smalls, an employee at an Amazon warehouse in Staten Island, N.Y., staged a walkout to protest these conditions and was subsequently fired (Hsu & Selyukh, 2022). Small formed the Amazon Labor Union without funding or connections to other organized labor groups. Smalls, a Black man, became the face of the modern-day labor movement but he was also subject to attacks by Amazon (Hsu & Selyukh, 2022). A leaked memo from Amazon's legal team about Smalls stated, "He's not smart, or articulate, and to the extent that the press wants to focus on us versus him, we will be in a much stronger PR position ..." (Blest, 2020).

Household Labor

While most attempts at labor organizing occurred, however quietly, in shared workplaces it was much more difficult for those in domestic work to unionize because of the long hours, isolation, and lack of support from established labor organizations (Phillips-Cunningham, 2021). However, domestic laborers have historically and continued to organize. In many homes domestic work was done by the women who resided there yet in the homes of the affluent or those striving toward some measure of affluence, housework was done by hired domestic workers, often Black women or immigrant women. Described by Hartman (2019) as the women who were "the ubiquitous figure of the captive maternal—conscripted to be friend, nurse, confidante, nanny, and bedwarmer" (p. 235). In 1897, Victoria Earle Matthews—a Black woman who had been born into slavery in Georgia, gave a speech before a mostly white audience titled "The Awakening of the Afro-American Woman." In her speech she put forth the importance of cause of Black women who were laboring in domestic and sharecropping insisting that they, too, deserved labor rights. She opened a lodging home for Black women domestics in New York City and was a staunch supporter of domestic service reform (Phillips-Cunningham, 2021).

More than any other group it was the labor of Black women that came to dominate the domestic workforce. However, this was not by accident as Hartman (2016) makes clear, "the systematic violence needed to conscript [B]lack women's domestic labor required locking them out of all other sectors in the labor market" (p. 170). In fact as Branch (2019) notes despite industrialization and regardless of geography, Black women experienced "occupational segregation" in more stark ways than either Black men or white women. In 1920 44 percent of Black women remained employed in domestic service, with another 29.5 percent laboring on farms (Branch, 2019, p. 107–8). Additionally, because there were often restrictions, especially in the south, on Black men's employment more Black women participated in the paid workforce (LeFlouria, 2011).

Domestic labor took many forms, while some Black women "lived-in" with the families who employed them, there was often more autonomy in "living out" and working as a laundress (LeFlouria, 2011). One of the earliest instances organizing on record came from a group of Black women in Jackson Mississippi (Kelly, 2022). In 1866, one year after emancipation, a group of Black washerwomen, whose wages were kept terribly low, co-signed a letter to the mayor of Jackson declaring their intent to charge a standard rate and stated their "desire to be able to live comfortably if possible from the fruits of our labors." These women signed the letter "The Washerwomen of Jackson" and in so doing they became an early example of organized labor in Mississippi (Kelly, 2022).

In the years immediately following emancipation more than 90 percent of Black women workers in Atlanta were employed in domestic work (LeFlouria, 2011). In 1932 a young Black nine-year-old girl, Dorothy Lee Bolden, joined her mother in domestic work in Atlanta and would ultimately spend nearly 50 years as a domestic worker. In 1963 she held the first meeting of the National Domestic Workers Union with programs specifically targeting Black women she required every member to be a registered voter and worked to assuage the concerns many Black folks had of organized labor due to their historic exclusion from unions. As Kelly (2022) notes, "within the first two years of NDWU's existence, Atlanta's domestic workers saw their daily wages rise from less than $5 to an average of $13.50–$15" (p. 144). In 1942, the FBI opened an investigation into groups of Black maids throughout the United States who had allegedly formed "Elanor Clubs" ascribing to the motto, "no colored maid in the kitchen by Christmas." This was meant to highlight their refusal to respond when addressed by their first names, wear servants uniforms, and work unlimited hours (Cobb Jr., 2014, p. 66).

By 1850 in New York City, 75 percent of domestic workers were Irish-American, Stansell (1986) termed this the "Irishization" of the field of domestic labor. Phillips-Cunningham (2021) highlights the parallels between Irish immigrant women and Black southern women in the homes of affluent northeastern families. Irish domestic workers occasionally organized with other women laborers including factory workers but because domestic work was not recognized by the government as "real" work there was little success in changing their working conditions. However, this did not stop them from taking out newspaper ads to support higher wages and time off (Phillips-Cunningham, 2021).

Another facet of domestic labor centers on the work of home health care workers. In Chicago in 1984 a group of homecare workers began the work of what would become the largest union in the Midwest. Made up of predominantly

Black and Brown women, the United Labor Unions Local 880, led by Irma Sherman, Doris Gould, Juanita Hill, and Mary, spent 18 months organizing their union and negotiating contracts with their a white-owned company who spent those months engaged in union-busting activities. Not only was their union successful but it became a template for future homecare organizers (Kelleher, 2024).

Today, the National Domestic Workers' Alliance (NDWA) represents 2.5 million nannies, housecleaners, and homecare workers, the majority of whom are women of Color (NDWA website). In 2010 NDWA was instrumental in the state of New York passing the Domestic Workers Bill of Rights which gave domestic workers the same lawful rights as employees in other sectors including vacation time and overtime pay (Americans Who Tell the Truth).

Present and Future Labor Organizing

The COVID-19 pandemic exacerbated and shed light on many of the safety issues facing various fields of labor as mentioned with Amazon workers. In 2019 Uber and Lyft drivers went on strike protesting poor treatment and low wages followed the next year by New York City taxi drivers (Kelly, 2022). Additionally, states that had previously written off as unable to organize have had some successes of late. In February 2024, Teamsters at Anheuser-Busch in Houston picketed and thousands threatened to walk off the job before reaching a tentative agreement on wages, job security, pensions, vacation, and retirement benefits (International Brotherhood of Teamsters). In April 2024 autoworkers at a Volkswagen plant in Chattanooga, Tennessee voted to unionize. This was a historic victory for workers who organized tirelessly in a region of the country that many have written off as unable to organize due to so-called "right-to-work" laws. Part of the success of this union vote, after two previously failed votes, was due to more diverse and younger workforce (Elk, 2024). In September 2024 Boeing factory workers in Seattle and Oregon voted 96.4 percent against a provisional labor deal that would have seen an increase in wages for its workers of over 25 percent over four years (Josephs, 2024; Kaye, 2024). Boeing workers noted that "the agreement didn't cover the cost of a living wage" (Josephs, 2024, para.9). These victories and near victories are especially important in the South as so-called right-to-work states have spent decades ensuring that unions gain no footing.

Union numbers and labor organizing have been on the decline for decades. However, United Autoworkers (UAW) President, Shawn Fain, has called on unions to join together for a general strike in 2028, "for the good of the entire working class" (Michels & Cox, 2024, para.2). In 2023, Fain stated, "We've not yet won racial and economic justice in the workplace for all of our members. We've not yet won retirement security and health care pensions for all" (Michels & Cox, 2024, para.21). While it would take a lot of organizing to get multiple unions organized to a general strike, many believe that organizing around the issue of healthcare could be an important through-line for various unions.

The Role of Education

It is also worth noting that within the history of this country, the value of the marginalized American has been rooted in their ability to contribute to the American labor movement (Croom & Alston, 2009; Kuelzer & Houser, 2019; Anderson, 1978, 1988). Within the structure of the American education system there has been a tremendous amount of attention given to preparing students to enter the workforce. The American education system has historically touted the ability to tailor its approach of education toward meeting the needs of society. For minority groups in this country, much of their educational experiences were tied to the needs of the country's labor source (Croom & Alston, 2009).

Moreover, the value of the oppressed has always been found in their ability to be of value to the oppressors (Du Bois, 1994; Robinson et al., 2019). For this reason, we have seen over the history of education and labor movements a focus on the inclusion of trade schools, vocational education, and the creation of higher education institutions that focus on manual labor (Larson, 2016). John Dewey, one of Americas most profound educational philosophers, knew the role that educational institutions hold within the American labor system (Dewey, 1916; Wang & King, 2009). While he opposed vocational education, he believed that future possibility of having different occupations excites students and causes them to be more interested in education (Dewey, 1916; Wang & King, 2009). Conversely, we also see an implicit focus on the training of minorities to operate within the workforce in the creation of the Hampton model. The Hampton model was created in an effort to increase the educational opportunities for Black Americans during Jim Crow segregation (Anderson, 1988). Through the creation of the Hampton model Samuel Armstrong and his apprentice Booker T. Washington aimed to provide educational opportunity for Black Americans that focused on a combination of vocational education, manual training, with a small percentage of the curriculum focusing on scholarly work (Anderson, 1988). These examples provide insight into the juxtaposition between the historic educational opportunities of the marginalized and the interests of labor organizations.

Furthermore, social studies courses hold the most potential when it comes to reframing labor history and educating students about their future rights once they enter the workforce. However, most social studies standards do an abysmal job at addressing labor and labor history choosing to focus on perspectives of business and capital while ignoring workers perspectives, especially in economics courses. Also, many states social studies standards contain a reference to "women's entry into the workforce" around World War II. This framing centers the experiences of white, middle-class women while overlooking the generations of labor by poor white women as well as all BIPOC women. As Symcox (2002, p. 32) states, the "myth of the non-laboring woman should be put to rest." This framing views labor as happening in factories or settings which had been traditionally dominated male workers and ignores domestic and unpaid labor of women at home. Furthermore, when addressing so-called "women's work" we must note that there is no universal woman's experience. Murray (1970) compared the laboring conditions of Black and white women, stating that the Black woman, "is in the labor market longer and in greater proportion, has less education, earns less, is widowed earlier, and carries a relatively heavier economic responsibility as family head than her white counterpart" (p. 194).

Conclusion

Of course, the stories in this chapter are but a drop in the bucket of the stories of labor organizing in the United States. Missing from these pages are the organizing efforts of railway porters, sex workers, teachers' unions, autoworkers, the organization of incarcerated workers, Teamsters, and numerous other groups large and small. Images of labor organizing in the United States are as diverse as the country itself but labor history is rarely depicted that way in curriculum or in the white imagination. As we have outlined, unions have not always or even often been welcoming environments to everyone. However, there are also countless instances where the support of unions was integral even when one might not expect it. In 1975, when Joni Christian left work at General Motors to receive gender-affirming surgery she returned to a hostile work environment but through the legal team provided by the United Autoworkers she was able to sue and retire from the factory after 30 years (Frank, 2014). Despite rarely having the support of, and in fact often having staunch opposition from, labor leaders and organizers-Black, Asian, Indigenous, Latinx, immigrant, white women, and queer folks have always organized and fought for themselves and their people in the places where they labor.

References

Americans who tell the truth (2024). *Ai-jen Poo: Organizer of domestic workers* https://americanswhotellthetruth.org/portraits/ai-jen-poo/

Anderson, J. D. (1978). Northern Foundations and the Shaping of Southern Black Rural Education, 1902–1935. History of Education Quarterly, 18(4), 371. https://doi.org/10.2307/367710

Anderson, J. D. (1988). The education of Blacks in the South, 1860-1935. University of North Carolina Press.

Baldwin, James. (1984, April). On Being White … and Other Lies. *Essence Magazine*. https://www.cwsworkshop.org/pdfs/CARC/Family_Herstories/2_On_Being_White.PDF

Beale, F. (1970/1995). Double jeopardy: To be Black and female. In Guy-Sheftall (Ed.) Words of fire: An anthology of African-American feminist thought. pp. 146–55

Blest, P. (2020, April 2). Leaked Amazon memo details plan to smear fired warehouse organizer: "He's not smart or articulate" Vice https://www.vice.com/en/article/leaked-amazon-memo-details-plan-to-smear-fired-warehouse-organizer-hes-not-smart-or-articulate/

Carstairs, C. (2001). Defining whiteness: race, class, and gender perspectives in North American history. *International Labor and Working-Class History, 60*, 203–6. JSTOR.

Cobb Jr., C. E. (2014). *This Nonviolent Stuff'll Get You Killed: How Guns Made the Civil Rights Movement Possible*. Duke University Press.

Croom, D. B., & Alston, A. (2009). The Problem of Agricultural and Industrial Education for African Americans: A Historical Inquiry. Journal of Agricultural Education, 50(3), 1–10. https://doi.org/10.5032/jae.2009.03001

Davis, A. (1981). Reflections on the black woman's role in the community of slaves. *The Black Scholar, 12*(6), 2–15. https://doi.org/10.1080/00064246.1981.11414214.

Dewey, J. (1916). Democracy and education: An introduction to the philosophy of education. Macmillan Publishing.

Dowd Hall, J. (1986). Disorderly women: Gender and labor militancy in the Appalachian south. *The Journal of American History, 73*(2), 354–82. https://doi.org/10.2307/1908226

Du Bois, W. E. B. (1935). *Black reconstruction in America: 1860–1880*. The Free Press.

Du Bois, W. E. B. (1994). The souls of Black folk. Dover.

Elk, M. (2024, April 19). After ten-year battle, a younger generation leads the way at Volkswagen. *The American Prospect.* https://prospect.org/labor/2024-04-19-ten-year-battle-younger-generation-leads-volkswagen/

Esty, K. (2022). "I told him to let me alone, that he hurt me": Black women and girls and the battle over labor and sexual consent in union-occupied territory. *Labor Studies in Working-Class History, 19*(1), 32–51. https://doi-org.libproxy.clemson.edu/10.1215/15476715-9475702

Farmworker Justice (2024). *Who are farmworkers?* https://www.farmworkerjustice.org/about-farmworker-justice/who-we-serve/#:~:text=An%20estimated%202.4%20million%20farmworkers,status%20under%20current%20U.S.%20laws

Flores, J. (1941). A Mexican American farmworker describes the importance of sticking together. In M. P. Johnson (Ed.) *Reading the American Past: Selected Historical Documents, Volume II: From 1865.* (4th ed., pp. 177–81).

Foner, P. S. (1983). Mother ones speaks: Speeches and writings of a working class fighter. Pathfinder.

Ford, C. (2012). From "superabundance" to dependency: Women agriculturalists and the negotiation of colonialism and capitalism for reservation-era Lummi. In C. Williams [Ed.] *Indigenous Women and Work: From Labor to Activism.* University of Illinois Press.

Frank, M. (2014). *Out in the union: A labor history of queer America.* Temple University Press.

Hartman, S. (2016). The belly of the world: A note on Black women's labors. Souls, 18(1), 166–73. https://doi.org/10.1080/10999949.2016.1162596

Hartman, S. (2019). *Wayward lives, beautiful experiments: Intimate histories of riotous Black girls, troublesome women, and queer radicals.* Norton & Co.

Haywood, W. D. (1929). *Bill Haywood's Book: The Autobiography of William D. Haywood.* International Publishers.

Hill, H. (1988). Myth-making as labor history: Herbert Gutman and the United Mine Workers of America. Politics, Culture, and Society, 2(2), 132–95.

Hill, H. (1996). The Problem of Race in American Labor History. *Reviews in American History, 24*(2), 189–208. JSTOR.

Hsu, A. & Selyukh (2022, April 2). He was fired by Amazon 2 years ago. Now he's the force behind the company's 1st union. NPR. https://www.npr.org/2022/04/02/1090353185/amazon-union-chris-smalls-organizer-staten-island

Josephs, L. (2024, September 13). Boeing factory workers strike for first time since 2008 after overwhelmingly rejecting contract. CNBC Online News. https://www.cnbc.com/2024/09/13/boeing-workers-strike-reject-contract.htmll

International Brotherhood of Teamsters (2024, February 28). Press Release. https://teamster.org/2024/02/teamsters-reach-major-new-agreement-with-anheuser-busch-boosting-wages-protecting-jobs/

Kaye, D. (2024, September 13). Here's What to Know About the Boeing Strike. The New York Times. https://www.nytimes.com/2024/09/13/business/boeing-strike-workers-explained.html?smid=url-share

Keiser, J. H. (1972). Strikebreakers and racism in Illinois, 1865-1900. *Journal of the Illinois State Historical Society*, *65*(3), 313–26.

Kelleher, K. (2024, February 13). How four black women changed labor organizing forever. *The Forge*. https://forgeorganizing.org/article/how-four-black-women-changed-labor-organizing-forever

Kelly, K., & Nelson, S. (2023). *Fight like hell: The untold history of American labor* (paperback edition). One Signal Publishers/Atria.

Kelley, R. D. (2020). Foreword: Why Black Marxism? Why Now? *Black Marxism: The Making of the Black Radical Tradition, 3rd Edn, Chapel Hill: The University of North Carolina Press*, pp Xi–Xxxiii.

Kuelzer, L., & Houser, N. (2019). Addressing the living history of oppression and emancipation in American education. Journal of Thought, 53(1 & 2), 38–54.

Larson, E. D. (2016). Black Lives Matter and bridge building: Labor education for a "New Jim Crow" era. Labor Studies Journal, 41(1), 36–66.

Lee, E. (2019). American for Americans: A history of xenophobia in the United States. Basic Books.

LeFlouria, T. (2011). "The hand that rocks the cradle cuts cordwood": Exploring Black women's lives and labor in Georgia's convict camps, 1865-1917. *Labor Studies in Working Class History of the Americas,* *8*(3), 47–63.

Library of Congress (n.d.). *Hawaii: Life in a plantation society.* https://www.loc.gov/classroom-materials/immigration/japanese/hawaii-life-in-a-plantation-society/

Mann, A. (1953). Gompers and the irony of racism. The Antioch Review, 13(2).

Martinez, V. (2016, October 10). Katsu Goto: Murder in Honoka'a. *Ke Kalahea.* https://hilo.hawaii.edu/news/kekalahea/KG-Murder.php

Michels, J. & Cox, W. (2024, March 31). The UAW's 2028 National Strike Should Center Medicare for All. Jacobin. https://jacobin.com/2024/03/uaw-general-strike-medicare-for-all

Murray, P. (1970). The liberation of Black women. In B. Guy-Sheftall (Ed.) *Words of Fire: An Anthology of African-American Feminist Thought* (pp. 185–97). The New Press.

National Domestic Worker's Alliance (2021). *About NDWA*. https://www.domesticworkers.org/about-ndwa/

New York Times (1911, March 16). 141 Men and girls die in waist factory fire; trapped high up in Washington Place Building; street strewn with bodies; piles of dead inside. Retrieved from: https://trianglefire.ilr.cornell.edu/primary/newspapersMagazines/nyt_032611.html

Phillips-Cunningham, D. (2021). Slaving Irish 'ladies' and black 'towers of strength in the labor world': Race and women's resistance in domestic service. *Women's History Review, 30*(2), 190–207. https://doi.org/10.1080/09612025.2020.1757864

Quan, H. L. T. (2005). Geniuses of resistance: Feminist consciousness and the Black radical tradition. *Race & Class, 47*(2), 39–53. https://doi.org/10.1177/0306396805058081

Robinson, C. J. (2000). *Black Marxism: The making of the Black radical tradition*. University of North Carolina Press.

Robinson, C. J., Quan, H. L. T., Gilmore, R. W., & Robinson, E. P. (2019). *Cedric J. Robinson: On racial capitalism, Black internationalism, and cultures of resistance*. Pluto Press.

Roediger, D. R. (1991/2007). *The wages of whiteness: Race and the Making of the American working class*. Verso.

Stansell, C. (1986). *City of women: Sex and class in New York, 1789-1860*. University of Illinois Press.

Spillers, H. J. (1987). *Mama's Baby, Papa's Maybe: An American Grammar Book. Diacritics, 17*(2), 65–81. JSTOR. https://doi.org/10.2307/464747

Symcox, L. (2002). *Whose history?: The struggle for national standards in American classrooms*. Teachers College Press.

Trumka, Richard. (2014, September 15). [Speech]. 2014 Missouri AFL-CIO Binnaul Convention, St. Louis, Mo. https://aflcio.org/speeches/trumka-our-brother-killed-our-sisters-son

Truth, S. (1851). *Ain't I a Woman?* [1851 Women's Rights Convention Speech]. 1851 Women's Rights Convention, Old Stone Church, Akron, Ohio.

U.S. Census Bureau (n.d.) Slave population of the United States. Retrieved September 15, 2024, from https://www2.census.gov/library/publications/decennial/1850/1850c/1850c-04.pdf

Wang, V. C. X., & King, K. P. (2009). Building workforce competencies in career and technical education. Information Age Pub.

Washerwomen of Jackson (1866, June 20). *Daily Clarion and Standard*.

Webster, M. (2024). *The Merriam-Webster dictionary* (Revised edition). Merriam-Webster, Incorporated.

Wells-Barnett, I. B. (2012). Southern horrors: Lynch law in all its phases. CreateSpace.

Wells-Barnett, I. B. (2015). The red record: Tabulated statistics and alleged causes of lynchings in the United States. Cavalier Classics.

Yoo, P. (2021). *From a whisper to a rallying cry: The killing of Vincent Chin and the trial that galvanized the Asian American movement.* Norton & Company.
Asian American movement. Norton & Company.

Appendix: Lesson Plan

1. Lesson Plan Title: Whose History is Labor History?
2. Theme: From the Washerwomen of Jackson to Chris Smalls: Labor History Dialog
3. Grade Level: 6–12 (middle/secondary)
4. Course: U.S. History
5. Time Required: 75 minutes
6. Essential and Supporting Questions:
   a. Whose history is Labor History?
   b. How did/do ordinary people organize their labor?
   c. How did/do people organize their labor across racial, ethnic, gender, geographic, and language differences?
   d. Who are some notable people who led labor movements?
7. Objectives:
   a. Students will able to evaluate how the historical events surrounding the history of American labor have largely influenced the narratives surrounding the American labor system.
   b. Student will be able to identify important individuals and groups in the fight for labor equality.
   c. Students will be able to analyze primary sources to build a narrative of labor history.
   d. Students will be able to discuss the power of collective action in comparison to individual action.
8. Standards (from the National Council for the Social Studies [NCSS]):
   a. NCSS: D2. His.1.9-12. Evaluate how historical events and developments were shaped by unique circumstances of time and place as well as broader historical contexts.
   b. NCSS: D2. His.3.9-12. Use questions generated about individuals and groups to assess how the significance of their actions changes over time and is shaped by the historical context.
9. Classroom Materials:
   a. Primary Source documents and materials
   b. Primary Source Analysis tool from the Library of Congress
   c. Video Clips
   d. Station Materials

10. Instructional Plan:
    a. Entry Task to Establish Context [time estimate 5 minutes—change based on time for class period]
        i. Open with problem-posing question: Have students turn and talk calling on their personal context of those who are in the workforce or who babysit or mow yards, etc. Ask them: Who is a laborer? What kinds of things do laborers need/want from their employers?
    b. Teacher-Directed Instruction
        i. Teacher should give a brief overview definition of labor, unions, strike, boycott, right-to-work states, and a timeline of labor organizing, and policies of Union exclusion as needed. Including this video as an example: (https://youtu.be/4LNzgpZ6_J8?si=RybQtLrTyzYCGVLH)
    c. Student-Centered/Engaged Learning (Student Inquiry Activity/Activities) [est. 30 minutes—change based on time for class period]
        i. Students will rotate through stations in small groups where they will have a folder of primary source materials for each of the following groups:
            1. Domestic Laborers
                a. the washerwomen of Jackson letter
            2. Coal-miners-
                a. speech to UMWA by Mother Jones
                b. Image of
            3. Farmworkers-
                a. Ceasar Chavez Wrath of Grapes speech excerpt
            4. Factory Workers
                a. -excerpt from Mother Jones Wail of the Children speech
                b. Viva La Huelga image
                c. Image of
            5. Local Labor Organizing (this section will need to be compiled by the teacher to recognize labor history of the local city or region)
            6. Current Labor Organizing efforts
        ii. Students will analyze the primary source at each station, completing the primary source analysis format.
    d. Exit Task for Summarizing Answer(s) to Essential and Supporting Questions: Write a brief history of labor organizing in the United States including

11. Assessment:
    Assessment Task:
    Students will choose one of these options that captures their understanding of the history of labor organizing in the United States and its relevance to modern labor movements. Components:
    1. Primary Source Analysis:
       - For each primary source station (e.g., Ceasar Chavez's "Wrath of Grapes" speech, Mother Jones's "Wail of the Children" excerpt, "Viva La Huelga" image, etc.), students will complete the primary source analysis format. This should include:
       - Description of the source
       - Context of its creation
       - Purpose and audience
       - Its role in the labor organizing history
    2. Local Labor History Report:
       - Research and include information about labor movements or organizing efforts specific to their city or region (guided by teacher-provided resources). This section should demonstrate connections between local efforts and broader national movements.
    3. Current Labor Organizing Analysis:
       - Investigate one modern labor organizing effort (e.g., unionization in tech industries, strikes in the service sector). Students must include:
       - A summary of the effort
       - Comparison to historical efforts analyzed in class
       - Implications for future labor movements
    4. Summary Response
       - Write a brief history of labor organizing in the United States that responds to the essential and supporting questions provided in class. This essay should synthesize their findings from the primary sources, local history, and current events.
         Grading Criteria:
         - Depth of analysis and critical thinking
         - Accuracy and relevance of historical content
         - Effectiveness in connecting historical and modern labor efforts
12. Community Engagement: By incorporating primary sources, local history, and current events into the curriculum, this lesson plan fosters meaningful community engagement. Students are encouraged to explore local examples

of labor organizing, which helps bridge classroom discussions with real-world relevance. The comparison between modern and historical efforts requires learners to engage critically with the social and economic dynamics within their own communities, promoting a deeper understanding of the factors influencing labor movements. This approach not only connects students to broader societal issues but also empowers them to consider their role in shaping future labor advocacy and community solidarity.

From Breaker Boys to Union Leaders: Labor Movements in the Coal Industry During the Second Industrial Revolution

Heather N. Hagan and Carolyn A. Weber

The coal mining industry in the early 1900s saw numerous labor conflicts and strikes. We will trace the history of coal mining and how the workers were exploited due to company coal towns and unsafe work conditions. These conditions led to multiple strikes in the late 1800s and early 1900s, including ones by the children who worked in the coal mines as "breaker boys." The included lesson plan is an inquiry designed to allow students to grapple with the compelling question "How did the working conditions in coal mines contribute to the rise of labor activism during the Second Industrial Revolution?" while focusing on supporting questions students are able to answer through exploration of both primary and secondary sources.

This chapter will include a review of scholarly secondary sources and an investigation into primary sources. The historical summary of the topic will be a starting point for the inquiry lesson which will allow students to explore secondary and primary sources, as well as young adult nonfiction books about the labor movement within the coal industry in the early 1900s.

Historical Context

Industrial Revolution

Coal mining was critical to the Second Industrial Revolution. Coal supported the growth of the railroad, factories, and numerous industries such as textiles, through its use in the production of iron and as an energy source (Jones, 2023). Burning coal, instead of charcoal, made iron production easier which, in turn, led to a growth in the railroad and increased use of steam engines which, in addition to being made of iron, used coal as its energy source. The steam engine was capable of powering large factories more efficiently. The increase in production efficiency, along with the strengthening of the railroad system, set the stage for a time of tremendous industrial growth.

Two types of coal, bituminous and anthracite, were produced in two types of mines in the eastern United States. Western Pennsylvania had the largest supply of anthracite (hard coal). Anthracite is harder to mine, but produces less smoke. It was frequently used for smelting iron and heating homes. West Virginia had the largest supply of bituminous (soft coal). It is softer and easier to mine. However, it produces more smoke and does not burn as hot (Cordery, 2010). While both types of mines had their share of strikes during the Second Industrial Revolution, the situations within the mining communities were not always the same.

A rise in coal usage also meant growth in the mining industry and the demand for thousands of workers (Kahle, 2023). This work was extremely dangerous and thousands died on the job from injury, disaster, or disease. The miners often worked for 12 hours or more per day for low wages (Cordery, 2010). Additionally, bituminous coalfields were often distant from industrial areas and had low local populations. Together, these factors contributed to the need to recruit miners to move to the coal camps to live and work in close proximity to the mine. Mining operations recruited men from distressed areas in Eastern and Southern Europe as well as Black workers from the South. In some cases, women and children were employed, as well.

Coal Mining Towns

Miners and their families often faced harsh living conditions in coal camps (Kahle, 2023). Mining companies ran almost every aspect of the camp. The housing conditions were poor and the only place to purchase goods was the company store which was often overpriced. Additionally, camp security was employed through the company guards who often supported the company over the rights and freedoms of the workers and residents.

Because anthracite mines tended to be closer to the larger industrial towns in eastern Pennsylvania, such as Pittsburgh, company towns were more common at bituminous mines which were found in more rural areas (Hindman, 2015). In these towns, housing and supplies were all controlled by the company. Because of the rural nature, other stores or housing opportunities did not exist. Coal companies, basically, received all the wages they paid out back through rent and store pricing. In fact, once a miner could not pay for supplies at the store, they were only paid their wages in scrip. Scrip could only be redeemed at the company store, making it nearly impossible for employees to leave the company town or mining industry (Hindman, 2015).

Workers organized unions in response to their working and living conditions (Grossman, 1974; Kahle, 2023; United Mine Workers of America [UMWA], n.d.). Beginning in 1890, several conflicts broke out between the mining operators and the miners. Collectively, this period known as the "mine wars," was marked by violent conflicts including a strike in Virginia in 1912 resulting in a declaration of martial law; a strike in Colorado known as the "1913 Ludlow massacre," which included the death of women and children; and a 1921 uprising in West

Virginia which resulted in more than 130 deaths. Notably, in 1902, the federal government, under the leadership of Theodore Roosevelt, stepped in to intervene in an anthracite mining strike in Pennsylvania. That same year, the well-known labor activist, Mary G. Harris, more commonly known as Mother Jones, helped to organize a strike in West Virginia, one of the most anti-union states until the New Deal Era (Cordery, 2010).

While striking was difficult in every mining town, due to the company's control of all levels of an employee's livelihood, West Virginia was even more of a challenge. Specifically, in West Virginia, the unity between the coal company and political figures made striking extremely difficult: "Coal company officials became political leaders—from sheriffs and district attorneys to senators and successive governors—with alarming regularity" (Cordery, 2010, p. 71). Additionally, West Virginia had the highest rate of fatalities and injuries in their mines compared to every other state (Cordery, 2010, p. 71).

Role of Children

At the time of the 1902 strike, the age limit for working above ground at the mine was 14 and for working below ground at the mine was 16. However, mines rarely asked for proof of ages before sending workers below ground into the mines (Hindman, 2015). During the strike, adult miners claimed that because their wages were so low, their young children had to go into the mines. Because of the use of child labor, their wages were then kept low with no opportunity to raise them (Hindman, 2015).

The most common role for children in the anthracite coal mines was that of Breaker Boy. Their job was to remove contaminants as they picked through anthracite coal that had been broken up in coal breakers (Hindman, 2015; Kahle, 2023). They were well-suited to this job because of their size and it was easier for them to hunch over the conveyor belts (Kahle, 2023).

Breaker Boys were only employed in the anthracite (hard-coal) mines and not in the bituminous (soft-coal) mines. In the bituminous coal mines there was no need to separate the impurities. However, other jobs existed in both types of mines. Young boys would also be employed as doorboys or drivers. Mines had a ventilation system which involved keeping doors closed within the mine. The door boys, also called "nippers" were in charge of waiting near a door until a mine cart pulled by mules, and later electrified, was ready to come through. They would open the door for the cart and then quickly close it. This allowed for fresh air to enter the mines. Door boys were expected to wait in darkness until a driver called out for the door to be open. If they were late or unresponsive, carts could run into each other or built-up methane could cause explosions in the mines (Hindman, 2015). Drivers existed in both anthracite and bituminous coal mines. These young boys were charged with bringing full carts up to the surface and bringing empty carts to be filled again. In larger mines, they usually drove mules who pulled the carts, but in smaller mines, the boys themselves drove the carts (Hindman, 2015).

The other difference between bituminous and anthracite mines was that the youngest boys in bituminous mines were often employed as loaders with adult men. Pennsylvania law in 1900 only specified that children as young as 12 could work in the bituminous coal mines as long as they were working with their fathers (Hindman, 2015). As Hindman (2015) explains,

> Miners were paid per ton of coal delivered to the tipple on the surface where the coal was loaded into railroad cars. The mine provided mules (and later electric haulage), cars, drivers, runners, couplers, and door boys to get the coal from the face to the tipple, but the miner was responsible for the coal face. He was responsible for cutting and blasting the coal, loading it into the car (while sorting dirt, shale, and rock), and, in these early days, building his own bracing to protect himself from roof falls. Time spent away from cutting coal was money out of the miner's paycheck. So, fathers took their sons in as loaders (p. 97).

Because most people worked in their mines for their entire lives, the career trajectory was similar. Starting as either Breaker Boys in anthracite mines, or loaders with their fathers in bituminous mines, then continuing to be door boys, followed by drivers. They then ended up back as loaders when they reached the age to do "men's work" (Hindman, 2015, p. 98). Sometimes in anthracite mines, older men returned to work as Breakers when they could not continue as loaders. This became more common as child labor laws were passed and enforced (Hindman, 2015).

After the 1902 strike, Pennsylvania law required owners of the mines to have potential workers provide an affidavit of their ages. In 1905, Owne Lovejoy of The National Child Labor Commission (NCLC), which was founded in 1904, investigated mines in eastern Pennsylvania. He found that at least 9,000 boys and possibly as many as 12,800 boys under 14 were employed by the mines. However, the Pennsylvania Department of Mines disagreed with those numbers and suggested there were less than 2,000 illegal workers in the mines, also arguing that the children's parents had signed affidavits claiming their children were older (Hindman, 2015). Lovejoy was able to fight back by proving that his numbers were actually on the conservative side and there were potentially even more underage boys employed by the mines throughout the region (Hindman, 2015).

Dangers to Children

Working in mines was dangerous work for adults, and especially children. NCLC estimated that children under the age of 16 were three times more likely than those over 16 to have an accident or be injured on the job. While they did not offer specific data to support this number particularly for mining, this came to be an accepted reasonable estimate (Hindman, 2015). Between 1880 and 1923, 70,000 people died while working in the mines. This number does not include those who died of mine-related illnesses outside of the mines (Kahle, 2023).

There were many dangers to adults and children, such as breathing in the coal dust and losing hearing due to the loud sounds within the mines. However, danger to the Breaker Boys also had to do with the dangers of sitting on a wooden bench above a conveyor belt moving quickly down. Breaker boys were known to fall off their benches and be smothered or burned (Hindman, 2015). In both types of mines, door boys faced other dangers as approaching drivers faced uneven pathways and the inability to control the mules at times. They could also be crushed between carts. Additionally, loaders were in danger of explosions and roof collapses as they worked at the coal face. Because, in bituminous mines, young boys often worked as loaders with their fathers, they were in danger from these collapses (Hindman, 2015).

Finally, while the boys might have an accident or be injured on the job through dangerous activities, the fact was that just starting this arduous work at a young age could have disastrous effects on their overall health. As Hindman (2015) explains, "During the great anthracite strike of 1902, the U.S. Navy sent a Lieutenant J. P. Ryan to recruit sailors from among the idled miners. After a short stay in the region, he was ordered to leave for the following reason: One curious outcome of the recruiting was that very few of the strikers who applied for enlistment could pass the physical requirements. Lieutenant Ryan found that nearly all of those who were willing to go into the navy are under size, weak-chested and round-shouldered, and physically undesirable in nearly every way. This is attributed to going to work at an early age, lack of nourishment, and hard labor in unsanitary surroundings" (p. 102).

Importance and Implications

The hazardous working conditions, child labor, and difficult living conditions created tension between operators and miners, sparking "mine wars" in the late nineteenth and early twentieth centuries. During the "mine wars," numerous conflicts arose between workers and mining companies. The harsh working and living conditions led to the organization of labor unions in response

(Grossman, 1974; Kahle, 2023; UMWA, n.d.) including United Mine Workers of America, the Progressive Miners Union, and the National Union of Mineworkers. Although there were some federal government efforts to increase safety and the Bureau of Mines was created in 1910, most reforms required mine inspections but the insufficient number of inspectors, "corruption, market pressures, intimidation, and weak enforcement mechanisms limited their utility in preventing accidents" (Kahle, 2023).

The "mine wars" were an important time in U.S. labor history. Because miners were often brought in from outside the local area, including from the south and various countries in Europe, this period was marked by the unionization of a racially and ethnically diverse labor force frequently facing language barriers (Grossman, 1974). Despite the difficulties created by these differences, unions persisted and several strikes, frequently violent, occurred during this time (Kahle, 2023).

Although this list is not exhaustive, the following is a brief description of several labor conflicts in the coal industry at the time.

1891 Coal Creek War—Miners in Tennessee seized a group of convict miners on October 31, 1891 in protest to the "convict-lease system," where prisoners, mostly African Americans, were leased to private companies for labor (Zinn Education Project, n.d., para.2). The miners sent a train car full of 40 convicts and their guards to the governor in Knoxville who responded by accompanying the militia to Coal Creek (Coal Creek Watershed Foundation & Inc, n.d.). Governor Buchanan met with the free miners but failed to convince them of the benefits of convict-lease mining. When mine inspections showed unsafe conditions; the free miners captured more convict miners and sent them to Knoxville by train; and the governor sent in more militia and eventually built Fort Anderson. Convict-lease mining officially ended in Tennessee when the next governor abolished it. However, he established the Brushy Mountain Mine and Prison, a profitable state-run mine that used prisoners for its labor until 1938.

1897 Lattimer Strike—In Pennsylvania, European immigrants provided plenty of laborers to operate mines and keep wages low (Shackel, 2019). However, "English-speaking" miners native to the United States, were concerned with protecting their own job and wages. In 1897, the Campbell Act required each coal operator to pay a 3-cent-a-day sales tax for each non-U.S. citizen miner. The UMWA supported this measure, but immigrant miners were already being paid less than native miners and decided to strike. About 400 immigrant miners peacefully marched carrying the American flag, though about 150 carried weapons. Deputies and coal company police ordered them to stop. As they continued to march, they were fired on for about two minutes. Around 20 men died that day. Deputies were tried for one striker's death, but found innocent. The event set the stage for a more inclusive union.

1902 Anthracite Coal Strike of 1902—In May 1902 Pennsylvania anthracite miners requested "better wages, a shorter work week, and recognition of their union" (Theodore Roosevelt Center at Dickinson State University, n.d., para.1). Neither side was stepping down and union leaders brought in female activist Mother Jones (Arnold, 2014; Cordery, 2010). Coal operators worked with local officials to write injunctions against union organizers and arrested several (Cordery, 2010). As the strike went on, President Roosevelt became concerned. He became involved in efforts to resolve the strike on behalf of the American public and commissioned a government investigation of the strike. This marked a tremendous shift in government policy. The strike ended in October 1902 when both parties agreed to abide by the commission report.

1912 Painted Creek-Cabin Creek Strike—Workers in West Virginia struck for higher pay and they were soon backed by the union who sent in labor organizer Mary "Mother" Jones (Donaldson, 2021; Kahle, 2023). Coal operators evicted workers, hired strikebreakers, and called in a private security agency to break the strike. In response, miners armed themselves and marched to the state capitol (Kahle, 2023). The governor declared martial law with the clear intention of breaking the strike. Although fighting paused, 200 strikers were imprisoned while guards and operators faced no punishment. Throughout the 13-month struggle, 12 strikers and 13 company men died.

1913 Ludlow Strike—Colorado's coal industry employed nearly 7,000 workers and had almost double the national death rate for coal miners (National Park Service [NPS], n.d.). The United Mine Workers of America (UMWA) presented several demands to the Colorado Fuel and Iron Company including "the enforcement of an 8-hour workday and the right to choose their own housing and doctors" (NPS, n.d., para.2). Miners were evicted from company housing and established a tent colony for their families. UMWA members armed themselves. On April 20, 1914, the colony was attacked with machine guns and set ablaze (PBS, n.d.). Twenty-one people were killed in what became known as the "Ludlow Massacre." After ten days of fighting, President Woodrow Wilson sent in Federal Troops to end the violence and disarm both sides. A congressional investigation of the events produced a report which later aided in the promotion of child labor laws and enforcement of the eight-hour workday (NPS, n.d.).

Governmental Policy

Initially, these strikes were seen as disputes between labor and private industry. As part of a capitalist economy, state and federal governments played a limited role in labor conflict. However, as time progressed, states began taking action, often on behalf of the operators. Eventually, the presidents' involvement set the stage for federal regulation to protect workers.

State government involvement. States sometimes became involved in strikes when called upon by the operators to maintain order or when they felt it necessary to protect their property. State governments stepped into some of the strikes described above for various reasons and implemented a few different interventions. In the 1891 Coal Creek War in Virginia, the governor allowed convicts to be leased to mines in order to undercut labor costs. The governor sent in militia to protect the convicts, tried to convince miners of the advantages of convict-lease mining, and, eventually, ended the convict-lease program. Shortly thereafter Virginia bought their own mines and, again, used convicts as free labor. In this case, the state's involvement sought economic advantage.

It was not uncommon for states to send in military troops to intervene. The 1912 Painted Creek-Cabin Creek Strike in West Virginia saw state involvement when the governor declared martial law. In this case, the operators hired private security and the miners armed themselves in response so the governor sent in troops to settle the conflict. Although military intervention stopped the strike, the outcome favored the operators who faced no punishment though about 200 strikers were imprisoned.

Some states also resorted to legal action and arrests. One notable incident occurred in Virginia where mine operators enlisted the help of circuit-court judges to file injunctions (Cordery, 2010). Operators hoped that without union organizers to lead them, miners would lose resolve. Judges filed orders to prohibit union organizers from meeting with workers saying that unions were "engaged in an illegal conspiracy to hurt the companies by forcing them to accept only unionized miners" (Cordery, 2010, p. 73). This was quite a blow for union organizers who now ran the risk of arrest if they spoke to miners at rallies on company grounds. The initial injunction was only applicable in the county where the mine was located so union organizers rented grounds nearby. However, a subsequent injunction crossed county lines so holding rallies anywhere within the state became illegal. During a 1902 rally in Virginia, male organizers were arrested for violating the injunction. Immediately after the arrests, Mother Jones refused to stop when being told she was in violation with the injunction. She and the male organizers were all imprisoned. State government involvement had limited impact, usually to suppress a strike. Any action taken on behalf of states did not impact the mining industry, as a whole. Operators in other states could continue "business as usual," and conditions in mines and towns were not usually improved as a result of a single strike.

Federal government involvement. During the Second Industrial Revolution, in a capitalist economy, the federal government's role in labor disputes was considered to be limited. The U.S. government was hesitant to get involved in labor conflicts and, when it did, it often took on the role of a strikebreaker sending in troops, such as in 1834, 1877, and 1894. There were also a few attempts to ease labor tensions neutrally through the establishment of the Bureau of Labor in

1884 and a few laws. The 1902 anthracite strike in Pennsylvania marked a shift in governmental policies in labor relations.

Anthracite coal mining was a monopoly. The coal itself was found in one location, only a few hundred square miles of Pennsylvania (Grossman, 1974; Moss, 2017). Additionally, the mining operations were controlled by only a handful of operators, railroaders, and bankers. This concentration of power gave the owners an upper hand. Local anthracite coal unions began forming in Pennsylvania in the1860 and, in 1869, these consolidated to form the General Council of the Workingmen's Associations of the Anthracite Coal Fields of Pennsylvania or WBA (Moss, 2017, p. 331). Though these organizations morphed several times, in 1899 anthracite miners began joining the bituminous mining union, the United Mine Workers (Moss, 2017). John Mitchell, the president of the United Mine Workers, understood the nation's dependence on anthracite.

In 1900, the United Mine Workers called for a meeting with mine operators (Grossman, 1974; Moss, 2017). When the operators refused, the workers declared a strike. Mitchell hoped that this conflict would end in the worker's favor as an 1897 bituminous coal strike had recently ended in an agreement that was profitable for both workers and operators. Fortunately for the miners, the 1900 strike coincided with an upcoming election between President William McKinnley and William Jennings Bryan (Grossman, 1974; Moss, 2017). Republican Senator Marcus A. Hanna noted the necessity of coal for the railroad industry and worked with railroad presidents to persuade coal operators to increase pay. He warned that a prolonged strike would impede their party and the re-election of McKinnley. A week before the election, coal operators agreed to increase pay and implement a grievance procedure but they never formally recognized the union (Moss, 2017). Settling the strike set the stage for McKinnley's win just a week later and also paved the way for the U.S. government to work as a peacemaker in future labor struggles. Operators, however, were unhappy with their hand being forced for political reasons.

In 1902, anthracite miners again made demands, this time for more pay, shorter hours, and recognition of their union (Grossman, 1974; Moss, 2017). Operators refused to negotiate and the union requested a special session of Congress. The 1900 government involvement was fresh in the minds of operators and they rebuffed the idea of further governmental involvement. A 1902 letter from President Theodore Roosevelt to Senator Henry Cabot Lodge explained that "One of the greatest troubles in dealing with the operators is … their avowed determination … to do away with what they regard as the damage done to them by submitting interference for political reasons in 1900. From the outset they have said that they are never going to submit again to having their laborers given a triumph over them for political purposes" (Roosevelt, 1902 a). Mine operators were trying to remedy the "damage" done by the previous strike.

The union requested mediation but the two parties could not agree on an acceptable group to moderate the process. On May 12, 1902, the miners went on strike. At first, it was only the miners on strike, but maintenance crews, including firemen, engineers, and pumpmen joined the strike just a few weeks later on June 2 (Grossman, 1974). In all, the Labor Commissioner, Carroll D. Wright, reported that 147,000 workers went on strike.

Later that month, Roosevelt sent Labor Commissioner Wright to investigate (Berfield, 2020; Grossman, 1974; Wright, 1902). However, Wright went to New York instead of the mines, reporting that he felt "his presence would do more harm than good." While in New York, he interviewed coal road presidents, mine operators, foremen, superintendents, and financiers. He also invited union president John Mitchell to hear the miner's side. Wright's report was sent to the president 12 days after he arrived in the city. His report provided an in-depth description of both sides (Wright, 1902). He concluded with several "Suggestions that seem Reasonable and Just," including an anthracite coal miner's union independent from the United Mine Workers and American Federation of Labor, a six-month trial of nine-hour work days, the formation of a joint committee on conciliation composed of both anthracite union representatives and mine operators, an investigation into "all conditions relative to mining anthracite coal" conducted by the conciliatory commission, the weighing and payment for coal be completed by two independent inspectors representing the mine operators and the miners until the commission can report, protection of non-union workers, and all bargaining be done within the rules created by the commission (Wright, 1902).

Roosevelt consulted Philander Knox, his attorney general, about the report and how to proceed with the strike. Knox maintained that the president should not get involved because it was outside his office (Moss, 2017). But, Roosevelt (1902 a) was unsure how to proceed writing to Cabot Lodge "There is literally nothing … the national government has any power to do … I am at wit's end how to proceed."

In early October 1902(e), Roosevelt wrote that he "could no more see misery and death come to great masses of people in our large cities and sit by idly" (Roosevelt, 1902e). He intervened on behalf of a third party, the public. At this time in history, many citizens were dependent upon anthracite coal for heating and the shortage threatened their wellbeing as winter approached (Grossman, 1974).

He called the miners and operators to Washington, D.C. to negotiate on October 3. Neither side backed down. The union viewed the meeting

(Grossman, 1974) as an official recognition and in a letter to Robert Bacon, Roosevelt (1902c) wrote that Mitchell, the union president and representative, "was dignified and moderate and straightforward...[But] The operators ... used insolent and abusive language about him; and in at least two cases assumed an attitude toward me which was one of insolence." The meeting ended without resolution. Roosevelt (1902c) told Bacon "the situation is bad, especially because it is possible it may grow infinitely worse. If when the severe weather comes on there is a coal famine I dread to think of the suffering ... and I fear there will be fuel riots of as bad a type as any bread riots we have ever seen." This concern for the wellbeing and safety of the general public led to Roosevelt's (1902c) conclusion that "there is certainly right and wrong on both sides...[but] whatever, with my limited powers, I can do toward securing a peaceful settlement, if possible in the interests of both parties, at least in the interests of the general public, will be done." Despite an unclear role and disagreement about the president's power in the dispute, without an allegiance to either side, Roosevelt was compelled to action on behalf of the nation's people.

Roosevelt attempted to appeal to the miners by promising another investigation if they returned to work, but Mitchell refused, citing that the mine operators were untrustworthy and that a return to work would be seen as surrender. The mine operators called for Roosevelt to send in troops to break the strike but he refused to do so knowing the strikers had not interfered with any government property (Roosevelt, 1902b). Roosevelt was "exasperated" (1902b) by the mining operators.

Root, the secretary of war and personal friend of J. P. Morgan, was concerned about the anthracite strike and met with Morgan to draft a proposal for the miners to return to work while a commission investigated (Grossman, 1974). Unlike the similar proposals before this, operators were willing to abide by the Root-Morgan Proposal because the operators and employers would present their grievances to the commission rather than the union. The mining operators suggested five members of the commission: a member of the army or navy, a judge, a sociologist, a practical mining engineer, and an individual familiar with anthracite mining and selling (Roosevelt, 1902 d) while John Mitchell reported that the miners did not wish to influence the president's decision but trusted him to represent them fairly. After meeting with Roosevelt to discuss the list, Mitchell (1902 a) agreed that the union would stand by the agreement if Roosevelt added a Roman-Catholic clergyman and a representative for the workers. In the end, Roosevelt wrote to J. P. Morgan that he would appoint seven men to the commission, five in accordance with the operators' suggestions with the exception of former President Grover Cleveland in place of the army or navy representative, plus two men who were "familiar with the interests of the wage-workers" (1902 d), a Bishop and the Grand Chief of the Order of Railway Conductors. According to Roosevelt (1902 d) "it would be well-nigh impossible to get a commission of abler men more certain to approach the whole subject in a spirit of fearlessness and sober good sense and of resolute purpose to do even-handed justice." At the time of Roosevelt's letter, Mitchell had already agreed to the commission and Roosevelt concluded his letter to Morgan by saying "surely there can be no good reason for refusing such a commission" (1902 d). In the end, former president Cleveland was replaced by a retired Army General and Anthracite Coal Strike Commission and Labor Commissioner Wright was added as a recorder (Cortelyou, 1902). The operators did not want a "labor-man," on the commission, but agreed to include the Grand Chief of the Order of Railway Conductors if he was named as the "Sociologist." Both sides agreed to abide by the findings of the Anthracite Coal Strike Commission.

On October 21, 1902 John Mitchell (b) sent a telegram to President Roosevelt notifying him that the UMWA delegate convention voted to accept the commission. They would return to work on October 23, 1902 and the commission would meet for the first time on October 24. Roosevelt (1902f) directed the commission "to investigate and decide on all points at issue between the two parties and also to advise action to be taken which will prevent the recurrence of such a calamity in the future." In the end, the commission, essentially, "split the difference" between the miners and operators (Grossman, 1974) by awarding a 9 hour workday, shortened from 10 hours; 10 percent wage increase, though miners demanded 20 percent (United States Anthracite Coal Strike Commission, 1903, pp. 80–1); and the formation of a conciliatory committee comprised of three representatives of the workers and three representatives of the operators to negotiate disagreements (pp. 65–8).

Roosevelt's involvement in the strike marked a turning point in U.S. labor relations. He initiated the role of the U.S. government saying that he "speak[s] for neither the operators nor the miners but for the general public" and "that the party, the great public, had vital interests and overshadowing rights" (Grossman, 1974). Although the government had played the peacemaker role in 1900, that administration was prompted to action by the upcoming election and McKinnley's campaign. The operators in the 1900 strike gave in to demands in order to preserve their party in the White House. Roosevelt, on the other hand, was less motivated by politics and, instead, moved on behalf of the general public for its welfare. The 1902 Anthracite Coal Strike marked the first time the federal government intervened "to resolve a strike both without force and without such a clear legal justification" (Moss, 331) and set the stage for additional action in the future.

Federal labor laws. The 1902 Anthracite Strike opened the door for more federal involvement in labor relations. Once President Roosevelt intervened on behalf of the public, the federal government's role was no longer just on behalf of business interests or as a strikebreaker. National laws were written and agencies were created to better support and protect labor, especially children.

In 1903, Lillian Wald, suggested a Federal Children's Bureau to address the wellbeing of children in the United States (Brown, 2011). Although the process took 9 years, the Bureau is still active. It not only provides grants and programs to provide for the needs of children and families but collects data on numerous child and family concerns. Originally the Bureau focused research on infant mortality. Today, it collects data on adoption, child abuse and neglect, child welfare services, equity, foster care, guardianship, and services provided to children and families in foster care as a part of the Administration for Children and Families (Children's Bureau, 2024).

Census data reported that in 1900 more than 1.75 million 10- to 15-year-olds were working (Paul, 2017). Reformers took note of this and, at the 1903 National Conference of Charities and Corrections, child labor was a frequent topic of presentations. Shortly after, in 1904, the National Child Labor Committee (NCLC) was formed (Paul, 2017). There had been several state and regional organizations, but the NCLC became one of the largest social welfare societies of the twentieth century (Paul, 2017). The organization researched and documented child labor conditions across industries and states and was chartered by Congress in 1907. Famously, the organization hired Lewis Hines as a photographer in 1908 to document and report on child labor (National Archives, 2022; Paul, 2017). The organization also advocated for the 1924 Child Labor Amendment to the Constitution which was passed but never ratified.

Hines' reporting brought children's working conditions into public knowledge (National Archives, 2022). This increased attention to the dangerous conditions and the Keating-Owen Act was passed by Congress in 1916. Products from any factory, shop, or cannery where children under 14 worked were prohibited from sale. Additionally, products from mines employing children under 16 could not be sold, nor could products from any business that employed children under 16 at night or required children to work for more than 8 hours per day. Although President Woodrow Wilson signed the Act into law, in 1918 the *Hammer v. Dagenhart* Supreme Court ruling declared it unconstitutional because Congress could not regulate interstate commerce.

Many fair working regulations were not established until much later. President Franklin D. Roosevelt signed the National Labor Relations Act, also known as the Wagner Act, on July 5, 1935 (National Archives, 2021). This act gave workers "the right to self-organization, to form, join, or assist labor organizations, to bargain collectively through representatives of their own choosing, and to engage in concerted activities for the purpose of collective bargaining or other mutual aid and protection" (Section 7). To protect these rights, the act established the National Labor Relations Board which protects the rights and safety of workers to unionize and collectively bargain. This board may arbitrate in labor disputes and penalize employers for interfering in labor activities. Perhaps one of the most influential laws was the 1938 Fair Labor Standards Act (Library of Congress, n.d.) signed into effect by President Franklin D. Roosevelt. This act established a federal minimum wage of $0.25 per hour, overtime pay for working more than 40 hours per week, and established a minimum working wage of 16 for most industries (Grossman, 1978).

The Second Industrial Revolution was a period of rapid economic changes. Although the history of the coal labor struggle presented in this chapter is far from exhaustive, the "mine wars" are indicative of an era of widespread labor conflict. Coal was only one of the many industries that saw developments that benefited the owners without the workers seeing conditions improve. However, workers in the coal industry, as well as other industries, fought back and set the stage for many of the labor rights and regulations we have today.

Main Teaching/Learning Strategy

The inquiry-based lesson plan presented in this chapter focuses on the coal mining strikes during the late 1800s and early 1900s and uses an adaptation of the framework developed by Weber and Hagan (2023). The inquiry for high school students focuses on the compelling question "How did the working conditions in coal mines contribute to the rise of labor activism during the Second Industrial Revolution?" and is carried out over the course of several lessons. Students use a variety of sources including nonfiction literature, interactive maps, information from the National Park Service, primary sources from the Library of Congress and National Archives, and videos, primarily from PBS's American Experience.

Following Weber and Hagan's (2023) framework, the first step will be for students to be introduced to the topic through a video from PBS's American Experience about coal mining in the 1900s, specifically about Coal Towns. The class will also examine maps of Pennsylvania, West Virginia, and Colorado to discuss the physical location of mines within each state and how that impacted the mining industry. Second, the students will hear the compelling question for the first time and be given an opportunity to write a hypothesis based on their prior knowledge and the brief introduction. Next, students will delve into each supporting question through the sources provided (books, primary sources, and more videos) and be asked to revise their hypothesis based on the evidence, learning, and answer to the supporting question. The development of a hypothesis helps students activate their prior knowledge and its continuous revision supports the organization of their thinking into a conclusion as well as promoting flexible thinking as they learn new information.

Each supporting question will involve three stations and we recommend spending a full class period on each supporting question. The first supporting question asks students to examine the working conditions of both adults and children in coal mines and they will analyze photographs of child and adult miners as well as mining towns and scrip. The second question explores how workers and unions fought for better working conditions by looking at three incidents that were part of the "Mine Wars" through articles and videos. The final supporting question asks students to consider the lasting impact of the coal mining strikes by investigating the government response to these labor struggles as well as child labor laws and general labor laws that were eventually enacted. Finally, students will be asked to write a final response to the compelling question, focusing on evidence they gained from each of the supporting questions and sources.

After formalizing their conclusion, students are given the opportunity to connect their learning about the coal labor struggles of the Second Industrial Revolution with their community today. Because this lesson will be implemented in a variety of contexts, students are given a few options. They could develop their own inquiry questions to research your community's connection to a local union and its local impact. If feasible, we encourage students to interview a local labor union representative or community member involved in a strike, union, or the connected industry.

References

Arnold, A. B. (2014). *Fueling the Gilded Age: Railroads, miners, and disorder in Pennsylvania coal country*. New York University Press.

Berfield, S. (2020, July 14). *The coal strike that defined Theodore Roosevelt's presidency*. Smithsonian Magazine. https://www.smithsonianmag.com/history/when-roosevelt-and-jp-morgan-fixed-coal-mine-strike-180975311/

Brown, A. (2011). *Brief history of the Federal Children's Bureau: (1912–1935)*. Social Welfare History Project. https://socialwelfare.library.vcu.edu/programs/child-welfarechild-labor/childrens-bureau-a-brief-history-resources/

Coal Creek Watershed Foundation, Inc. (n.d.). *Coal Creek: War and disasters.* https://www.coalcreekaml.com/Legacy.htm

Cordery, S. (2010). *Mother Jones: Raising Cain and Consciousness.* University of New Mexico Press.

Cortelyou, C. (1902, October 16). *Anthracite Coal Strike Commission news release.* https://www.theodorerooseveltcenter.org/Research/Digital-Library/Record?libID=o39356

Daniel, P. (1975). *The Tennessee Convict War.* Tennessee Historical Quarterly, 34(3), 273–92. http://www.jstor.org/stable/42623533

Donaldson, R. (2021). *Paint Creek and Cabin Creek strikes.* West Virginia Mine Wars. https://www.nps.gov/articles/000/paint-creek-and-cabin-creek-strikes.htm

Children's Bureau. (2024). *Data & research.* The Administration for Children and Families. https://www.acf.hhs.gov/cb/data-research

Grossman, B. D. (1974). *Talk.* Vocational Guidance Quarterly, 22(3), 188. https://www.dol.gov/general/aboutdol/history/coalstrike

Grossman, B. D. (1978). *Fair Labor Standards Act of 1938: Maximum struggle for a minimum wage.* Department of Labor. https://www.dol.gov/general/aboutdol/history/flsa1938#

Jones, C. (2023). *Overview: Rise of coal in the nineteenth-century United States.* Energy History Online. https://energyhistory.yale.edu/rise-of-coal-in-the-nineteenth-century-united-states/

Kahle, T. (2023). *Overview: Coal mining and labor conflict.* Energy History Online. Yale University. https://energyhistory.yale.edu/coal-mining-and-labor-conflict/

Hindman, H. D. (2015). *Child labor: An American history.* Routledge.

Library of Congress (n.d.). *Fair Labor Standards Act signed.* Research guides: This month in business history. https://guides.loc.gov/this-month-in-business-history/june/fair-labor-standards-act-signed

Mitchell, J. (1902 a, October 16). *Letter from John Mitchell to Theodore Roosevelt.* Theodore Roosevelt Papers. https://www.theodorerooseveltcenter.org/Research/Digital-Library/Record?libID=o39429

Mitchell, J. (1902b, October 21). *Telegram from John Mitchell and W. B. Wilson to Theodore Roosevelt.* Theodore Roosevelt Papers. https://www.theodorerooseveltcenter.org/Research/Digital-Library/Record?libID=o39493

Moss, D. A. (2017). Labor, capital, and government: The anthracite coal strike of 1902. In *Democracy: A Case Study* (pp. 330–64). Harvard University Press. https://doi.org/10.2307/j.ctv31xf5x1.14

National Archives. (2022, February 28). *Keating-Owen Child Labor Act (1916).* Millstone Documents. https://www.archives.gov/milestone-documents/keating-owen-child-labor-act

National Archives. (2021, November 22). *National Labor Relations Act (1935).* Millstone Documents. https://www.archives.gov/milestone-documents/national-labor-relations-act

National Park Service. (n.d.). *War in the Coalfields: The "Ludlow Massacre" and its Impact on the Eight-hour workday.* 2024 Preservation Planning Grants Highlights. https://home.nps.gov/articles/000/war-in-the-coalfields-the-ludlow-massacre-and-its-impact-on-the-eight-hour-workday.htm

Paul, C. A. (2017). *National Child Labor Committee (NCLC).* Social Welfare History Project. https://socialwelfare.library.vcu.edu/programs/child-welfarechild-labor/national-child-labor-committee/

PBS. (n.d.). *The Ludlow Massacre.* American Experience. https://www.pbs.org/wgbh/americanexperience/features/rockefellers-ludlow/

Roosevelt, T. (1902 a, September 27). *Letter from Theodore Roosevelt to Henry Cabot Lodge.* https://www.theodorerooseveltcenter.org/Research/Digital-Library/Record?libID=o294205

Roosevelt, T. (1902b, October 5). *Letter from Theodore Roosevelt to Grover Cleveland.* https://www.theodorerooseveltcenter.org/Research/Digital-Library/Record?libID=o26618

Roosevelt, T. (1902c, October 5). *Letter from Theodore Roosevelt to Robert Bacon.* https://www.theodorerooseveltcenter.org/Research/Digital-Library/Record?libID=o183194

Roosevelt, T. (1902 d, October 15). *Letter from Theodore Roosevelt to J. Pierpont Morgan.* https://www.theodorerooseveltcenter.org/Research/Digital-Library/Record?libID=o26616

Roosevelt, T. (1902e, October 16). *Letter from Theodore Roosevelt to Anna Roosevelt Cowles.*

https://www.theodorerooseveltcenter.org/Research/Digital-Library/Record?libID=o285946

Roosevelt, T. (1902f, October 22). *Letter from Theodore Roosevelt to Winthrop Murray Crane.* https://www.theodorerooseveltcenter.org/Research/Digital-Library/Record?libID=o18338

Shackel, P. A. (2019). *How a 1897 massacre of Pennsylvania coal miners morphed from a galvanizing crisis to forgotten history.* Smithsonian Magazine. https://www.smithsonianmag.com/history/how-1897-massacre-pennsylvania-coal-miners-morphed-galvanizing-crisis-forgotten-history-180971695/

Theodore Roosevelt Center at Dickinson State University. (n.d.). *Anthracite coal strike.* TR Encyclopedia. https://www.theodorerooseveltcenter.org/Learn-About-TR/TR-Encyclopedia/Capitalism-and-Labor/Anthracite-Coal-Strike

United Mine Workers of America. (n.d.). *United Mine Workers of America history.* History. https://umwa.org/about/history/

United States Anthracite Coal Strike Commission. (1903). *Report to the President on the Anthracite Coal Strike of May-October, 1902, by the Anthracite Coal Strike Commission*. Government Printing Office. https://librarycollections.law.umn.edu/documents/darrow/Report%20Anthracite%20Comm.pdf

Weber, C. A. & Hagan, H. N. (2023). *Integrating inquiry in Social Studies classrooms.* Routledge.

Wright, C. D. (1902, June 20). *Report from the Commissioner of Labor on the Anthracite Coal Strike*.https://www.theodorerooseveltcenter.org/Research/Digital-Library/Record?libID=o38311&from=https%3A%2F%2F

Zinn Education Project. (n.d.). *This day in history: Oct. 31, 1891: Coal Creek war.* Zinn Education Project: Teaching People's History. https://www.zinnedproject.org/news/tdih/coal-creek-war/

Appendix

Lesson Plan

1. Lesson Plan Title: From Breaker Boys to Union Leaders: Labor Movements in the Coal Industry During the Second Industrial Revolution.
2. Theme: This lesson focuses on the labor movement specifically in coal mines during the Second Industrial Revolution. Students will focus on the working conditions which led to the development of unions in the coal industry. Next, they will dive into three strikes from the early twentieth century. On the third day, students will delve into the government's response to those three events and how labor laws were passed. On day four, students will respond to the compelling questions and identify questions they still have. Finally, students will have the opportunity to find how their communities have been impacted by recent labor negotiations.
3. Grade Level: 9–12.
4. Course: U.S. History.
5. Time Required: The instructional portions of this lesson will take five days to complete (with 40- to 50-minute class periods each day). One class is designed as the introduction to the lesson, then there are three days for inquiry, and the last day for the assessment. Additionally, the next one to two days could be spent on the community engagement activity.
6. Essential and Supporting Questions:
    a. Essential/Compelling Question: How did the working conditions in coal mines contribute to the rise of labor activism during the Second Industrial Revolution?
    b. Supporting questions:
        1. What were the working conditions for adults and children at coal mines during the Second Industrial Revolution?
        2. How did workers and unions fight to change working conditions of mines during the Second Industrial Revolution?
        3. What has been the lasting impact of the coal mining strikes?
7. Objectives:
    a. Students will be able to analyze primary and secondary sources to determine how mine workers during the Second Industrial Revolution changed working conditions.
    b. Students will be able to generate questions for further research based on their analysis into the conditions of coal workers during the Second Industrial Revolution.

8. Standards (from the National Council for the Social Studies [NCSS]):
   a. D2. Civ.5.9-12: Evaluate citizens and institutions effectiveness in addressing social and political problems at the local, state, tribal, national, and/or international level.
   b. D2. Civ.14.9-12: Analyze historical, contemporary, and emerging means of changing societies, and promoting the common good and protecting rights.
   c. D2.His.12.9-12: Use questions generated about multiple historical sources to pursue further inquiry and investigate additional sources.
9. Classroom Materials:

   Note: These are listed in the order they are used in the lesson.

   PBS (n.d). The Coal Town System. *The Mine Wars.* https://iowa.pbslearningmedia.org/resource/amex28mw-soc-minetown/the-coal-town-system-the-mine-wars/

   American Geoscience Institute (2024). Interactive Atlas of Historical Coal Mine Maps in Pennsylvania. https://www.americangeosciences.org/critical-issues/maps/interactive-atlas-historical-coal-mine-maps-pennsylvania

   American Geoscience Institute (2024). Interactive Map of Coal Mines in West Virginia. https://www.americangeosciences.org/critical-issues/maps/interactive-map-coal-mines-west-virginia

   American Geoscience Institute (2024). Interactive Map of Coal Mines in Colorado. https://www.americangeosciences.org/critical-issues/maps/interactive-map-mines-colorado

   Yale University (n.d). *Child labor, Pennsylvania coal mines.* Energy History Online. Yale University. https://energyhistory.yale.edu/child-labor-pennsylvania-coal-mines-gallery/

   Yale University (n.d). *Coal miners working inside the mine, early twentieth century.* Energy History Online. Yale University. https://energyhistory.yale.edu/coal-miners-working-inside-the-mine-1908-gallery/

   Yale University (n.d). *Stonega Coal Mines and Company Camp, 1915-1930.* Energy History Online. Yale University. https://energyhistory.yale.edu/stonega-coal-mines-and-company-camp-1915-1930-gallery/

   Yale University (n.d). *Arthur Kilgore Mine Scrip Collection.* Energy History Online. Yale University. https://energyhistory.yale.edu/arthur-kilgore-mine-scrip-collection/

   Yale University (n.d). *Blank coal labor contract, 1920s.* Energy History Online. Yale University. https://energyhistory.yale.edu/blank-coal-labor-contract-1920s/

   National Park Service. (n.d.). *War in the Coalfields: The "Ludlow Massacre" and its Impact on the Eight-hour workday.* 2024 Preservation Planning Grants

Highlights. https://home.nps.gov/articles/000/war-in-the-coalfields-the-ludlow-massacre-and-its-impact-on-the-eight-hour-workday.htm

PBS. (n.d.). *The Ludlow Massacre*. American Experience. https://www.pbs.org/wgbh/americanexperience/features/rockefellers-ludlow/

Mauk, B (April 18, 2014). *The Ludlow Massacre still matters.* The New Yorker. https://www.newyorker.com/business/currency/the-ludlow-massacre-still-matters

Donaldson, R. (2021). *Paint Creek and Cabin Creek strikes.* West Virginia Mine Wars. https://www.nps.gov/articles/000/paint-creek-and-cabin-creek-strikes.htm

PBS (n.d.) *Paint Creek and the Mine War.* The Mine Wars. https://iowa.pbslearningmedia.org/resource/09060936-263e-4214-8ef4-071319f8e29f/paint-creek-and-the-mine-wars/

West Virginia Public Broadcasting (June 10, 2020). *June 10, 1913: Paint Creek-Cabin Creek Hearings Begin.* West Virginia Public Broadcasting. https://wvpublic.org/june-10-1913-paint-creek-cabin-creek-hearings-begin/

Burns, K. (2014) *United Mine Workers Strike.* The Roosevelts an Intimate History [Film]. https://iowa.pbslearningmedia.org/resource/united-mine-strike/ken-burns-the-roosevelts/

Bartoletti, S. C. (1999). *Kids on Strike!* MA: Houghton Mifflin Company. Chapter 4: I'll be a Johnny Mitchell Man: The Anthracite Coal Strikes Pennsylvania (1897, 1900, and 1902).

Bartoletti, S. C. (1996). *Growing Up in Coal Country.* MA: Houghton Mifflin Books. Chapter 8:

Grossman, J. (n.d). The Coal Strikes of 1902. *US Department of Labor.* https://www.dol.gov/general/aboutdol/history/coalstrike

Berfied, S. (2020, July 14). *The Coal Strike that Defined Theodore Roosevelt's Presidency.* Smithsonian Magazine. https://www.smithsonianmag.com/history/when-roosevelt-and-jp-morgan-fixed-coal-mine-strike-180975311/

National Archives. (2022, February 28). *Keating-Owen Child Labor Act (1916).* Millstone Documents. https://www.archives.gov/milestone-documents/keating-owen-child-labor-act

Brown, A. (2011). *Brief history of the Federal Children's Bureau: (1912–1935).* Social Welfare History Project. https://socialwelfare.library.vcu.edu/programs/child-welfarechild-labor/childrens-bureau-a-brief-history-resources/

National Archives. (2021, November 22). *National Labor Relations Act (1935).* Millstone Documents. https://www.archives.gov/milestone-documents/national-labor-relations-act

Library of Congress (n.d.). *Fair Labor Standards Act signed.* Research guides: This month in business history. https://guides.loc.gov/this-month-in-business-history/june/fair-labor-standards-act-signed

10. Instructional Plan (all links for resources are found earlier):
    a. Entry Task to Establish Context: Teacher will begin by asking students what they know about coal mining communities during the Second Industrial Revolution. After a few minutes discussion, the teacher will show the PBS video: Coal Town System which explains about coal mining and coal mining towns.
    b. Teacher-Directed Instruction: After viewing the video, ask students to list some of the working conditions described in the video.
    Allow students time to explore the interactive map tools for Pennsylvania, West Virginia, and Colorado.
    Teacher Note: The West Virginia and Colorado interactive maps display current mine locations; however, these are similar geographic areas to the locations of mines during the Second Industrial Revolution.
    Ask the following questions:
    - What do you notice about the three interactive maps?
    - What are some similarities and differences between the three states?
    - How do you think the geographic locations of coal impacted these states?

    Introduce students to the compelling question:
    How did the working conditions in coal mines contribute to the rise of labor activism during the Second Industrial Revolution?
    Give students a few minutes to write a response based on their prior knowledge, the PBS video, and the three interactive maps.
    After students are able to write their hypothesis, explain that you will be focusing on labor relations during the Second Industrial Revolution for the next three days. Each day, students will receive a new supporting question and they will interact with three stations (described in detail later). At the end of each day, they will have the opportunity to revise their hypothesis to the compelling question based on the resources they explored during class. After answering all three supporting questions, students will write a formal response to the compelling question.
    c. Student-Centered/Engaged Learning (Student Inquiry Activity/Activities):
    At the beginning of the next 3 days, students will be given a supporting question. They will then visit three stations to help them answer that question. At the end of the day, they will revisit their hypothesis for the compelling question.

Day 1: Supporting Question: What were the working conditions for adults and children at coal mines during the Second Industrial Revolution?

Station 1 a: Child labor photographs from Pennsylvania Coal Mines

Resources (links provided earlier):

Yale University (n.d.). *Child Labor Pennsylvania Coal Mines Picture Gallery*

Directions: Read the information about the *Child Labor, Pennsylvania Coal Mines* picture gallery. Look closely at each picture and read the captions. Use the information to answer the supporting questions for this station. Remember you will use this information at the end of the day to revise your hypothesis to the compelling question.

Station 1b: Adult labor photographs from Pennsylvania Coal mines

Resources:

Yale University (n.d). *Coal Miners Working Inside the Mine, early twentieth century.*

Directions: Read the information about the *Coal miners working inside the mine, early twentieth century* picture gallery. Look closely at each picture and read the captions. Use the information to answer the supporting questions for this station. Remember you will use this information at the end of the day to revise your hypothesis to the compelling question.

Station 1c: Mining towns and scrip

Resources:

Yale University (n.d). *Stonega Coal Mines and Company Camp, 1915–1930.*

Yale University (n.d). *Arthur Kilgore Mine Scrip Collection.*

Yale University (n.d). *Blank Coal Labor Contract, 1920s.*

Directions: Read the description for each picture. Think about what mining towns provided and how they were used by mining companies. Use the information to answer the supporting questions for this station. Remember you will use this information at the end of the day to revise your hypothesis to the compelling question.

At the conclusion of day 1, ask students to review the supporting question and evidence. Encourage them to make notes based on their findings, learning, and evidence from today's stations that will help them respond to the compelling question as they write their conclusion on day 4.

Day 2:

Supporting Question: How did workers and unions fight to change the working conditions of miners during the Second Industrial Revolution?

Station 2a: Ludlow Massacre

Resources:

National Park Service. (n.d.). *War in the Coalfields: The "Ludlow Massacre" and its Impact on the Eight-hour workday.*

PBS. (n.d.) *The Ludlow Massacre.*

Directions: Look at the two resources about the massacre in Ludlow, Colorado in 1914. The National Park Service website describes what happened. The PBS website provides communications from the time period. Use the information from both websites to answer the supporting question.

Station 2b: West Virginia Mine Wars: Paint Creek

Donaldson, R. (2021). *Paint Creek and Cabin Creek strikes.*

PBS (n.d.) *Paint Creek and the Mine War.*

Directions: Read the Donaldson article and watch the PBS video. The NPS article and PBS video give an overview of what happened. Use the information in order to answer the day's supporting question.

Station 2c: Anthracite Strike of 1902

Resources:

PBS (n.d.) *United Mine Workers Strike.*

Bartoletti, S. C. (1999). Kids on Strike! MA: Houghton Mifflin Company. Chapter 4: I'll be a Johnny Mitchell Man: The Anthracite Coal Strikes Pennsylvania (1897, 1900, and 1902).

OR

Bartoletti, S. C. (1996). Growing Up in Coal Country. MA: Houghton Mifflin Books. Chapter 8: Strike!

Note: Both chapters are high-quality, in-depth resources. However, due to time constraints, teachers may find it necessary to direct students to any particular sections they choose to focus on.

Directions: Watch the PBS video and read the book chapters about the Anthracite Strike of 1902. Use these resources to answer the supporting question.

At the conclusion of day 2, ask students to review the supporting question and evidence. Encourage them to make notes based on their findings, learning, and evidence from today's stations that will help them respond to the compelling question as they write their conclusion on day 4.

Day 3: Lasting Impact

Supporting Question: What has been the lasting impact of the coal mining strikes?

Station 3 a: Government Response

Anthracite Strike:

Grossman, J. (n.d).

Berfied, S. (July 15, 2020).

Ludlow Massacre:

Mauk, B. (April 18, 2014).

Note: This resource was published in 2014 and the context of mining and labor has changed since then. However, we chose to include this article because it includes pertinent, historical information that is accessible to students.

West Virginia:

West Virginia Public Broadcasting (June 10, 2020).

Directions: Read the three articles which detail how governments responded to the strikes you read about yesterday. Some of the articles are about the federal government's response and some are about the state's response. Use these articles to respond to the supporting question.

Station 3b: Child Labor Laws

Child Labor Laws:

National Archives. (2022, February 28). *Keating-Owen Child Labor Act (1916).*

Creating the Children's Bureau:

Brown, A. (2011).

Directions: Read the introduction at the National Archives website about the Keating-Owen Child Labor Act. This gives an overview of the first federal law passed to protect children at work. It also explains how the courts overruled many of its provisions. Read Brown's article which is about how the US government set up a children's bureau to investigate child labor throughout the country.

Station 3c: Labor Laws

National Labor Relations Act:

National Archives. (2021, November 22). *National Labor Relations Act (1935).* Fair Labor Standards Act:

Library of Congress (n.d.). *Fair Labor Standards Act signed.*

Directions: Read the National Archives introduction to the *National Labor Relations Act* and the Library of Congress story about the *Fair Labor Standards Act.*

At the conclusion of day 3, ask students to review the supporting question and evidence. Encourage them to make notes based on their findings, learning, and evidence from today's stations that will help them respond to the compelling question as they write their conclusion on day 4.

d. Exit Task for Summarizing Answer(s) to Essential and Supporting Questions
After you have answered each of the supporting questions using the resources found at the nine stations over 3 lessons, take a few minutes to finalize your response to the compelling question. Make sure you are using specific examples from each of the stations to support your response.
After you have written your response to the compelling question, write down additional questions that you have about the labor movement and coal mines. How could you find the answers to these questions?

11. Assessment:
Checklist for students' responses to the compelling question:
Do students address how working conditions in coal mines contribute to the rise of labor activism during the Second Industrial Revolution?
Did students cite a source from each station; therefore making sure to include examples from the Ludlow Massacre in Colorado, the Pennsylvania Anthracite Strikes, and the Paint Creek Strike in West Virginia and government responses?
Did students address the lasting impact of the coal mine strikes?
Did students identify further research questions and possible places to find the answers?

12. Community Engagement: Have students research a local strike and/or contact a local labor union representative. As a class, develop questions about the local union connection and its impact on your community. If feasible, interview the union representative or a community member involved in the strike or the connected industry.

Echoes of Engagement: Amplifying *Voces Cívicas* Through Chicano Narratives. *Ecos de Compromiso: Amplificando* Voces Cívicas *a través de Narrativas Chicanas*

Debora V. Saavedra-Winch and Tina Lane Heafner

In classrooms across Central America, students weren't just learning; they were becoming revolutionaries. Imagine it, January 9, 1964, in the Panama Canal Zone. A group of Panamanian high schoolers marched in, dead set on raising their Panamanian flag right next to the American one, even though President Lyndon B. Johnson had explicitly ordered it to stay down (McPherson, 2009). These kids knew what they were doing, it wasn't just about hoisting a piece of cloth. It was a huge moment of defiance, a stand against imperialism, showing the power of youth who are *educated* and *aware*. This kind of patriotism in schools? It's not just about flags and pledges, it's about teaching young people that they have a stake in their country's future.

And it wasn't just Panama. The 1960s and 1970s were full of these moments across Latin America, with students rising up everywhere. The Cuban Revolution had lit a fire, and students from Nicaragua to Guatemala weren't afraid to confront their governments. On September 26, 1970, students at Universidad Centroamericana in Nicaragua protested the Somoza dictatorship (Rueda, 2019). In Guatemala, students from the Universidad de San Carlos de Guatemala pushed back against Jorge Ubico's military regime (Johnson, 2018). These young people weren't just angry at their own governments, they were also standing up against foreign interference. What history witnessed was a wave of activism that empowered a generation to say, "No more."

Now, similar actions occurred in our backyard, in Los Angeles. The 1968 East LA walkouts, where thousands of Chicano students marched out of their classrooms, weren't all that different. Just like the students in Latin America, these young people were fed up. They wanted better schools, better teachers, and they wanted to learn their *own* history. Until then, schools ignored Mexican American history, treating these students like they didn't belong. This act of historical erasure stems from the Treaty of Guadalupe Hidalgo in 1848, which usurped land and rights from Mexicans, leaving generations of Mexican Americans with a deep feeling of being outsiders in their own land. This sense of displacement, the feeling that you're part of the country but not really "of" the country, became fuel for the Chicano Movement. It became the response of a group of people who found themselves misplaced, and it wasn't just about making sure kids had books and better teachers. It was about identity, reclaiming space in a country that denied their culture and history. These students knew that education was the battleground for cultural survival; a fight which continues in every classroom today, whether we realize it or not.

Now, here's where history finds its songs. As students protested in the streets of LA, music became their rallying cry. In this spirit of Broadway versions of history (e.g., *Hamilton*), imagine the Carnaval del Barrio scene from *The Heights*. There is a community that feels displaced, like they don't fully belong anywhere, and then—bam!—the music starts. It's vibrant, it's powerful, and suddenly, everyone's connected. Even if they don't have a homeland they can point to music as giving them that sense of place. It's like saying, "Hey, we belong here, and we're going to sing it loud enough so everyone knows."

Music has that power, right? Think about the song you played at your wedding, the one that marked your high school graduation, or the song you played on repeat after your first heartbreak. Music taps into something deeper, it creates a strong connection between emotion and identity, grounding us in moments that define who we are. Music transcends borders, connects people, and becomes a way of claiming space, even when *physical* land has been taken or denied. The Chicano students were doing that in their walkouts—through their protests and their music, they were saying, "We exist. Our culture exists." And this is something we see over and over throughout history: identity shaped and strengthened through music, with songs that speak across boundaries and bring people together.

These examples reveal an undeniable truth: classrooms are not just places of learning; they are where activism is born. Here, students are not passive vessels waiting to be filled with knowledge, they are active participants, shaping and challenging their environment. Civic participation begins right here, within the walls of our schools, where students discover that their voices have power, and their ideas can spark change. But what happens when these students are uprooted, when they leave behind their countries, their cultures, and their languages, and find themselves navigating the unknown in a foreign land?

As educators in the United States, many of us have students who bring with them rich legacies of resistance and activism. They are the children of those who fled political instability in El Salvador, those who survived the aftermath of Daniel Ortega's reign in Nicaragua, or those who escaped the dictatorship of Manuel Antonio Noriega in Panama. These students arrive in our classrooms carrying the weight of their histories, histories filled with struggle, resilience, and the fight for justice. Yet, when they step into American schools, they are often met with a new challenge: a curriculum that does not reflect *their stories*, their past, or their potential for civic engagement. Instead of empowering them, the system can become yet another barrier, distancing them from the very participation they once knew.

This is where we, as educators, have a critical role to play. How do we bridge that gap? How do we help these students reclaim the sense of agency and community activism that may feel so distant in their new environment? One of the most powerful ways to do this is through stories and music that resonate deeply with their cultural identities. Chicano music, in particular, serves as a vivid example of how art can be a dynamic force for civic engagement. Songs like "Cantos de mi Cantón" don't just fill the air, they ignite the soul. They carry the struggles and triumphs of a people, connecting listeners to their heritage and to movements greater than themselves. These songs remind us, and our students, that activism can begin with a melody, a verse, and a rhythm. It can start in the classroom, with us, the teachers.

This chapter invites you to explore how Chicano music, especially "Cantos de mi Cantón," can serve as a spark for civic engagement and cultural pride within our classrooms. We, as educators, have the power to transform our students' understanding of their histories, their identities, and their roles in society. Imagine a classroom where students—many from marginalized or minority communities—hear music that reflects their lives, their challenges, and their potential to create change. Imagine the energy that comes alive when students realize they can take the lessons from the Chicano Movement and apply them to their own communities, to issues they care deeply about.

In this chapter, we will delve into how engaging with narratives from the past, particularly those found in Chicano music, can open up spaces of activism and participation for our students. Can the stories of the Chicano Movement help them see themselves as agents of change? Can we, as educators, use music to inspire the kind of civic engagement that not only informs but also empowers? The answer, we believe, is a resounding yes—and it starts with us, the teachers. Together, we can harness the power of music and storytelling to create classrooms where every student feels a sense of belonging, cultural pride, and the drive to fight for social justice.

Historical Context: Understanding the Chicano Movement

In 2015, The Huffington Post published an article titled "Teaching Hip Hop Illegally Promotes Ethnic Solidarity, Arizona Official Says," highlighting a controversy over including Mexican American and African American perspectives in public school curricula. Arizona State Superintendent John Huppenthal accused

Tucson Unified School District of violating a 2010 law prohibiting the promotion of ethnic solidarity and the overthrow of the U.S. government (Planas, 2015). Huppenthal criticized the teaching of "Tú eres mi otro yo" ("You are my other me"), an Indigenous philosophy emphasizing interconnectedness, particularly within Mayan culture.

> Tú eres mi otro yo. (You are my other me.)
> Si te hago daño a ti, (If I do harm to you)
> Me hago daño a mi mismo. (I do harm to myself)
> Si te amo y respeto, (If I love and respect you)
> Me amo y respeto yo. (I love and respect myself).

This interconnectedness contrasts with the American schooling system, which historically aimed to create a unified culture, language, and tradition (Castagno, 2008). The term "Chicano" emerged as a byproduct of exclusion, with Mexican Americans feeling rejected by both Mexico and the United States. The Chicano civil rights movement of the 1960s and 1970s responded to systemic discrimination and social exclusion. Mexican American youth reclaimed "Chicano," a term originally meant to diminish them, transforming it into a symbol of pride (La Blue Kombi, 2021).

A major focus of the Chicano Movement was labor rights, particularly in the agricultural sector, where Mexican American farmworkers faced exploitation, low wages, and harsh conditions (Chappell, 2023; Isaac & Christiansen, 2002). However, the movement also addressed broader issues of identity, inequality, and cultural suppression (Rodriguez, 2019).

Key figures like Dolores Huerta and Cesar Chavez, co-founders of the United Farm Workers (UFW), organized strikes, boycotts, and marches, drawing national attention to farmworkers' struggles and achieving significant labor reforms. Inspired by the Black civil rights movement, both emphasized nonviolent resistance and demonstrated the interconnectedness of marginalized groups' social justice movements (Jensen & Hammerback, 1980; Ortiz, 2018). Huerta's rallying cry, "Sí, se puede" ("Yes, we can"), became a symbol of empowerment for workers and marginalized communities (Broadhurst, 2014). The movement's blend of labor struggles and cultural resistance united diverse communities in a collective fight for justice (Rodriguez, 2017).

Music also played a pivotal role in the movement, serving as both cultural expression and political resistance. Artists like Agustin Lira, co-founder of El Teatro Campesino, used music to raise awareness of Mexican American labor struggles and inspire civic engagement. Lira's song "Cantos de mi Cantón" exemplifies how Chicano music was a tool for mobilization (American Folklife Center & Library of Congress, 2011). The fusion of art and activism, often called Chicanismo, connected cultural pride with poltical action (Rodriguez, 2019). Music became a unifying force for the Chicano community, galvanizing them in the fight for justice (Isaac & Christiansen, 2002).

Through the efforts of leaders like Huerta, Chavez, and Lira, the Chicano Movement became not only a labor and civil rights movement but also a cultural renaissance, reclaiming Mexican American identity and instilling pride and resilience within the community (Dunbar-Ortiz, 2021). The artistic expressions, particularly music, helped preserve Mexican American heritage, fostering solidarity and leaving a lasting legacy for future generations (Rodriguez, 2019). This movement's emphasis on labor rights, education reform, and cultural affirmation laid the foundation for future activism, demonstrating how music and social movements are deeply intertwined.

The purpose of this chapter is to explore the powerful role that Chicano music played in the activism and social change of the 1960s and 1970s. By focusing on songs like "Cantos de mi Cantón," this chapter will examine how music served as a catalyst for civic engagement and a reflection of the broader Chicano Movement. Music was not only a means of expressing the struggles of the Chicano community, but it also inspired collective action and brought people together in the fight for justice (American Folklife Center & Library of Congress, 2011). As Chappell (2023) argues, the cultural and educational importance of music during the Chicano Movement extended into various aspects of community-building, from street protests to educational reforms.

Purpose of this Chapter

This chapter will investigate the ways in which Chicano music, especially the work of Agustin Lira, contributed to the empowerment of the Chicano community and the fight for labor and civil rights. It will also explore how these musical traditions can be used in modern educational practices to engage students in discussions about activism, identity, and social justice (Rhodes, 2011). The main questions this chapter will address are:

1. How did Chicano music, particularly Agustin Lira's work, act as a catalyst for civic engagement and activism within the Chicano Movement?
2. In what ways can music be integrated into the classroom to inspire student activism and foster a deeper understanding of social justice?

3. How can the lessons of the Chicano civil rights movement, as expressed through music, be applied to contemporary struggles for equality and civil rights?

By addressing these questions, the chapter aims to provide educators with strategies to use music as a tool for teaching civic engagement, cultural pride, and the importance of social justice in today's classrooms.

The Historical and Cultural Significance of Chicano Music

Gerald Wilson's move to Los Angeles during the Great Migration immersed him in the city's jazz scene and sparked his interest in Mexican culture through his marriage to Josefina Villasenor. This cultural fusion inspired his composition "Viva Tirado," a tribute to bullfighter José Ramón Tirado. The 1962 piece gained iconic status, reinterpreted by the Chicano band El Chicano in 1970 and sampled by Kid Frost in his 1990 hit "La Raza." Despite growing segregation, music like "Viva Tirado" united Black and Latino communities in postwar Los Angeles. El Chicano's version became an anthem of the Chicano Movement, while Kid Frost's sampling bridged Chicano identity with hip-hop, illustrating music's power to transcend boundaries and foster collaboration (Wang, 2010).

Music is not merely a reflection of identity; it is an active process through which individuals engage with their cultural surroundings (Connell & Gibson, 2003). Chicano music incorporates traditional and contemporary influences, creating a complex tapestry that reflects Chicano identity. It provides a platform for individuals to express their experiences and resist marginalization (Madsen, 2020). This is evident in the rise of mariachi programs in U.S. schools during the 1960s and 1970s, when the Chicano Movement amplified pride in Mexican heritage (Chappell, 2023). Educators like Zeke Castro used mariachi to instill pride and cultural self-worth in students, even for those not fluent in Spanish (Chappell, 2023).

The historical context of Chicano music underscores its significance in identity formation. Figures like Luis Valdez and Teatro Campesino used music and performance to critique social injustices and foster ethnic solidarity during the civil rights movements of the 1960s and 1970s (Rodriguez, 2007). The evolution of programs like Castro's mariachi education highlights the enduring impact of Chicano music in shaping identity and activism (Chappell, 2023).

Beyond representation, Chicano music serves as a tool for cultural learning and self-exploration. It empowers individuals to assert their identity in a society that often seeks to undermine it. Chicano music continues to inspire a sense of collective identity, bridging personal and collective memory in a multicultural context (Chappell, 2023).

Research indicates that music plays a formative role in developing cultural identity, especially among young ethnic minorities (Bennett, 2017). Chicano youth engage with their musical heritage as a means of cultural learning and self-exploration, with active participation in music fostering a sense of agency and belonging. This process is essential for identity development, connecting personal experiences with collective history.

Music as a Voice for the Voiceless

Chicano music has historically served as a critical vehicle for political expression and social justice, providing a voice for marginalized Mexican Americans. It addresses conditions of exploitation, racism, and social inequities faced by Chicano communities. As Ulibarri (2018) explains, Chicano music not only expresses cultural identity but also serves as political mobilization and protest against oppressive structures. Leaders like Cesar Chavez and Dolores Huerta played key roles in merging music with activism. Songs such as "Corrido de César Chávez" and "De Colores" became central to the United Farm Workers' strikes and protests (Chavez, 2000).

Chicano music shares strong connections to other social movements, like the African American civil rights movement. Both used music to inspire and mobilize communities toward activism. The lyrics of Chicano protest music often mirrored those of African American spirituals, expressing oppression and resistance (Ortiz, 2018). Music provided marginalized groups with a platform to articulate their struggles when other forms of communication were inaccessible. Artists like Agustin Lira used music to highlight the plight of farmworkers, creating a shared cultural experience that empowered and united the community. Lira's contributions underscored the importance of music as a tool for cultural preservation and political activism.

"Cantos de mi Cantón"

Agustin Lira's "Cantos de mi Cantón" is an essential piece in the Chicano musical canon, reflecting the collective struggles of the farmworkers' movement during the 1960s. Sung by Patricia Solórzano, the song is part of the album *Que hubo raza*, which is archived in the Library of Congress. This piece, rooted in the spirit of the farmworkers' movement, captures the essence of Chicano resilience, unity, and the fight for justice. Written during a period when laborers were organizing for better wages, working conditions, and basic human rights, "Cantos de mi Cantón" not only celebrates the victories achieved through solidarity but also serves as a reminder of the ongoing struggle for equity among marginalized communities.

Two poignant lyrics in particular reflect the deeper emotional and cultural context of this struggle: "La sangre de mi gente / Ha regado este suelo" ("The blood of my people / Has watered this soil") and "Aquí seguimos firmes / Sin que nadie nos derrumbe" ("Here we stand firm / Without letting anyone bring us down"). These two lines illustrate the contrasting emotions of sacrifice and endurance, highlighting the hardships faced by the Chicano community while also underscoring their unwavering resolve. Together, they emphasize how the Chicano Movement was both a reflection of historical suffering and a testament to the community's determination to fight for justice and dignity, aligning with the chapter's broader themes of resilience and collective empowerment. These powerful lyrics set the tone for the broader message of "Cantos de mi Cantón," capturing the dual essence of sacrifice and resilience. As the song unfolds, it expresses several significant themes that reflect the heart of the Chicano Movement and its fight for justice.

Themes in "Cantos de mi Cantón"

The song's lyrical content delves into several significant themes: freedom and liberation, reflection and nostalgia, cultural identity and heritage, and struggle and hardship. These themes provide an avenue to explore the broader sociopolitical context of the Chicano Movement.

Freedom and Liberation

The theme of freedom is central to "Cantos de mi Cantón." The song highlights collective struggles, with references to historical moments that shaped Chicano identity, such as the signing of the Treaty of Guadalupe Hidalgo in 1848, which resulted in the loss of Mexican lands to the United States. This reference underscores the long history of broken promises and the continued fight for civil rights. As analyzed through thematic coding, the song emphasizes freedom not only as a political goal but as a cultural aspiration. The lyrics connect the Chicano Movement's collective efforts to secure freedom for future generations to the liberation struggles of Indigenous ancestors. Lira's message speaks directly to the audience of the 1960s, urging them to remember the past as a way to fuel present activism.

The line "Pa' liberar a nuestra gente / Y hasta morir por nuestras tierras" ("To liberate our people / And even die for our lands") expresses a deep commitment to freedom, justice, and the defense of land and community central to the Chicano Movement. The phrase *liberar a nuestra gente* speaks to the fight to free Mexican Americans from systemic oppression, exploitation, and marginalization. In the context of farmworkers and labor rights, it reflects the struggle for fair wages, safe working conditions, and dignity in the face of exploitation. This line underscores that the movement's goal is not just political or economic reform but a broader quest for social and cultural liberation. The reference to "our people" signals that this fight is communal—one that encompasses the entire Chicano community and is driven by a deep sense of solidarity and shared purpose. The second part of the line, *Y hasta morir por nuestras tierras*, highlights the ultimate sacrifice many are willing to make in defense of their land and identity. The word *tierras* is both literal and symbolic, representing not only the physical land Mexican Americans labored on but also the cultural and historical roots tied to that land. The willingness to "die for our lands" connects the movement to the long-standing struggle of Indigenous peoples and figures like Emiliano Zapata, whose revolutionary fight for land and justice in Mexico resonates deeply with the Chicano cause. This lyric emphasizes the moral duty to protect both the land and the community's future, symbolizing a profound connection between cultural identity, historical memory, and the collective fight for justice.

Reflection and Nostalgia

Reflection and nostalgia are deeply embedded in the narrative of "Cantos de mi Cantón," as the song looks back on key historical events, such as the Treaty of Guadalupe Hidalgo, to frame the present-day struggles of the Chicano community. The Treaty of Guadalupe Hidalgo, signed in 1848, which ended the Mexican-American War and resulted in Mexico ceding a vast portion of its territory—including present-day California, Arizona, New Mexico, and parts of Colorado, Utah, and Nevada—to the United States. The lyrics serve as a means of reflecting on the collective experience of betrayal and injustice that began with the treaty's signing. For many Mexican Americans, this treaty marked the start of their marginalization in the United States, despite promises of citizenship and property rights. The song captures the lingering sense of injustice, reminding listeners that the Chicano community's current struggles are deeply tied to historical events that have shaped their identity. The reflection on the treaty allows the song to create a bridge between the past and present, showing how the wounds of history still affect the community's fight for justice today.

The line *No'mbre que mentirosos cuando firmaron el tratado los americanos* ("Man, how they lied when the Americans signed the treaty") is particularly powerful in expressing this sentiment. the Treaty of Guadalupe Hidalgo, signed in 1848, which ended the Mexican-American War and resulted in Mexico ceding a vast portion of its territory—including present-day California, Arizona, New Mexico, and parts of Colorado, Utah, and Nevada—to the United States. It encapsulates the anger and bitterness felt by generations of Mexican Americans who were promised equality and protection under the law, only to face systemic disenfranchisement and land dispossession. The use of the word *mentirosos* (liars) highlights the betrayal felt by the Chicano community, whose trust was shattered when the promises of the Treaty of Guadalupe Hidalgo were broken. This reflection on the past evokes not just anger, but a deep sense of loss and disappointment, reminding the community of how their rights were disregarded, and their lands were taken from them. In this way, the song channels both historical memory and emotional resonance, making it a poignant tool for both mourning and mobilization.

This reflection also carries with it a deep sense of nostalgia, as the song longs for a time when the promises of equality and justice could have been fulfilled. This yearning is not just for the lands and rights that were lost, but for a vision of a more just and equitable future that was never realized. The nostalgia evoked in the song is not merely about remembering the past, but also about reclaiming the dignity and agency that were stolen. This combination of reflection and nostalgia allows the song to serve as a powerful vehicle for historical awareness and collective action, encouraging the Chicano community to remember their past while continuing to fight for the justice that has long been denied to them.

Cultural Identity and Heritage

Cultural identity is a key theme throughout "Cantos de mi Cantón." The song reaffirms the Indigenous heritage of Chicano people by mentioning groups such as *chichimecas, zapotecas, y de los yaquis*, and referencing revolutionary figures like Emiliano Zapata and Pancho Villa. These allusions to Indigenous and revolutionary roots serve to strengthen Chicano identity, reinforcing the idea that their struggle is a continuation of historical resistance against colonization and cultural assimilation. This celebration of cultural heritage is a vital element of the Chicano Movement, which sought not only to secure labor rights but also to foster a deeper understanding and pride in Mexican American history and culture. As Dunbar-Ortiz (2021) notes, Chicanidad has evolved into a symbol of pride for those with Mexican Indian heritage, reclaiming a sense of belonging that was historically denied.

The line *Somos hijos de Zapata / Con el alma de la raza* ("We are the children of Zapata / With the soul of the people") from *Cantos de mi Cantón* is a declaration of cultural and revolutionary pride. This lyric connects the Chicano Movement to the legacy of Emiliano Zapata, one of Mexico's most iconic revolutionary figures. Zapata, a leader of the Mexican Revolution, fought for land reforms and the rights of the rural poor, particularly Indigenous people who had been dispossessed of their land by the wealthy elite. By invoking Zapata, the lyric ties the Chicano struggle to a larger history of resistance against oppression, highlighting the continuity of that fight for justice across generations and borders.

The phrase *hijos de Zapata* (children of Zapata) not only honors the revolutionary spirit of Zapata but also suggests that the Chicano community is his ideological and moral heir. It speaks to a collective identity that is rooted in a long history of resistance and defiance against colonialism, exploitation, and inequality. The line also emphasizes a strong connection to the land, as Zapata's central demand was *Tierra y Libertad* (Land and Liberty). For the Chicano Movement, which was deeply engaged in the fight for labor rights, particularly for farmworkers, this connection to Zapata is both symbolic and practical—tying the Chicano struggle for fair working conditions to the broader historical fight for land and dignity. The second part of the line, *Con el alma de la raza* (With the soul of the people), highlights the deep spiritual and cultural connection the Chicano community has with *la raza*—a term that refers to the collective identity of people of Mexican descent. This phrase emphasizes that their fight is not just political, but also cultural and spiritual. It underscores the idea that the movement is driven by a deep-seated pride in their shared heritage and the soul of their people, which persists despite centuries of colonization, discrimination, and hardship. The line embodies the essence of Chicanismo, which is not just a call for civil rights but a reclaiming of cultural and historical identity. It calls on the Chicano community to recognize that they are part of a larger legacy of resistance, carrying forward the dreams of figures like Zapata, who sought justice for the marginalized and oppressed.

Struggle and Hardship

The song also embodies the collective hardships endured by the Chicano community, particularly in the context of labor rights. "Cantos de mi Cantón" echoes the struggles of the farmworkers' movement, addressing the systemic injustices faced by laborers as a result of the Treaty of Guadalupe Hidalgo, with lyrics like *No'mbre que mentirosos cuando firmaron el tratado los americanos* (They lied when they signed the treaty). This captures the continued battle for land, justice, and rights. The song emphasizes the hardships of the Chicano people but simultaneously serves as a call to action, urging the community to persist in their fight against exploitation and oppression.

Similarly, the line *Nuestra lucha es de los pobres / No de ricos ni opresores* ("Our struggle is for the poor / Not for the rich or oppressors") carries profound meaning within the Chicano Movement. This lyric emphasizes the focus of the movement on advocating for the working class, particularly the Mexican American laborers who faced economic exploitation, systemic racism and oppression. The line draws a sharp contrast between the oppressed and the wealthy elite, illustrating that the fight for justice is rooted in uplifting the poor, not in serving the interests of the powerful or privileged. In this way, the line reflects a core element of Chicano activism: the desire to address and dismantle the structures of inequality that keep marginalized communities in poverty. It calls attention to the intersection of race and class, highlighting that the Chicano Movement was not only about ethnic identity but also about economic justice. This makes the song particularly resonant for farmworkers and other low-income individuals who saw themselves as part of a larger struggle against oppressive forces. The lyric channels the spirit of solidarity, uniting people under the banner of shared hardship and the pursuit of collective liberation. The communal nature of the melody reinforces the idea of collective struggle—*our* fight, not just an individual's battle.

Cultural Identity and Music: The Expression of Chicanismo

Chicanidad is a term that encapsulates the cultural, political, and social identity of Chicanos, individuals of Mexican descent living in the United States. It represents *a collective consciousness* that emerged in response to the historical and contemporary experiences of discrimination, marginalization, and cultural erasure faced by the immigrant community. The concept of Chicanidad is deeply rooted in the acknowledgment of Indigenous heritage and the reclamation of cultural identity, which asserts the Indigenous roots of Chicanos and emphasizes a connection to pre-Columbian civilizations.

Defining Chicanidad

Chicanidad is not a monolithic identity; it encompasses a spectrum of experiences and perspectives within the Chicano community. The complexities of Chicanidad are further enriched by intersections with other identities, such as sexuality and class. The Chicano Movement allowed for the collaboration of multiple social classes but it also allowed for women to become a primary actor in the mobilization process. While prominent male figures such as Rodolfo "Corky" Gonzales and César Chávez are well-recognized for their roles, the contributions of Chicana women, like Guadalupe Briseño, have been historically less visible. Chicana women played crucial roles in the movement, often working behind the scenes or in grassroots initiatives that were essential to the progress of the movement. They participated in organizing protests, educational reform, and cultural affirmation activities. These efforts were pivotal in establishing a sense of identity and community among people of Mexican descent in the U.S. Chicanas like Deborah Espinosa and Lisa Flores represent the multi-generational impact of el Movimiento. Espinosa, becoming involved during the height of the movement, found her cultural and racial identity within Chicanismo, the ideology of the Chicano Movement. The movement provided a framework for understanding and expressing her identity as a Mexican American woman, which was a powerful and empowering realization for many Chicanas at the time. For the subsequent generation, as represented by Lisa Flores, the Chicano Movement's legacy was ingrained from childhood. Raised with a strong Chicana identity, Flores exemplifies the movement's enduring influence on self-perception and cultural awareness among Mexican Americans. This intersectionality highlights the dynamic and often ambivalent nature of Chicano identity, where individuals navigate multiple layers of social and cultural expectations. The acknowledgment of such complexities is crucial for understanding how Chicanidad evolves and adapts in contemporary contexts, particularly in relation to broader discourses on race and identity.

The significance of Chicanidad also lies in its role as a form of resistance against cultural assimilation and erasure. By embracing their unique heritage and asserting their identity, Chicanos challenge dominant narratives that seek to marginalize or homogenize their experiences. This resistance is not only cultural but also political, as Chicanidad has historically been linked to movements advocating for civil rights, social justice, and political representation. The term thus embodies a commitment to activism and social change, reflecting the ongoing struggles and aspirations of the Chicano community.

Music as a Reflection of Cultural Identity

Chicano music is a vital medium for preserving the language, traditions, and heritage of the Latino community in the United States. It reflects Chicano cultural identity while also serving as a platform for social activism. Bands like *Los Tigres del Norte* highlight issues such as discrimination and marginalization faced by Mexican migrants. Through storytelling, Chicano music communicates the community's experiences across generations, resonating with both young and old.

Music connects communities to their cultural traditions, preserving practices and deepening pride and continuity (McGrath & Brennan, 2011). For Chicanos, it has been a key tool in maintaining cultural identity amid pressures to assimilate. Music reinforces linguistic and historical bonds, making it not just entertainment but a form of cultural resilience. Songs like *corridos* act as historical records and emotional testimonies, offering insights into social conditions and fostering a collective memory that ties the Chicano community to its roots (Gomez, 2024).

Corridos, in particular, have been a cornerstone of Chicano music, serving as narrative ballads that tell stories of struggle, resistance, and heroism. These songs often reflect the lived experiences of Mexican Americans and their battles with systemic oppression, much like they did during the Mexican Revolution and continue to do in modern social movements. As a reflection of cultural identity, *corridos* allow the community to assert its voice, offering a means of resistance and solidarity in the face of marginalization (Smithsonian Institution, 2023). This tradition of storytelling through music helps to preserve the cultural history of the Chicano community, ensuring that future generations remain connected to their roots.

Furthermore, the use of music in the Chicano Movement extends beyond the cultural. It serves as a direct form of political engagement, with songs addressing issues such as land dispossession, labor exploitation, and civil rights. For example, the popular use of *huelga* songs during the farmworkers' movement, led by figures like César Chávez and Dolores Huerta, underscores how music was instrumental in mobilizing communities and sustaining morale during difficult times (Smithsonian Institution, 2023). These songs were not only reflections of cultural identity but also calls to action, empowering the Chicano community to take ownership of their struggles and resist oppression through collective solidarity. In this way, Chicano music transcends its role as an art form, becoming a vital medium for political expression and community-building. It continues to serve as a voice for the voiceless, enabling the community to articulate its desires for justice, equality, and recognition, while remaining firmly rooted in its cultural heritage. This blend of cultural pride and political engagement makes Chicano music a powerful reflection of the community's ongoing fight for self-determination and social justice.

Defining Chicanismo

Chicanismo is a deeply personal concept which represents a powerful, multifaceted identity born out of the Chicano Movement of the 1960s–1970s, where Mexican Americans sought to reclaim their cultural heritage and resist systemic marginalization. It is not just a cultural affirmation but also a political ideology that resists assimilation into dominant U.S. society. This identity embraces the Indigenous and mestizo roots of the Mexican American community, asserting pride in Mexican American history while remaining grounded in resistance to colonization and continued struggles for justice (Chavez, 2004). Chicanismo critiques both historical and contemporary forms of oppression, emphasizing self-determination, social justice, and cultural pride. The concept of chicanismo is not monolithic but reflects various perspectives and evolving ideas within the Mexican American community. This fluidity is essential for understanding how Chicanismo responded to diverse issues like labor rights, education reform, and community empowerment during the Chicano Movement. Thus, Chicanismo is an identity that recognizes the struggles of the past and the ongoing fight for justice in the present.

Music played a crucial role in shaping and celebrating this identity. Through the sounds of *corridos*, *mariachi*, and *huelga* music, the Chicano community connected with their cultural roots, using music to tell their stories of struggle and resistance. Artists like Agustin Lira, with his iconic song, "Cantos de mi Cantón," transformed music into a tool of political empowerment. Chicano music became the soundtrack of a movement by expressing the collective struggles of laborers, students, and activists while also celebrating the rich traditions of Mexican American identity. As the movement grew, music provided a unifying force, echoing the spirit of Chicanismo by bridging the personal and the political.

Music as a Reflection of Cultural Identity

Chicano music has historically functioned as a means of preserving the language, traditions, and heritage of the Latino/Mexican American community, particularly in the context of the United States. It is through music that stories of struggle, resistance, resilience are told, and these narratives help shape and strengthen cultural identity. For example, in "*Cantos de mi Cantón*," Lira expresses themes of liberation, cultural pride, and the hardships faced by Mexican American laborers. The lyrics and melodies convey a sense of belonging and solidarity among the Chicano community. The use of music allowed Mexican Americans to maintain and transmit their cultural identity across generations, particularly at a time when efforts to assimilate into white American society were prevalent. Chicano music maintained connections to ancestral roots while simultaneously critiquing the structures that oppressed Mexican Americans.

Connecting the Personal to the Political

Chicano music allows individuals to bridge the gap between personal struggles and broader social issues, transforming deeply personal experiences into collective expressions of political activism. As the farmworkers' movement led by Cesar Chavez and Dolores Huerta, music was instrumental in uniting individuals around common causes and inspiring action. Songs like *De Colores* and *No Nos Moverán* became rallying cries for those fighting for labor rights and civic justice. The interrelationship between cultural pride and political activism is at the core of Chicano music. Through songs, individuals are not only able to express their own personal hardships, such as labor exploitation or cultural erasure, but also contribute to the broader movement for change. As noted in studies on the Chicano Movement, cultural nationalism was articulated through Chicanismo, a form of cultural and political language which found expression in music (Chavez, 2000). Thus, Chicano music serves as a form of protest, a celebration of identity, and a source of hope. By using music to articulate calls for justice and equality, Chicano music not only fosters a legacy of resilience and unity within the Chicano community, but also ensures that the Chicano Movement's message would resonate across generations.

The Role of Music in the Classroom: Educational Approaches

Incorporating Chicano music into the social studies curriculum can be transformative. Music is more than just entertainment; it serves as a cultural lens through which Generation Z and Generation Alpha understand and interact with the world. As educators, it's essential to adapt teaching practices to meet the evolving needs of our students in a changing society (Seemiller, 2017). Today's students are constantly connected to music through streaming services, TikTok trends, and social media movements, making music an accessible and impactful teaching tool. By using music in the classroom, teachers can tap into this connection. For instance, songs are more than melodies—they tell stories that reveal the struggles and triumphs of communities. One effective approach is to create lessons that explore how songs reflect the social and political contexts of their time, encouraging students to make connections to the social movements they witness today. This helps bridge the gap between historical movements like the Chicano Movement and contemporary issues that students care about, highlighting music's ongoing role as a force for change.

To deepen these lessons, focus on how music has historically fueled activism. For example, after analyzing *Cantos de mi Cantón*, students can explore its themes of resistance and community action, and draw connections to current social issues they encounter. Music has evolved as a form of expression, and Generation Z and Generation Alpha are especially attuned to its role in shaping perspectives and sparking movements. By leveraging this energy, educators can encourage students to reflect on how Chicano music not only inspired activism in the past but can also motivate them to take action in the present. This approach transforms the classroom into a space where students see the direct link between the arts and activism, empowering them to engage with social justice in meaningful ways.

Case Study in the Classroom: *Cantos de mi Cantón*

When you teach *Cantos de mi Cantón,* start by playing the song and encouraging your students to really listen to the lyrics. What do they hear? What emotions does it evoke? Guide them to think critically about how these songs represented the struggles of Chicano laborers during the farmworkers strikes and how it was used to unite a community of people. Break down the lyrics, focusing on key ideas that emerged from the text: oppression, resilience, hope, displacement. After engaging the students in discussion about how music, like this song, can give a voice to those who feel voiceless, you can also guide students in thinking about modern day parallels: What songs today carry similar messages of resistance or community-building?

Once groundwork is laid, divide students into small groups and assign each group an activity. They could analyze another Chicano song or even create their own lyrics that reflect an issue they care about. Consider extending this process through the usage of images that can create a mental picture of what the struggle looked like for this particular population. In order to bring it full circle, connect their ideas to the concept of civic engagement, by asking, How does music inspire action, and how can they use it in their own lives? The objective is to not only help students understand the Chicano Movement, but also empower students to see how something as simple as a song can spark meaningful change.

Civic Action Through Music Education

One of the most powerful things about teaching Chicano music is how it inspires students to become active participants in their own communities. Gen Z and Gen Alpha are already tuned into the issues that matter to them, and music is one of the ways they can express that. Whether it is climate change, immigration, racial justice, music can motivate students to engage in the issues they care about. In your lesson, move learning into action by encouraging students to take what they have learned and apply it to their own communities. This can be presented through the creation of a video of their neighborhood, highlighting local murals or music that reflects their community's struggles and strengths. They might write their own song addressing a specific issue they see in their own town. The goal is to show students that music is more than just entertainment, it's a tool for advocacy and a way to take informed action. By the end of the lesson, they will not only have a deeper understanding of Chicano music and its impact, but also feel empowered to use their own voices to create change. Through empowering students to use music as a tool for advocacy and action within their own communities, we move beyond passive learning and encourage real-world engagement. This transition from learning to action highlights the unique power of music, not only as a form of personal expression but also as an impactful primary source in the social studies classroom. Music's ability to evoke sensory and emotional responses makes it an ideal medium for students to connect deeply with historical events and social movements, bridging the gap between the past and the present in meaningful ways.

Music and Social Studies: The Perfect Melody

Music's sensory and emotional value makes it a uniquely effective tool for social studies learning, bridging the gap between past and present experiences. Music can act as a cultural definer of political beliefs, class values, and economic life (Heafner et al., 2014). Unlike text-based primary sources, music immediately engages multiple senses—hearing, feeling, and even movement—triggering emotional responses that can bring historical events to life in a visceral way (Logeswaran & Bhattacharya, 2009). The emotional power of songs such as *Cantos de mi Cantón* allows students to connect more deeply with the struggles and triumphs of the Chicano community, making abstract historical concepts like oppression, resistance, and empowerment more relatable. The same emotional and sensory engagement which mobilized and inspired the Chicano Movement, when utilized in the classroom, can encourage students to critically assess not just the content of the music but also the socio-political contexts that influenced its creation. This multisensory learning with music enables students to explore history not just as a series of events but as lived emotional experiences, offering them a more personal understanding of historical movements and their relevance to today's social issues (Mangram & Weber, 2012).

Music also fosters a unique connection between students' understanding of the present and the past, helping them draw parallels between historical struggles and contemporary social movements. Chicano protest songs, for instance, reflect issues of labor rights and cultural identity that are still relevant today, such as the fight for immigrant rights and social justice. This direct emotional and sensory engagement with historical music helps students recognize how the lessons of the past continue to shape current events, encouraging them to think critically about their own roles as civic actors. Moreover, music's timeless nature allows students to revisit historical eras through sound, helping them understand how cultural and political expressions of different time periods influence contemporary thought and activism (Cohen, 2012; Pellegrino & Lee, 2012). The songs of the Chicano Movement were not just reflections of cultural pride; they were deeply embedded in the socio-political struggles of the time, helping to unite disparate groups within the movement and providing a platform for resistance (Mariscal, 2004). This is crucial for students to grasp as they explore how past movements inform present-day activism. By engaging with music as a primary source, students can critically examine how cultural and political expressions from different time periods influence contemporary thought and civic participation

What makes music particularly valuable in the social studies classroom is its ability to foster empathy and historical understanding. Songs from the Chicano Movement, like many other protest songs, are emotionally charged artifacts that reflect not only the cultural heritage of a community but also its ongoing struggles. As students listen to and analyze these songs, they are invited to explore history through the personal experiences of those who lived it, creating a bridge between historical content and their present-day realities. By integrating music as a primary source, teachers can help students develop a deeper emotional and sensory connection to historical events, making learning both relevant and transformative. Furthermore, the emotional power of Chicano music was central to mobilizing communities and inspiring collective action. Mariscal's (2004) work on César Chavez highlights how the United Farm Workers (UFW) and other Chicano activists used music to connect with and galvanize marginalized communities during boycotts and marches. The cultural resonance of Chicano music made it an effective tool for organizing, and when used in the classroom, it can help students understand how music operates as both an emotion and political artifact.

Expanding Civic Engagement: Chicano Music as a Global Influence

Chicano Music's Influence Beyond Borders

Chicano music has had a significant impact not only within the United States but also across various global movements, where its themes of social justice, cultural pride, and resistance have been embraced and adapted by marginalized communities. One of the most striking examples of this is in Latin America, where musicians have long drawn inspiration from the Chicano Movement's commitment to cultural identity and collective action. The 1973 song *El Pueblo Unido Jamás Será Vencido* by Sergio Ortega and the Chilean folk group Quilapayún became an anthem of resistance against the oppressive regime of Augusto Pinochet and is emblematic of the deep connections between music and political activism (Karmy & Farias, 2023). In this song, the powerful lyrics, "El pueblo unido jamás será vencido" ("The people united will never be defeated"), encapsulate the collective strength and determination of the Chicano Movement, reinforcing the importance of unity in fighting systemic oppression (Chappell, 2023). This song echoed the calls for unity and justice heard in Chicano protest music, showcasing how shared themes of empowerment through music resonate in different cultural contexts (BBC News Mundo, 2019).

Another example of Chicano music's influence can be found in Brazil and Argentina, where musicians used music as a form of resistance against dictatorial regimes during the 1960s and 1970s. Protest songs during this time carried messages of political and social resistance, much like the *corridos* and *huelga* songs of the Chicano Movement, underscoring the universality of music as a tool for mobilization and advocacy for human rights (Risinger, 2012). In both Latin American and U.S. contexts, these protest songs served as vehicles for preserving cultural memory while inspiring political action. Much like Chicano music's focus on justice for laborers and farmworkers, Latin American protest music became a unifying force that empowered oppressed communities to fight against social inequalities. Chicano music's emphasis on reclaiming Indigenous heritage and resisting assimilation resonates strongly with these groups, as they too seek to protect their cultural identity and assert their rights (Ortiz, 2018). This cross-cultural exchange, rooted in shared experiences of oppression, has helped foster solidarity between different marginalized communities across national borders.

Beyond Latin America, Indigenous communities across the Americas have also adopted themes from Chicano music, particularly its emphasis on reclaiming cultural heritage. In Bolivia, musicians have combined Indigenous instruments and languages with themes of resistance that parallel the Chicano Movement's message of empowerment for marginalized peoples (Karmy & Farias, 2023). This cross-cultural exchange has reinforced Chicano music's global influence as a medium for promoting solidarity and creating a shared narrative of resistance. In Canada, for example, Indigenous activists have also drawn on similar themes, using music to resist cultural erasure and assert their rights and identity in the face of ongoing colonialism. These connections underscore the profound role Chicano music has played in inspiring and informing global movements for justice and equity. Its blend of cultural pride and political activism provides a universal framework that resonates with marginalized communities, enabling them to assert their identities and demand change. By fostering a sense of solidarity across borders, Chicano music has become a powerful tool for uniting diverse groups under a common cause of resistance and empowerment.

Songs of Freedom, Redemption Songs

> Music doesn't lie. If there is something to be changed in this world, then it can only happen through music.
>
> —Jimi Hendrix

Chicano music shares many commonalities with other global protest music genres, such as Bob Marley's reggae, Jimi Hendrix's protest songs, or Woody Guthrie's folk ballads, all of which have deeply impacted social movements worldwide. Bob Marley's reggae, for instance, became a voice for the oppressed people of Jamaica and later for marginalized communities across the globe. His songs like "Get Up, Stand Up" and "Redemption Song" paralleled Chicano music in their calls for liberation and justice. "Redemption Song," in particular, is a poignant reflection on emancipation from mental and physical slavery, and Marley's lyrics urge listeners to "emancipate yourselves from mental slavery," a sentiment that resonates deeply with the goals of Chicano music, which also calls for liberation from societal oppression (Marley, 1980). Marley's music, much like *huelga* songs, was grounded in both personal and political struggles, making it a powerful medium for inspiring civic engagement and social change. As Paul Ortiz (2018) argues, the fusion of Black and Latinx struggles in the United States has long been intertwined with cultural forms like music, which provided a means for expressing both resilience and resistance against systemic oppression. Ortiz highlights how music, in the context of both African American and Latinx communities, served as a cultural weapon in their respective fights for civil rights and social justice, strengthening solidarity within and across communities (Ortiz, 2018).

Jimi Hendrix, on the other hand, used his music to comment on the social and political turmoil of the United States during the 1960s, especially with songs like *Machine Gun* and his famous rendition of "The Star-Spangled Banner." Hendrix's distortion of the national anthem at Woodstock was a radical expression of discontent, reflecting the same spirit of defiance present in Chicano protest music. Both Hendrix and Chicano musicians utilized their art to challenge dominant narratives and call for societal transformation, weaving together cultural pride and activism. Ortiz (2018) notes that the shared histories of resistance between Black and Latinx communities are often reflected in their cultural productions, including music. Chicano music, much like African American spirituals and blues, transcends its role as entertainment, becoming a repository for collective memory and a force for mobilizing action against injustice. This connection between music and activism underscores how vital cultural expression has been in shaping both identity and political resistance in marginalized communities.

Woody Guthrie's music shares significant thematic parallels with Chicano protest music, particularly in its focus on social justice, resistance, and empowerment. Guthrie, known for his iconic song "This Land Is Your Land," gave voice to the disenfranchised during the Great Depression and the Dust Bowl migrations, much like Chicano musicians did for Mexican American farmworkers during the labor movements of the 1960s and 1970s. Guthrie's folk ballads, like those in the *corridos* tradition, reflect the struggles of the working class and marginalized communities, offering narratives of resilience against systemic injustices. His songs, infused with populist and socialist ideals, often called for collective action and solidarity, aligning closely with the spirit of Chicano music (Cohen, 2012). As with Chicano music, Guthrie's songs served as a repository for collective memory, documenting the hardships and hopes of rural and working-class Americans. Guthrie's influence extended beyond U.S. borders, as his music inspired various global movements, echoing the use of Chicano music in Latin America to resist oppressive regimes. The common thread in Guthrie's music and Chicano protest songs is the emphasis on the dignity of labor and the fight for civil rights, underscoring their shared goal of using cultural expression as a form of resistance and empowerment (Cohen, 2012; Smithsonian Folkways, 2015).

At the heart of these musical traditions—whether Chicano, reggae, rock, or folk—are the themes of resistance, identity, and empowerment. Resistance is evident in how artists confront systems of oppression, whether through lyrics that speak directly to injustices or through the very act of preserving cultural traditions in the face of erasure. In Chicano music, for example, preserving Indigenous and Mexican heritage through *corridos* and *huelga* songs was an act of defiance against cultural assimilation and erasure (Risinger, 2012). Similarly, Marley's use of reggae was a form of cultural resistance, pushing back against the colonial legacy in Jamaica and promoting Rastafarianism as a spiritual and political identity. Hendrix's music, though less tied to a specific ethnic identity, resonated with the counterculture and civil rights movements in America, offering a radical critique of U.S. militarism and racism.

Identity is another common thread running through these genres. Chicano music's focus on reclaiming Mexican American and Indigenous identity mirrors Marley's championing of Black identity and pride in Rastafarian culture. Both traditions sought to empower their communities by affirming their unique cultural and historical experiences, offering an alternative narrative to the dominant, often oppressive, societal structures. Hendrix's music, though less ethnically rooted, offered a powerful expression of countercultural identity, aligning with the broader anti-establishment sentiment of the 1960s. Empowerment is the final shared theme, as all these musical forms encouraged their listeners to take action, whether by fighting for civil rights, resisting exploitation, or reclaiming cultural heritage. Chicano music's role in the farmworkers' movement, much like Marley's role in promoting political action in Jamaica or Hendrix's influence on the U.S. anti-war movement, highlights how music can galvanize individuals and communities to stand up against injustice and demand change. As Ortiz (2018) emphasizes, music provided a way for marginalized communities to articulate their visions of liberation, creating an avenue for activism and solidarity across borders.

Chicano music, much like other activist music around the world, is more than just a form of cultural expression—it is a tool for empowerment, identity formation, and resistance. By drawing on the rich traditions of Mexican American and Indigenous cultures, Chicano music has created a powerful platform for social and political engagement, influencing both local and global movements. Whether through the soulful rhythms of *corridos* or the urgent cries of *huelga* songs, Chicano music continues to inspire activism and foster a sense of solidarity among oppressed communities across the globe.

Conclusion

In the classrooms of the Chicano Movement, music was never just background noise; it was a heartbeat, a rallying cry, a call to action. Imagine the scene–workers gathered after long hours in the fields, their hands calloused from labor, lifting their voices together to songs like *Cantos de mi Cantón*. This wasn't just music; it was a declaration of identity, a refusal to be invisible. Agustin Lira's lyrics became more than entertainment–they transformed into anthems of resistance, reminding listeners of their strength, their roots, and their power to fight back. Just as students marched in Los Angeles during the 1968 walkouts, Chicano music gave voice to those fighting for justice. It was the sound of solidarity, a force that bridged the gap between personal struggle and political activism.

Today, as the fastest-growing genre (Contreras, 2024), Latin music—rooted in deep historical and cultural traditions—pulses through the lives of new generations, echoing not only across the nation but also reverberating in the digital world. Contemporary musicians, such as those within the rising genre of Música Mexicana, have adapted the spirit of Chicano protest music, infusing it with modern influences while continuing to address issues like immigration rights, social justice, and identity (Contreras, 2024). These musicians, much like their predecessors, use their art to give voice to the voiceless and to remind the broader public of the ongoing struggles faced by Mexican Americans and other marginalized groups. In this way, Chicano music remains a living tradition, one that not only preserves cultural heritage but also engages with contemporary social and political issues.

Chicano music, a vital thread in this rich tapestry, serves as more than just entertainment; it connects students to their history, reminding them of the ongoing battles for labor rights, immigrant reform, and cultural preservation. This is where we, as educators, hold a critical role—bridging the past and present, and guiding students to see how these musical legacies empower them to engage with the struggles of their time. Our classrooms can be places where those echoes of activism are amplified. Chicano music offers us a unique tool to make these lessons tangible and deeply meaningful. When students hear songs that reflect their lived experiences, songs like *Cantos de mi Cantón*, they are reminded that they, too, are part of a legacy of resistance and empowerment. They realize that they, too, have a voice that can shape the future. Music connects them, not just to the struggles of their ancestors, but to the social movements of today.

As we look to the future, the role of music in student activism becomes increasingly crucial. By engaging with Chicano music and its themes of resistance and cultural pride, students can draw direct connections to contemporary civic education debates, such as North Carolina's HB 10, which seeks to limit discussions of race and equity in the classroom. Just as Chicano music gave voice to social justice movements in the past, it now empowers students to stand against policies that threaten to undermine inclusive education and equity. This ongoing relevance highlights how music, as both a cultural and political artifact, continues to shape activism and challenge oppression.

In conclusion, this chapter challenges us to tap into that power and imagine the potential in a classroom where music isn't just something students listen to on the way to school but is instead woven into the very fabric of their history and social studies learning. Our classrooms can be where they dissect the lyrics of *Cantos de mi Cantón* to uncover the deep sense of belonging and resilience that the Chicano Movement embodied. It can be a space where students reflect on how songs of past movements still resonate with the issues they care about today–whether it's racial justice, environmental sustainability, or workers' rights. By making music central to our teaching, we create classrooms where students from historically marginalized communities feel seen, heard, valued, and empowered to continue the long fight for justice. Just like in the fields and streets of the 1960s and 1970s, their activism can begin with a melody.

References

American Folklife Center & Library of Congress. (2011). *Songs of the Chicano Movement.* Washington, D.C.

BBC News Mundo. (2019, December 16). The story of the song "The people united will never be defeated." Retrieved from https://www.t13.cl/noticia/tendencias/bbc/la-historia-de-el-pueblo-unido-jamas-sera-vencido-el-emblematico-himno-de-protesta-que-volvio-a-ser-protagonista-en-chile

Bennett, A. (2017). *Music, space and place: popular music and cultural identity.* Routledge.

Castagno, A. E. (2008). "I don't want to hear that!": Legitimating whiteness through silence in schools. *Anthropology & Education Quarterly, 39*(3), 314–33.

Chappell, K. (2023). The Life and Career of Mariachi Educator Zeke Castro. *Journal of Historical Research in Music Education, 45*(2), 172–92.

Chavez, E. (2000). Imagining the Mexican Immigrant Worker: (Inter) Nationalism, Identity, and Insurgency in the Chicano Movement in Los Angeles. *Aztlán: The Journal of Chicano Studies, 25*(2), 109–21.

Cohen, R. D. (2012). *Woody Guthrie: Writing America's Songs*. Routledge.

Contreras, J. P. (2024, July 18). Latin music growth in the U.S.: Música Mexicana artists like Fuerza Regida and Peso Pluma are leading the way. *Los Angeles Times*. https://www.latimes.com/delos/story/2024-07-18/latin-music-growth-us-musica-mexicana-fuerza-regida-peso-pluma

Connell, J., & Gibson, C. (2003). *Sound tracks: Popular music identity and place*. Routledge.

Dunbar-Ortiz, R. (2021). *Not "a nation of immigrants": Settler colonialism, white supremacy, and a history of erasure and exclusion.* Boston: Beacon Press.

del Barco, M. (2018, July 6). Chicano protests and celebrity portraits: George Rodriguez's Los Angeles. *NPR*. https://www.npr.org/sections/pictureshow/2018/07/06/625414088/chicano-protests-and-celebrity-portraits-george-rodriguezs-los-angeles

Gomez, A. (2024). Sonidos de Aztlán: A historical analysis of Chicano music (Capstone Project). California State University, Monterey Bay. Digital Commons @ CSUMB. https://digitalcommons.csumb.edu/caps_thes_all

Heafner, T. L., Groce, E., & Finnell, A. (2014). *Springsteen's Born in the U.S.A.: Promoting historical inquiry through music. Social Studies Research and Practice,* 9(3), 118–37.

Isaac, A., & Christiansen, R. (2002). Chicano Music and the Chicano Movement. *Journal of Chicano Studies, 28*(1), 37–49.

Jensen, R. J., & Hammerback, J. C. (1980). The Rhetorical Worlds of Cesar Chavez and Reies Tijerina. *Western Journal of Speech Communication, 44,* 166–76.

Johnson, C. (2018). Introduction: Transitional, Transnational, and Distributive Justice in Post-War Guatemala. In C. JOHNSON & S. HENIGHAN (Eds.), *Human and Environmental Justice in Guatemala* (pp. 3–33). University of Toronto Press. http://www.jstor.org/stable/10.3138/j.ctv2fjwz0n.5

Kallen, S. A. (2010). *We Are Not Beasts of Burden: Cesar Chavez and the Delano Grape Strike, California, 1965–197.* Twenty-First Century Books.

Karmy, E., & Farias, M. (2023). A people's anthem: 50 years of the song "The people united will never be defeated." *REVUELTAS*, 8(2023), 40–66. https://www.revistarevueltas.cl/ojs/index.php/revueltas/article/view/156

La Blue Kombi. (2021, September 16). Inside Chicano culture in Los Angeles | East LA [Video]. YouTube. https://www.youtube.com/watch?v=l_zQEh77cpc&t=103s

Logeswaran, R., & Bhattacharya, J. (2009). Crossmodal transfer of emotion by music. *Neuroscience Letters, 455*(2), 129–33.

Madsen, D. L. (2000). *Understanding contemporary Chicana literature*. Univ of South Carolina Press.

Marley, B. (1980). *Redemption Song.* On Uprising [Vinyl]. Island Records.

Mangram, J. A. & Weber, R. L. (2012). Incorporating music into the social studies classroom: A qualitative study of secondary social studies teachers. *The Journal of Social Studies Research, 36*(1), 3–21.

Mariscal, J. (2004). Negotiating César: César Chavez in the Chicano Movement. *Aztlán: The Journal of Chicano Studies, 29*(1), 21–3.

McPherson, Alan. "From 'Punks' to Geopoliticians: U. S. and Panamanian Teenagers and the 1964 Canal Zone Riots." *The Americas*58, no. 3 (2002): 395–418. https://www.jstor.org/stable/1007860.

McGrath, B., & Brennan, M. A. (2011). Tradition, cultures and communities: exploring the potentials of music and the arts for community development in Appalachia. *Community Development*, *42*(3), 340–58.

Ortiz, P. (2018). *An African American and Latinx history of the United States.* Beacon Press.

Pellegrino, A. M. & Lee, C. D. (2012). *Let the music play! Harnessing the power of music in the social studies classroom.* Charlotte, NC: Information Age Press.

Planas, R. (2015, January 5). *Teaching hip hop illegally promotes ethnic solidarity, Arizona official says.* HuffPost. https://www.huffpost.com/entry/teaching-hip-hop-illegally-promotes-ethnic-solidarity-arizona-official-says

Risinger, C. F. (2012). Integrating art and music into social studies instruction. *Social Education*, *76*(3), 157–8.

Rhodes, M. (2011). Chicano Protest Music in the Classroom: A Pedagogical Guide. *Latino Studies Journal*, *9*(3), 18–22.

Rodríguez, M. (2007). "*We ARE America!" cultural politics and Chicano movement legacies in the work of Los Tigres del Norte and El Vez* (Doctoral dissertation).

Rodriguez, R. (2017). In Lak'Ech and Panche Be: The Roots of Social Justice in Mexican American Studies. *Journal of Latinos and Education, 18*(2), 126–33.

Rodriguez, R. (2019). No Revolution Without Poets: The Role of Artists in the Chicano Movement. *Western Journal of Speech Communication, 46*(1), 72–91.

Rodriguez, G. (1970). *Chicano Moratorium, Boyle Heights, 1970.*

Rodriguez, G. (1970s). *City Terrace, 1970s.*

Smithsonian Institution. (2023). *Estoy aquí: Music of the Chicano Movement:* A Smithsonian Folkways music pathway for students in Grades 6–8. Smithsonian Folkways.

Rueda, C. (2019). The Origins of Student Anti-Somoza Consciousness, 1937–1944. In *Students of Revolution: Youth, Protest, and Coalition Building in Somoza-Era Nicaragua* (pp. 21–40). University of Texas Press. http://www.jstor.org/stable/10.7560/319307.6

Seemiller, C., & Grace, M. (2017). Generation Z: Educating and engaging the next generation of students. *About campus, 22*(3), 21–6.

Smithsonian Folkways. (2015). *Classic American Ballads*. Smithsonian Folkways Recordings.

Ulibarri, J. (2018). Chicano movement: Paths to power. *The Social Studies, 102*(1), 25–32.

Varela, M. (1968). *A young Chicanita hawks La Raza newspapers at the Poor People's Campaign, Washington, D.C. May–July 1968.*

Wang, O. (2010). *The Journey of 'Viva Tirado': A Musical Conversation Within Afro-Chicano Los Angeles*. Journal of Popular Music Studies, 22(4), 348–66.

Apendix A

"Que hubo raza"

El Mexicano no se quiere hacer gringo

Bueno pues Cuba
Como les va
Que lindo dia para cantar
Noticias que han llegado
Que han llegado del nuevo mexico
1848, pues fue firmado el gran tratado de guadalupe Hidalgo
Prometiendo justicia y libertad,
A tierras y terrenos, de gente indigena
No'mbre que mentirosos cuando firmaron el tratado los americanos
El mexicano se hace gringo
No puede ni quiere
El mexicano se hace gringo
No puede ni sera
Porque en sus venas lleva la sangre
De los chichimecas, zapotecas, y de los yaquis, cochimíes, y de los mayas.
En su cuerpo lleva la sangre de Cuauhtémoc, de los morenos, de Zapata, y del famoso Pancho Villa.
Texas, Utah, California, Wyoming, Colorado, y Nuevo México
Todas estas tierras fueron robadas
Y ahora nos encontramos pidiéndole al gobierno

Reyes y Lopez, Tijerans el nuevo Mexico.
A levantado armas, sus tierras reclamo.
Ahi esta aqui nos tienen, nuestra cultura aplastada
Y hablando "english."
El mexicano se hace gringo
No puede ni quiere
El mexicano se hace gringo
No puede ni sera

Appendix B:

"Ser como el aire"

Ser como el aire libre
No mas se pasa volando
Ser como la paloma
Tambien se pasa volando
Cuando yo era chico
Mii madrecita deica
Cuidate mi hijito
No te metas en lio
Ser como el aire libre
No mas se pasa libre
Ser como la paloma
Tambien se pasa volando
Cuando yo era chico
Esas pabras me duelen
Porque la vida es larga
Y yo la paso llorando
Ser como el aire libre
No mas se pasa libre
Ser como la paloma
Tambien se pasa volando

Ser como el mar tan lindo
Tambien es libre su canto.

Lesson Plan Title: Voices of Change: Exploring Civic Engagement and Cultural Identity through Chicano Music

1. **Theme:** This lesson explores how Chicano music, particularly the song "Cantos de mi Cantón," serves as a catalyst for civic engagement and cultural awareness within the Latino community. It examines the role of music in fostering activism and social change and integrates this understanding into educational practices.
2. **Grade Level:** 11th–12th Grade (High School).
3. **Course:** Social Studies/Civics, Ethnic Studies, or History.
4. **Time Required:** 3 class periods (approximately 45 minutes each).
5. **Teacher Historical Context:**
    a. Teachers should be familiar with the historical significance of Chicano music in cultural and political movements. Key events include the Chicano civil rights movement of the 1960s and 1970s.
    b. Essential figures include Dolores Huerta, Cesar Chavez, and Agustin Lira.
    c. Refer to "Habla Loud: The Chicano Identity and Student Agency" for detailed historical background on the Chicano music scene and its impact on social justice and community activism.
6. **Essential and Supporting Questions:**
    a. How did Chicano music become a cultural awakening of individual rights and community activism? (Compelling Question)
    b. How does Chicano music, particularly the song "Cantos de mi Cantón," serve as a catalyst for civic engagement and cultural awareness within the Latino community?
    c. How does Chicano music inspire activism and social change?
7. **Objectives:**
    a. Analyze how Chicano music, specifically "Cantos de mi Cantón," acts as a catalyst for civic engagement and cultural awareness within the Latino community.
    b. Explore how this understanding can inspire activism and social change in students' communities.
8. Standards (from the National Council for the Social Studies [NCSS]):
    a. Dimension 1: Developing Questions and Planning Inquiries
        i. D1.4.9-12. Explain how supporting questions contribute to an inquiry and how, through engaging source work, new compelling and supporting questions emerge.

   b. Dimension 2: Applying Disciplinary Concepts and Tools
      i. D2.Civ.2.9-12. Analyze the role of citizens in the U.S. political system, with attention to various theories of democracy, changes in Americans' participation over time, and alternative models from other countries, past and present.
   c. Dimension 3: Evaluating Sources and Using Evidence
      i. D3.1.9-12. Gather relevant information from multiple sources representing a wide range of views while using the origin, authority, structure, context, and corroborative value of the sources to guide the selection.
   d. Dimension 4: Communicating Conclusions and Taking Informed Action
      i. D4.7.9-12. Assess options for individual and collective action to address local, regional, and global problems by engaging in self-reflection, strategy identification, and complex causal reasoning.
9. Classroom Materials:
   a. "Dolores Huerta: The Civil Rights Icon Who Showed Farmworkers 'Sí Se Puede'" (Source: Dolores Huerta Biography)
      i. https://www.npr.org/sections/thesalt/2017/09/17/551490281/dolores-huerta-the-civil-rights-icon-who-showed-farmworkers-si-se-puede
   b. "Cantos de mi Cantón" (Library of Congress)
      i. https://www.loc.gov/item/2021688731/
   c. "Singing through the Past" (Observation Sheet)
      i. https://docs.google.com/document/d/1P1sjQnfdiUjvjtdUnbMbDZa47d_usWtmrrY3TyYP7HM/edit?usp=sharing
   d. Photographs (Optional resource)
      i. https://www.npr.org/sections/pictureshow/2018/07/06/625414088/chicano-protests-and-celebrity-portraits-george-rodriguezs-los-angeles
   e. Video: "Voces" PBS Short (Source: PBS—Voces)
      i. https://www.pbs.org/video/chicano-rights-movement-y13qkx/
   f. Sample video: "Chicanidad in Japan" (Post-Lesson)
      i. https://www.youtube.com/watch?v=r8bMLcCxxAA
10. Entry Task to Establish Context
   a. Time Estimate: 5 minutes
   b. Activity:
      i. Discuss how music has personal meaning and evokes emotions.
      ii. Students select a song that evokes strong emotions for them.

  iii. Pair-share activity to discuss the emotions and context of their selected songs.
  c. Distribute and read about Dolores Huerta.
    i. Comprehension Questions:
      1. How does the phrase "Sí se puede" reflect the themes of empowerment and resistance?
      2. What were the conditions of farmworkers as described by Dolores Huerta, and how did these inspire activism?
      3. How did gender and cultural identity influence Huerta's role?
      4. How do Huerta's experiences relate to the issues addressed in Chicano music?
      5. How can Huerta's story help us understand Chicano music as a tool for civic engagement?

11. Teacher-Guided Instruction:
  a. Time Estimate: 5–10 minutes
  b. Activity:
    i. Analyze "Cantos de mi Cantón" in the context of Chicano music's role in civic engagement and cultural awareness.
    ii. Student-Centered/Engaged Learning (Student Inquiry Activity/Activities)
  c. Time Estimate: 30 minutes
  d. Activity:
  e. Primary source analysis: Photographs
  f. Visual inventory using student inquiry questions.
  g. Use the Database of Hispanic Photographs and short texts as a museum exhibit.
12. Teacher-Directed Instruction
  a. Time Estimate: 10 minutes
  b. Activity:
    i. Discuss how common suffering leads to cultural awakening and recognition of individual rights.
13. Student-Centered/Engaged Learning (Student Inquiry Activity/Activities)
  a. Time Estimate: 30 minutes
  b. Activity:
  c. Small group analysis of Chicano music, focusing on its role in inspiring activism and social change.
14. Exit Task for Summarizing Answer(s) to Essential and Supporting Questions
  a. Time Estimate: 5 minutes
  b. Activity:

15. Write lyrics for a song that represents Chicano activism and its impact on the community.
    a. Assessment:
    b. Task:
        i. Write lyrics for a song representative of Chicano activism. Identify local movements and common concerns in their community.
16. Reflect on how music can serve as a political weapon and inspire activism.
    a. Community Engagement:
    b. Activity:
        i. Explore if Chicanidad is present in the community.
        ii. Create a video walk of the community demonstrating this presence.
        iii. Engage in critical service learning and informed action by exploring local art, music, murals, and cultural celebrations.
        iv. Write lyrics related to a specific issue in their community.
17. Additional Resources:
    a. "Ser como el aire"
    b. "Que hubo raza"
    c. Extensions: Connections to Bob Marley, Jimi Hendrix, and other influential musicians.
    d. Documentary: Singing Our Way to Freedom SINGING OUR WAY TO FREEDOM (chunkyfilm.com)

Teaching LGBTQ+ Labor History through Sociological Perspectives

Niklaus Ryker K. Christensen and Adam I. Attwood

Introduction

This chapter addresses LGBTQ+ labor history in twentieth-century America through the sociological perspectives of "la/beling" theory, conflict theory, and the "glass ceiling" theory for use in social studies education. These perspectives may inform historical context of perceptions of LGBTQ+ inclusion in labor movements of the twentieth century. Being "out" has long been an internal debate among LGBTQ+ workers because of sociocultural norms that have historically made it dangerous in the twentieth century for many LGBTQ+ workers to be out about their minority sexual orientation or gender identity. That history has continued to influence labor movements into the twenty-first century, especially in how some civil rights leaders, such as Bayard Rustin, have been underrepresented or excluded in many K-12 history textbooks. This chapter highlights Rustin's role in the Civil Rights Movement of the twentieth century, especially his work as an "out" gay man who was a main organizer of the 1963 March on Washington for Jobs and Freedom. This chapter may be used by teachers in designing lessons to promote gender and sexual orientation equality and get youth to understand labor equality among LGBTQ+ people.

Sociohistorical Perspectives

Labeling theory is a sociological theory that posits that state leaders—those with power to make laws—create labels that cause people's perception of individuals and groups to change or reinforce a certain perception. Labeling theory may be summarized to emphasize the argument that "powerful individuals and the state create crime by labeling some behaviours as inappropriate" (Skaggs, 2024, para.3). Those state officials who have the power to label people may, therefore, control popular perception of groups per the labels they have applied. This concept, then, may help to explain why certain minority groups, such as LGBTQ+ people, faced discrimination, because they were not in power. LGBTQ+ people have historically faced disproportionate inequality and lack of access to positions of power in legislatures which further reinforced the majority's subjugation of LGBTQ+ people. In applying labeling theory, Skaggs (2024) further explained that:

> As members in society begin to treat these individuals on the basis of their labels, the individuals begin to accept the labels themselves. In other words, an individual engages in a behaviour that is deemed by others as inappropriate, others label that person to be deviant, and eventually the individual internalizes and accepts this label. (para.3).

Labeling theory, then, impacted employment law.

The labeling of people by people in power then influences people in all levels of society who use the labels that those in power use. People who are not in positions of power, such as peer-to-peer level interaction, also use labels against people who they perceive as being outside of their social norm. Teachers and students, for example, can replicate problematic labels that enforce their view of social norms. This prompts the question: Who determines what "normal" is? Changing a label can be difficult for individuals with less influence. Negative labels could adversely impact a group's access to employment and career advancement and mobility (Davies & Tanner, 2003).

For example, it was not until 1973 that "homosexuality" was removed from the Diagnostic and Statistical Manual (DSM) of the American Psychiatric Association (Drescher, 2015). Changing that label helped LGBTQ+ people and their allies to advocate more for themselves in the culture of the majority and help to change laws to be less oppressive toward LGBTQ+ people. Proactive protections began to be implemented at the federal level. For example, on June 26, 2015, the *Obergefell v. Hodges* decision guaranteed same-sex couples the right to marriage. On June 15, 2020, the U.S. Supreme Court further affirmed the prohibition on sex discrimination in Title VII of the Civil Rights Act of 1964 with their decision in *Bostock v. Clayton County* (U.S. Equal Opportunity Commission, n.d.).

Conflict theory, as with most sociological theories, are contested. Nevertheless, conflict theory may provide insight into some of the history of LGBTQ+ labor access and participation in the U.S. Civil Rights Movement. In an analysis of conflict theory, Athens (2013) outlined the steps of the theory:

> First, we must view all conflicts as taking some form of dominative encounters. Second, we must identify the different sequence of stages through which both completed and uncompleted dominative encounters pass. Third, we must identify the factors that prevent and foster the completion of dominative encounters and, thereby, differentiate inchoate from completed ones. Fourth, we must distinguish power from domination so that we can better understand both why and how dominative encounters are fought and who wins and [loses] them. Finally, we must not be reluctant to apply the notions of

> wars and revolutions to all dominative disputes in which they are applicable, no matter whether the combatants are small or large acting units. (p. 84)

These steps may be applied to a sociological analysis of labor history. When considering the heteronormative dominance in culture throughout history, conflict theory may be relevant to the study of LGBTQ+ labor history. Sexual orientation minorities, for example, may have had to navigate a complex social web where the dominant majority culture and the laws were not supportive and tried to change the narrative and the majority's collective mind one person at a time that equality was the American way. Eventually, laws were changed by individuals taking action to make changes in society, even at great personal risk. This power dynamic, as outlined by Athens (2013), may help to explain the process by which LGBTQ+ people and their allies in the dominant majority tried to advance labor access equality.

The glass ceiling concept is a theory that was originally used to explain why women did not advance in higher leadership roles in their career even with qualifications equal to men in similar roles for advancement. Purcell et al. (2010) further suggested that the "glass ceiling does not refer to all gender disparities, but rather to those that are more pronounced at higher levels of an organizational hierarchy than they are at lower levels" (p. 706). This theory has also been linked to some arguments for why some LGBTQ+ workers have struggled to advance to senior leadership positions in some employment sectors; because it has been argued that they have faced discrimination for their minority sexual orientation or gender identity (Gill, 2023).

According to the Human Rights Campaign (2021):

> LGBTQ+ workers earn approximately 89 cents for every dollar earned in a week by the typical worker in the United States. Disparities were even more pronounced for LGBTQ+ women, transgender men and women, and LGBTQ+ people of color. Though we did not assess the underlying reasons for this disparity, it is likely that discrimination is playing a role. One-third (36%) of LGBTQ+ workers say they have experienced discrimination in the workplace, with 29% of LGBTQ+ people, 37% Black respondents, and more than half of transgender respondents saying this discrimination had significantly impacted their financial well-being. (para.9)

In 2022, women typically earned 82 cents for every dollar earned by a man; in 2002, it was 80 cents; and in 1982 it was 65 cents. While that is a substantial improvement between 1982 and 2002, there was only an improvement of 2 cents between 2002 and 2022 (Kochhar, 2023).

Bayard Rustin as a Case Study in Social Change in the Civil Rights Movement

Bayard Rustin—a civil rights leader and an openly gay man—did not fit the social mold for most men in the 1960s, which was being a heterosexual family man, regardless of race (Miller, 2022). This was a form of conflict in that there was tension between the ideas of what being a "family man" was at that time. Sociological perspectives may inform historical understanding. Integrating sociological theories such as labeling theory, conflict theory, and the glass ceiling theory, may help students understand why some groups and individuals were underrepresented and why the Civil Rights Movement was especially important for trying to uphold the ideals of the U.S. Declaration of Independence and the U.S. Constitution. Integrating those sociological theories (DeCesare, 2005). Demographic data and statistics of economic access by group, for example, can be part of the social science of LGBTQ+ inclusion in the labor rights movement. Analyzing speeches, interviews, and discussion of conceptual frameworks can be part of the humanities art of analysis and discussion to advance understanding. In 2018, for example, Lewis (2018) observed:

> Despite the substantial strides in equality that the LGBT community has made over the past ten years, including the nationwide establishment of marriage equality in 2015, the study reveals that LGBT workers still experience discrimination substantial enough to prevent people from feeling comfortable enough to come out to their colleagues. (para.2)

This was after decades of work by LGBTQ+ people advocating for their rights while under threat of losing their jobs where employment law was not updated to protect sexual orientation and gender identity (Krupat & McCreery, 2001; Lewis, 2018).

The "gay glass ceiling" was encountered by many LGBTQ+ people throughout their careers (Gill, 2023; Lewis, 2018). Bayard Rustin's experience highlights the gay glass ceiling, but his advocacy helped to open the doors for others to advance employment opportunities through representation. Some of the many examples of LGBTQ+ people being at risk for losing their jobs because of their LGBTQ+ sexual orientation or gender identity were the "Don't Ask Don't Tell" policy in the U.S. military that was in effect from 1994 to 2011, the lack of federal marriage equality law until 2015, and many states lacking employment protections for workers who were gay or lesbian (Gill, 2023; Krupat & McCreery, 2001; Lewis, 2018). These affected all sectors of employment from the public sector to the private sector. The gay glass ceiling affected many people because they felt that they had to hide their sexual orientation and relationships because of policies or laws that put them at risk for losing their jobs because of who they were.

Bayard Rustin was a gay African American man in the Civil Rights Movement who worked alongside Martin Luther King Jr. (Miller, 2022; Schraeder, 2019). He was an advisor to Martin Luther King Jr. and one of the main organizers of the Civil Rights Movement throughout the 1940s through the 1960s. Among his accomplishments was being one of the leading organizers of the 1963 March on Washington for Jobs and Freedom, which was the event where Martin Luther King delivered his famous "I Have a Dream" speech (Martin Luther King Jr. Research and Educational Institute, n.d.a). However, Rustin was not given the credit he should have at the time because he was openly gay. In 1953, he was arrested for a consensual same-sex relationship with another man in California. At the time, same-sex relationships could be prosecuted by the state. It was not until 2023 that Rustin was posthumously pardoned by Governor Newsom (Katz, 2020).

In the 1960s, society labeled individuals such as Bayard Rustin as an outlier because of his sexual orientation and being openly gay. Katz (2020) noted: "In 1951, in fact, FBI Director J. Edgar Hoover launched an initiative deliberately targeting 'sex deviates'" (para.6). Consensual same-sex sexual relationships were legalized in California in 1976. The delay in equal rights was indicative of heterosexism—an ideological system that denigrates nonheterosexual identities and nonheterosexual romantic relationships—that was a pervasive component of society during that time (Hebl et al., 2010). Having LGBTQ+ representation in positions of power, such as in legislatures, has been crucial in securing civil rights. This includes employment rights and protections. According to Katz (2020), Rustin's posthumous pardon by Governor Newsom was secured largely by the advocacy of Scott Wiener, chair of the California Legislative LGBTQ Caucus, and Shirley Weber, chair of the California Legislative Black Caucus:

> "Rustin was a great American who was both gay and black at a time when the sheer fact of being either or both could land you in jail," says Weber in a statement. "This pardon assures his place in history and the Governor's ongoing commitment to addressing similar convictions shows that California is finally addressing a great injustice." (Katz, 2020, para.4)

It is because of LGBTQ+ legislators and allies that labels such as "sex deviate" had been removed from same-sex couples. This was a first step in giving openly LGBTQ+ people access to jobs and career advancement in places such as California.

As one of the main organizers of the 1963 March on Washington for Jobs and Freedom, Rustin had a substantial impact on securing more civil rights for multiple groups of Americans, such as LGBTQ+ people and racial minorities who had been historically underrepresented (Martin Luther King Jr. Research and Educational Institute, n.d.b). However, he was not included in many K-12 history textbooks. In researching Rustin's role in securing more civil rights in the United States, Miller (2022) noted:

> To continue bringing Rustin out of the footnotes of the civil rights narrative, I reconsider the rhetoric ahead of the march and King's famous speech, foregrounding Rustin and his sexuality. On August 13, two weeks before the march, Senator Strom Thurmond outed Rustin on the Senate floor. (p. 45)

More than 200,000 people showed up to demonstrate in the 1963 March on Washington for Jobs and Freedom, so opponents of the Civil Rights Movement, such as Senator Strom Thurmond targeted organizers such as Rustin. Homophobia was a major problem in the United States and Thurmond used that bigotry to try to negatively influence the public against Rustin and omit him from K-12 history textbooks for the remainder of the twentieth century (Miller, 2022; Schraeder, 2019).

The 1963 March on Washington for Jobs and Freedom, as indicated in the name of the civil rights advocacy march itself, was focused in part on labor rights. Securing people's right to employment and improving labor conditions was part of Rustin's goals for improving economic access for historically underrepresented and underserved groups in the United States. By improving access to employment and career mobility and advancement, people's quality of life would improve (Krupat & McCreery, 2001).

Toward a Representative LGBTQ+ Community after the 1960s Civil Rights Movement

Following the 1963 Civil Rights Movement event the March on Washington for Jobs and Freedom was another major movement at the end of that decade known as the Stonewall Uprising. This was a reaction toward the unequal treatment of the LGBTQ+ community in New York City. The Stonewall Uprising was the spark that erupted the movement for equal rights movement and ending the social discrimination of members of LGBTQ community. Just prior to this event, individuals who identified as homosexuals were at risk of being arrested, harassed and jailed for their sexuality. Members of the LGBTQ community united in New York City in the Greenwich village—more particularly, the Stonewall Inn—to seek "freedom" by taking a stand for more civil rights to be openly LGTBQ+ in the workplace and public spaces. As more people of the LGBTQ community became more prominent in this neighborhood, police forces began to conduct raids in Greenwich Village. The constant raids on those premises eventually led to a pushback from the community, thus, sparking another social movement toward LGBTQ equality that would set a precedent for social justice advocacy (Arcidiacono & Carbone, 2021).

The Stonewall Uprising put a national focus on inequality of LGBTQ. This encouraged individuals in other communities across the United States to continue to advocate for equality and has been the apex of the gay rights movement. This event gained national news attention which expanded interest beyond the LGBT community generating conversations across America, which heightened awareness of LGBTQ social issues for equality. By winning the public relations fight against inequality of LGBTQ persons in New York City at Stonewall, this led to the 1970 first Gay Pride event in New York City (Library of Congress, n.d.). Every year since then, United States has had a celebration of LGBTQ identity known today as Pride Month. For the last 54 years, June has become the month to represent Gay Pride month across the entirety of United States. It is important for young queer people to understand the importance of what Pride Month stands for. By introducing this small excerpt of historical events, people can finally understand the importance of Pride Month (Arcidiacono & Carbone, 2021).

Two years after the first Pride parade, a new law got introduced into the American education system, known as Title IX. Title IX was introduced in 1972, and it was designed to protect individuals against sex discrimination. This includes gender identity, as far as educational institutions this meant that everyone could receive financial aid. It is important to note that this was not only reflected in academia, but also applied toward school athletics programs. In athletics, it had expanded to female athletes in a way that has increased the promotion and participation of women in sports programs. Since Title IX, girls and women achieved equality in sports in school and outside of school in the professional leagues. Title IX supported equal access and equitable representation to participate in athletic events of all types, from sports such as soccer, softball, football, hockey, and any others. While the state power was instrumental in achieving this equality, it is at the grassroots that cultural change occurs in enduring ways so that equity in sports continues (Hextrum & Sethi, 2022).

Prior to Title IX, many people were frequently subject to stereotyping in sports and employment access. The mentality of stereotyping ties into labeling theory in sociology because of the sex assigned at birth often determining societal expectations and social reinforcement of gendered roles along masculine and feminine options. The labeling theory regarding Title IX represented women as previously lacking legal equality with men—suggesting socially enforced inequality between the sexes before Title IX was enacted into law. However, once Title IX picked up traction, that sociohistorical inequality began to give way to social justice advocacy for equality and equity in sexuality and gender identity (Kimmel, 2016).

Furthermore, the Women's Armed Services Integration Act of 1948 was a major change to the law that officially allowed women to serve in the military and gave them regular and reserve status in all branches of the United States military. However, even though women were allowed to serve in the military, they were still partly discriminated against as service members. Women, while serving in the military forces, still sometimes had the label of caring and less "aggressive" than men, thus resulting in support roles in the military rather than combat roles. During this time up until the mid-2010s, women could certainly serve in the U.S. Armed Forces, but they were restricted from serving in a combat role. For example, women were barred from combat roles until 2013. In 2013, the U.S. military lifted its ban on women serving in direct ground combat roles, making both men and women eligible to serve in front-line combat. In 2015, Secretary of Defense Ash Carter opened all combat arms jobs to women which included all U.S. Special Forces, such as the U.S. Army Rangers (Vanden Brook, 2023).

Another historical event that took place, that resonates today and should be addressed in social studies curriculum related to the LGBTQ+ community was the murder of Matthew Sheppard. In 1998, an openly gay male, Matthew Shepard, was brutally murdered by three young men for his sexuality. This hate crime was the epitome of how devastating labeling can be. This is an important historical event because even though the government had become "open" to sexual identity, the country still had massive hurdles regarding sexual identity. His death, showcasing the physical danger that members of the LGBTQ still were present in the United States. Matthew Sheppard who was a student at University of Wyoming was an active member of an LGBTQ club, where there he was befriended by two men posing as gay. The evening of October 7, 1998, the two men posed as gay which they lured Matthew out of the club in which resulted in a brutal beating and resulted in his death four days later after being rushed to the hospital. Matthew Shepard's death brought attention not only to the town in which he resided in, but also across the country and the world. During that time, Wyoming did not have hate crime protection against persons sexual orientation, thus sparking the expansion of hate crime legislation (Parrott-Sheffer, 2024).

Nine years later following the death of Matthew Shepard, the law of hate crime was expanded to where sexual orientation became part of the law—later, it was renamed as the Matthew Shepard Act (Parrott-Sheffer, 2024). It is important to add that it was not until 2009 President Obama signed it officially as the Matthew Shepard Act. Visibility of LGBTQ inequality did not just expand in just academia but also within the ranks of the military. In 1993 President Bill Clinton signed into law the Don't Ask Don't Tell Act. This was fostered as a law when members of the Armed Forces were dishonorably discharge for being openly gay, as back then, it was erroneously believed that it might "hurt the morale and cause problems" within the military. Under this new policy, LGBTQ Americans could continue or serve in the military, as long as they kept their sexual identity secret. While the DADT was welcomed as a first step toward tolerance and acceptance, gay rights activists complained that serving in secrecy was more problematic, especially to those who were already in the military (Britannica, 2024).

During heightened opposition to DADT later in the first decade of the twenty-first century, President Barack Obama announced the repeal on September 10, 2011, ending the silence of LGBTQ+ members of the U.S. military. In doing so, members of the LGBTQ+ community who had been dishonorably discharged could appeal their discharge and change their discharge status to *honorable*. Prior to this historical event, soldiers were hiding behind the truth of their sexuality due to the fear of being discharged from the military, where many soldiers either lied about their true sexuality identity or remained in the "closet" as means to continue their service in the military. This issue is a great example regarding conflict theory because it highlights the inevitability of conflict within social groups due to their sexuality in a society that did not have equal protection laws, especially if these individuals were in position of leadership, creating an imbalance of power, especially when it came to distribution of responsibility and resources. LGBTQ+ advocates were crucial in advancing equality and getting the laws changed during the Obama administration (Frank, 2013).

Implications and Conclusions

Bayard Rustin's work organizing the 1963 March on Washington for Jobs and Freedom should receive greater attention. K-12 history textbooks should include Rustin for his civil rights advocacy in advancing representation of LGBTQ+ workers. Regardless of whether a high school textbook includes Rustin, social studies teachers should include a lesson on Rustin's work for LGBTQ+ representation in civil rights and employment access. While strides have been made for a more equal representation of equal pay, teachers can advance opportunities for equality in the workplace and not restrict people regardless of identity or social status. In the past, there had been substantial inequality in pay based on identity groups (e.g., race and gender).

Conflict theory can be applied to what some teachers and students may experience in some schools where there is a tension between what the teacher wants to teach about LGBTQ+ labor history and what the local school community leaders want taught. For example, a high school may have a sociology elective course for students that has approved Shepard and McTighe's (2014) *Sociology and You* as the textbook, but the sociology teacher is told by school administrators not to teach about LGBTQ+ issues or to expand on current events affecting that community. That indicates a tension in an unequal power dynamic in which an administrator can unilaterally pressure the teacher to not use a textbook that had already been approved by the school board because that administrator does not like the topic.

References

Arcidiacono, C., & Carbone, A. (2021). Stonewall Uprising: 50 years later—Emerging challenges for LGBTQ communities around the world. *Journal of Community & Applied Social Psychology, 31*(6), 639–43. https://doi.org/10.1002/casp.2584

Athens, L. (2013). Park's theory of conflict and his fall from grace in sociology. *Cultural Studies, Critical Methodologies, 13*(2), 75–87. https://doi.org/10.1177/1532708612471315

Britannica, The Editors of Encyclopaedia (2024, August 9). Don't Ask, Don't Tell. *Encyclopedia Britannica*. https://www.britannica.com/event/Dont-Ask-Dont-Tell

Davies, S., & Tanner, J. (2003). The long arm of the law: Effects of labeling on employment. *Sociological Quarterly, 44*(3), 385–404. https://doi.org/10.1111/j.1533-8525.2003.tb00538.x

DeCesare, M. (2005). 95 years of teaching high school sociology. *Teaching Sociology, 33*(3), 236–51. https://doi.org/10.1177/0092055x0503300301

Drescher J. (2015). Out of DSM: Depathologizing homosexuality. *Behavioral Sciences, 5*(4), 565–575. https://doi.org/10.3390/bs5040565

Frank, N. (2013). The President's pleasant surprise: How LGBT advocates ended Don't Ask, Don't Tell. *Journal of Homosexuality, 60*(2–3), 159–213. https://doi.org/10.1080/00918369.2013.744666

Gill, T. (2023, January 30). "Gay glass ceiling": Why more feminine men get passed over for leadership roles. *The Gaurdian*. https://www.theguardian.com/lifeandstyle/2023/jan/30/gay-glass-ceiling-why-effeminate-men-get-passed-over-for-leadership-roles

Hebl, M., Law, C., & King, E. (2010). Heterosexism. In J. F. Dovidio, M. Hewstone, P. Glick & V. M. Esses (Eds.), *The SAGE Handbook of Prejudice, Stereotyping and Discrimination* (pp. 345–60). SAGE Publications. https://doi.org/10.4135/9781446200919

Hextrum, K., & Sethi, S. (2022). Title IX at 50: Legitimating state domination of women's sport. *International Review for the Sociology of Sport, 57*(5), 655–72. https://doi.org/10.1177/10126902211037843

Human Rights Campaign. (2021). The wage gap among LGBTQ+ workers in the United States. https://www.hrc.org/resources/the-wage-gap-among-lgbtq-workers-in-the-united-states (Accessed August 7, 2024)

Katz, B. (2020, February 6). Gay civil rights leader Bayard Rustin posthumously pardoned in California. *Smithsonian Magazine*. https://www.smithsonianmag.com/smart-news/bayard-rustin-civil-rights-icon-tarnished-arrest-homosexual-encounter-pardoned-california-180974143/

Kimmel, A. P. (2016). Title IX: An imperfect but vital tool to stop bullying of LGBT students. *The Yale Law Journal, 125*(7), 2006–36.

Kochhar, R. (2023, March 1). The enduring grip of the gender pay gap. Pew Research Center. https://www.pewresearch.org/social-trends/2023/03/01/the-enduring-grip-of-the-gender-pay-gap/

Krupat, K., & McCreery, P. (2001). *Out at work: Building a gay-labor alliance* (1st ed.). University of Minnesota Press.

Lewis, M. G. (2018, June 25). Study reveals less than half of LGBT workers are out at work. *The Advocate*. https://www.advocate.com/business/2018/6/25/study-reveals-less-half-lgbt-workers-are-out-work

Library of Congress. (n.d.). 1969: The Stonewall Uprising. In *LGBTQIA+ Studies: A Resource Guide*. https://guides.loc.gov/lgbtq-studies/stonewall-era (Accessed August 16, 2024)

Martin Luther King Jr. Research and Educational Institute, The. (n.d.a). Rustin, Bayard. https://kinginstitute.stanford.edu/rustin-bayard

Martin Luther King Jr. Research and Educational Institute, The. (n.d.b). March on Washington for Jobs and Freedom. https://kinginstitute.stanford.edu/march-washington-jobs-and-freedom

Miller, J. H. (2022). Bolstering Bayard Rustin: Collaborative apologia, heteronormativity, and the 1963 March of Washington. *The Southern Communication Journal, 87*(1), 44–55. https://doi.org/10.1080/1041794X.2021.1995032

Parrott-Sheffer, C. (2024, August 1). Matthew Shepard. *Encyclopedia Britannica*. https://www.britannica.com/biography/Matthew-Shepard

Purcell, D., MacArthur, K. R., & Samblanet, S. (2010). Gender and the glass ceiling at work. *Sociology Compass, 4*(9), 705–17. https://doi.org/10.1111/j.1751-9020.2010.00304.x

Schraeder, E. F. (2019). Invisible rainbow: Notes for educators and librarians. *Radical Teacher, 114*, 84–86. https://doi.org/10.5195/rt.2019.547

Shepard, J., & McTighe, J. (2014). *Sociology and You*. McGraw-Hill.

Skaggs, S. L. (2024, July 24). Labeling theory. *Encyclopedia Britannica*. https://www.britannica.com/topic/labeling-theory

US Equal Opportunity Commission. (n.d.). Protections against employment discrimination based on sexual orientation or gender identity. https://www.eeoc.gov/laws/guidance/protections-against-employment-discrimination-based-sexual-orientation-or-gender

Vanden Brook, T. (2023, April 16). Just 10 years ago, women were banned from combat—Now, they're on the front lines, climbing the ranks. *USA Today*. https://www.usatoday.com/story/news/politics/2023/04/16/women-in-combat-military-progress/11548931002/

Lesson Plan

1. Lesson Plan Title: LGBTQ+ labor history and Bayard Rustin
2. Theme: This lesson highlights Rustin's role in the civil rights movement of the twentieth century, especially his work as an "out" gay man who was a main organizer of the 1963 March on Washington for Jobs and Freedom. This chapter may be used by teachers in designing lessons to promote gender and sexual orientation equality and get youth to understand labor equality among LGBTQ+ people.
3. Grade Level: 12
4. Course: Sociology or History elective
5. Time Required: 55 minutes
6. Essential and Supporting Questions:
    a. Who determines what "normal" is?
    b. What was Bayard Rustin's contribution to LGBTQ+ history?
    c. Why is the 1963 March on Washington for Jobs and Freedom an important part of LGBTQ+ history?
7. Objectives:
    a. Students will be able to explain the importance of Bayard Rustin for LGBTQ+ representation in advancing access to employment.
8. Standards (from the National Council for the Social Studies [NCSS]):
    a. NCSS: D1.4.9-12. Explain how supporting questions contribute to an inquiry and how, through engaging source work, new compelling and supporting questions emerge.
    b. NCSS: D3.3.9-12. Identify evidence that draws information directly and substantively from multiple sources to detect inconsistencies in evidence in order to revise or strengthen claims.
9. Classroom Materials: PowerPoint, summaries of articles cited in this chapter.
10. Instructional Plan:
    a. Entry Task to Establish Context [time estimate 5 minutes]
        i. Students watch PBS YouTube video (3:36), "The story of Bayard Rustin, openly gay leader in the civil rights movement," https://youtu.be/KwNBLgMVhPs?si=oIq14MHAJNlAix0n
        ii. Students answer question: What is something you learned about Bayard Rustin?
    b. Teacher-Directed Instruction [est. 15 minutes]
        i. Give students handout summarizing labeling theory, conflict theory, and the glass ceiling concept (may use summaries in this chapter)
        ii. Lead discussion with students about Bayard Rustin based on the Entry Task. Integrate the sociological theories/concepts in this chapter into the discussion.

c. Student-Centered/Engaged Learning (Student Inquiry Activity/Activities) [est. 30 minutes]
   i. Place students in pairs. Using the handout on sociological theories/concepts, the PBS YouTube video on Bayard Rustin from the Entry Task, and a handout summarizing Bayard Rustin's contributions (may use this chapter), have student discuss in pairs and write their answers to these questions:
      1. Who determines what "normal" is?
      2. What was Bayard Rustin's contribution to LGBTQ+ history?
      3. Why is the 1963 March on Washington for Jobs and Freedom an important part of LGBTQ+ history?
d. Exit Task for Summarizing Answer(s) to Essential and Supporting Questions [est. 5 minutes]
   i. Ask students to volunteer the highlights of their discussions.
   ii. Students submit their written responses to the three questions.

11. Assessment: Entry Task (students write answer), written responses to the three questions.
12. Community Engagement: During the discussion, the teacher discusses students' comments about who determines what "normal" is and how that relates to their individual roles in changing or reinforcing social norms.

Contextualizing the "Lavender Scare" with Critical Human Rights Education

Sean Corrigan

In the wake of the Second World War, after playing a central role in founding the United Nations to promote peace and global standards of human dignity, the United States government engaged in systematic discrimination against the LGBTQ+ community. At the same time American officials were drafting the Universal Declaration of Human Rights (1948), it was purging the State Department of gay and lesbian members, arguing that dimensions of their sexuality made them communist sympathizers and/or vulnerable to blackmail. These blatant human rights violations, in what would later be named the Lavender Scare, fueled workplace discrimination across the United States, as state and local governments used federal precedents to institutionalize homophobic policies. This dark era in American labor history was central to LGBTQ+ activism during the Civil Rights Movement. Despite the fact that well known civil rights leaders, such as Malcolm X and Martin Luther King Jr., and lesser-known LGBTQ+ rights advocates, such as Stonewall Uprising icon Storme DeLarverie, explicitly linked struggles for decency and equality in the United States to human rights concepts, social studies teachers rarely make these connections in their classrooms (Grant & Gibson, 2013; Corrigan, 2023).

This chapter uses human rights education (HRE) to frame the Lavender Scare and associated discriminatory practices to demonstrate how teachers can critically approach issues of discrimination and social justice in their classrooms. The focus on this episode of LGBTQ+ history promotes the inclusion of a historically marginalized group in social studies curriculum and the teaching of labor history. The Lavender Scare illuminates important narratives in the Civil Rights era and American labor history by highlighting personal stories amidst systematic oppression perpetrated by the United States government that still reverberate today. This chapter is also a response to two position statements by the National Council for the Social Studies (NCSS) about the need for history teachers to better contextualize LGBTQ+ history (2019) and the "importance of teaching and learning about human rights" in social justice education (2021). The included lesson is explicitly connected to human rights concepts, NCSS Curriculum Standards, and the C3 Framework. It is organized using an Inquiry Design Model (IDM) to scaffold critical instruction about a key event in LGBTQ+ and labor history in the United States.

Human Rights Education

Human rights education (HRE) provides an important critical, analytical, and practical approach to the Lavender Scare. HRE is learning that develops knowledge, advocacy skills, and values that center human rights. HRE prompts students to examine their own experiences and actions from a human rights perspective and incorporate human rights concepts into their personal values and decision-making processes (Osler, 2016). While HRE frameworks vary, scholars agree that HRE includes education *about rights*, and education *for rights*. Education *about rights* includes knowledge of human rights discourse, such as treaties, declarations, legislation, or debates about what constitutes a human right. Education *for rights* includes skill-building and attitudinal orientations, which use human rights aims to promote advocacy and other forms of civic participation. Such dispositions and reflective action are important in a world where individual and/or community actions can have far-reaching impacts. Consequently, a HRE approach ensures that students consider their rights and responsibilities to all humans. The cultivation of such a disposition has the potential to create a more just society where members recognize that their actions have implications beyond their immediate surroundings, and teachers can play an enormous role in moving the needle in this direction. A human rights approach to social studies instruction also offers a number of pedagogical benefits for teachers and students. HRE can provide a conceptual tool for teachers to frame "bad events" in history curriculum, address sensitive or controversial topics, compare rights issues across time and place, promote global citizenship, and build empathy by emphasizing our shared humanity (Corrigan, 2022).

Social studies classrooms often fail to frame rights issues, such as discrimination and/or homophobia, as human rights concerns. For example, Grant and Gibson (2013) argue that despite the use of human rights discourse by leaders of the Civil Rights Movement, these connections are rare in social studies classrooms. This omission is important because human rights-focused curriculum and pedagogy can provide counternarratives to versions of United States history that often ignore or downplay racism and other human rights violations (Bajaj, 2011; Zembylas, 2011). Instead, uncritical stories that emphasize American righteousness and exceptionalism are dominant. Social studies scholars have often noted the disconnect between these traditional narratives and the lived experiences of many Americans (Duncan & Murray-Everett, 2022). Furthermore, Nelson and Pang (2006) note, "Social studies curriculum does a poor job of examining the disparity between the American credo and pervasiveness of racism in the American experience (p. 129)." This observation is especially relevant for LGBTQ+ people that endured rampant homophobia while serving the same government that extolled and exercised its moral authority throughout the post-World War II world. In contrast to how the Civil Rights Movement is portrayed in U.S. social studies curricula, both Martin Luther King and Malcolm X intentionally used human rights discourse to frame their goals during the Civil Rights Movement. Meanwhile, the NAACP used passages from the Universal Declaration of Human Rights (UDHR) to shame the United States government into living up to a document it played a major role in creating. Moreover, Native Americans used human rights doctrines as grounds to pursue social justice and reparations during the 1960s and 1970s (Dunbar-Ortiz, 2015). Additionally, LGBTQ+ history has also been interpreted through a human rights lens (Corrigan, 2023), as have issues of sustainability (Kavanaugh, 2024) and children's rights (Bourke, 2024). According to Hahn (2020), these diverse narratives are important because human rights violations are often discussed by teachers in theoretical terms, as if they only happen far from home or in the distant past. HRE, however, has the potential to link rights discourses with social justice education in (and about) the United States. Human rights education connects specific rights-seeking groups to the larger human rights picture (Osler & Starkey, 2010). This means that human rights education can and should promote the rights of all minoritized people, since authentic human rights pursuits are universal. Ultimately, HRE in social studies classrooms can historicize and contextualize injustice in order to illuminate inequities and scaffold a path of informed democratic citizenship.

HRE and critical education

Human rights education is a key component of critical citizenship education and can reinforce key social studies concepts for students (Bajaj, 2011; Tolley, 2013). In fact, critical citizenship scholars, such as Banks (2004), have argued that human rights should underpin all citizenship education. Similarly, Carano and Clabough (2016) directly linked the study of human rights to global citizenship education, while Gaudelli and Fernekes (2004) have argued that social studies students who do not consider human rights issues in the context of global citizenship can be left with serious misconceptions of life outside of the United States. Furthermore, Andreotti (2014) argues that HRE has the potential to contribute to a critical approach to citizenship education because human rights discourse, and the UDHR in particular, have a universal appeal to proponents of equality and human dignity. Additionally, critical pedagogy aims to name and interrupt the power imbalances that are central to HRE and other frameworks that promote criticality. The goal of critical pedagogy is to build critical consciousness in order to encourage individuals to be agents of change through social critique and critical action (Freire, 1970; Giroux, 2007). HRE aims to use human rights concepts to illuminate injustice and serve as the basis for reform. Using HRE to raise critical consciousness supports the goals of critical pedagogy by facilitating social critique and framing action. This activism dimension also reinforces key components of social studies education, such as transformational citizenship.

This article references the Universal Declaration of Human Rights (UDHR), which is a central document to HRE. The UDHR is the most widely accepted and cited standard of human rights. It was codified by the United Nations on December 10, 1948, three years after the UN was chartered in 1945. Though not legally binding, the UDHR lists thirty individual rights meant to constitute the nucleus of human rights discourse worldwide. This document has been the source of critical citizenship since its inception, with advocacy organizations, such as Amnesty International and the NAACP, using passages from the UDHR to shame the United States government into living up to a document it played a major role in creating. Furthermore, the UDHR was written (1946-48) at the exact same time Executive 9836 was drafted (1947). The concurrent development and support for these documents represents blatant hypocrisy by U.S. government officials, and students have the opportunity to examine a clear example when institutions failed to live up to their stated moral and ethical stances. Consequently, scholars have advocated for the use of the UDHR in social studies classrooms to deepen learning about human rights issues and associated activism (Osler & Starkey, 2010; Alter & Fernekes, 2022; Oberman & Mallon, 2024). For example, Flowers and Magendzo (2022) assert that the UDHR is the defining feature of HRE, as it provides students with a heuristic for transformative education that centers justice and peace. Additionally, Gibson and Grant (2017) argue that the UDHR provides clarity in cross-cultural and historical analyses of oppression related rights movements. Building on these premises, Alter (2022) centered the UDHR to teach about homophobia, heteronormativity, and intersectional dimensions of identity development. Furthermore, Amnesty International (2012) found increased awareness on global themes of justice in resources that make the UDHR accessible to young students, with Oberman and Mallon (2024) noting that such resources were successful in raising student consciousness about human rights tied to environmental issues. Lastly, Corrigan (2022) outlined how the UDHR can help teachers frame antiracism and colonialism in social studies classrooms, as well as women's rights movements and contemporary feminism (Corrigan, 2024). The conceptual framework and lesson plan offered in this chapter build on prior HRE and social studies scholarship, which has found the UDHR to be an effective tool in promoting critical citizenship.

The UDHR contains what scholars refer to as both *negative* and *positive* rights. Negative rights are rights that oblige inaction, meaning these rights exist unless someone (or a group or government) takes them away. A negative right forbids others from acting against the holder of the right. Examples of negative rights include freedom of speech, freedom of religion, or freedom from slavery, and the right to life. Positive rights are rights that oblige action, meaning these rights will not exist unless an action is taken by a person, group, or government (Farinacci-Fernos, 2018). In order for a positive right to be exercised, someone else's action must be added to the equation. Examples of positive rights include the right to work, the right to an education, the right to food and housing, and the right to healthcare. The distinction between positive and negative rights has important implications when addressing advocacy issues, often called "transformative action" in social studies/citizenship education frameworks, as it helps focus activism. Also, since HRE seeks to promote rights-based advocacy, the concept of positive rights can expand possibilities for action beyond the more basic freedoms that fit into the category of negative rights. Furthermore, exactly how human rights (especially positive rights) are to be granted and ensured can generate engaging deliberations amongst students.

The Lavender Scare

The Lavender Scare refers to the mass dismissal of LGBTQ+ workers from government service in the late 1940s and early 1950s, and their continued discrimination in the workplace into the 1970s. Drawing parallels to the First Red Scare following World War I and coinciding with the Second Red Scare after World War II, in which Americans feared communist infiltration and subversion of key labor and political organizations, the Lavender Scare focused on the presence of LGBTQ+ people in government institutions. Many Americans believed that LGBTQ+ people serving the country would make their institutions weaker, as they might be more susceptible to blackmail or coercion, as well as be communist sympathizers. The manifestations of these fears began in 1947 when the US State Department cited security concerns in its imminent purge of LGBTQ+ workers from its ranks. The document central to the first wave of the Lavender Scare is Executive Order 9835. Often called the "Loyalty Order," President Truman signed this directive on March 21, 1947. Executive Order 9835 includes a preamble that explains the necessity of protecting the United States against the "infiltration of disloyal persons into the ranks of its employees." The order's six sections describe investigative procedures for any employee suspected of subversive activities. It is noteworthy, that while communist sympathies and associations are mentioned several times, there are no direct references to the LGBTQ+ community whatsoever. However, in practice LGBTQ+ workers were immediately targeted. Soon, thousands of job applicants were denied employment at government agencies due to allegations of homosexuality and current State Department employees suspected of LGBTQ+ sympathies were interrogated. This sanctioned discrimination resulted in a hostile workplace whereby LGBTQ+ workers suffered a range of indignities, from name-calling to physical violence. In short, the atmosphere of fear created around a communist infiltration of federal institutions that characterized the Red Scares was extended to include associations with the LGBTQ+ community.

After six years of increasingly severe discrimination in the workplace, Executive Order 10450 was issued by President Eisenhower in 1953. The second key presidential directive associated with the Lavender Scare, this order formally expanded security criteria to include sexual orientation as a pertinent consideration for all government positions, and grounds for termination. Until Executive Order 10450's reversal in 1973, approximately 5,000 LGBT people were fired from federal employment, often under hostile circumstances. Furthermore, similar state-level statutes across the United States also rid institutions of LGBTQ+ employees. For example, in the late 1950s, the Florida Legislative Investigative Committee turned its attention to LGBT people as targets for "subversive activity" when looking to undermine civil rights organizations after tying activists to communism proved difficult. Many students and professors at the University of Florida were forced to drop out or resign as a result of the committee's actions. During the federal and state proceedings that would lead to their dismissal, many LGBTQ+ people were publicly outed. This attention sometimes resulted in further economic and social consequences beyond the initial loss of employment.

HRE, labor, and LGBTQ+ discrimination

This chapter seeks to make connections between human rights concepts, labor history, and LGBTQ+ discrimination. demonstrating both their relationship and importance in social studies classrooms. For example, the right to dignified work was central to the Civil Rights Movement. When Martin Luther King was using the UDHR to illustrate the discrimination and dehumanization of Black Americans, he often did so by making arguments about labor issues. Dr. King was highly involved with the labor movement during the 1960s, believing that gains in labor rights were fundamental to bringing broader equality to Black Americans. In fact, it was a sanitation worker's strike that brought Dr. King to Memphis where he would be assassinated. Moreover, the same gainful and dignified employment desired by women and People of Color in the United States during the Civil Rights Movement was also an aspiration of the LGBTQ+ community. Despite the fact that the UDHR outlined the right to work (Article 23) and the right to take part in one's government (Article 21), policies of the United States government denied these rights to LGBTQ+ people during the Lavender Scare. Additionally, broader human rights issues in American labor history can be assessed with UDHR, such union membership, equal pay for equal work, and humane working conditions (protected by Article 23), as well as adequate living standards (Article 25) and limitations on work hours/paid time off (Article 24). Therefore, the Lavender Scare is central to understanding key dynamics in labor history, and HRE provides a framework to approach human rights issues raised by the discrimination inherent in the Lavender Scare. However, this lens can also be used to analyze the plight (past or present) of others who have struggled to have their rights protected in the workplace. This rights-focused approach also lends itself to intersectional solidarity in activism by providing clear aims and units of analysis.

Lesson Design

The lesson plan offered in this chapter asks students to use the Universal Declaration of Human Rights to evaluate federal workplace policies towards LGBTQ+ people from the late 1940s to the early 1970s. Students will examine primary and secondary sources, including legislation, congressional proceedings, media reports, and testimonies from those personally affected by discrimination. This lesson is explicitly aligned with two sets of NCSS standards, the *National Curriculum Standards for Social Studies* (2010) and the *College, Career, and Civic Life (C3) Framework* (2013). An Inquiry Design Model (IDM), which is an instructional support recommended by the creators of the *C3 Framework* for addressing their social studies standards, is provided. An IDM is a brief, simple representation of the key questions and sources that define a line of curricular inquiry. The compelling (or essential) question for this lesson is: What human rights issues are connected to the Lavender Scare? This question asks students to analyze the Lavender Scare through a human rights lens, synthesizing both the UDHR and the historical arc of LGBTQ+ discrimination in the United States.

This lesson opens with a short video that provides historical context for the Lavender Scare (PBS, 2020). The video describes the political atmosphere in the United States in the late 1940s and early 1950s, using Senator Joseph McCarthy's infamous speech in Wheeling, West Virginia to make connections between key dynamics at the time. These events include the emerging Cold War and arms race with the Soviet Union, the Chinese Communist Revolution and the rising influence of Mao Zedong, and the discovery of spies working in the United States government. In his 1950 speech, Joseph McCarthy claimed that 205 communists were working in the United States State Department, and that many of these employees were selling secrets to American competition abroad, particularly the Soviet Union and its communist allies. These salacious allegations garnered national headlines immediately and propelled what is now known as the Second Red Scare. McCarthy and many of his Senate colleagues created a moral panic about a communist infiltration of the U.S. government which soon put the LGBTQ+ community in its crosshairs. This video demonstrates how the Lavender Scare was related to the better-known Red Scare. This pedagogical approach allows teachers to connect prior knowledge and instruction to the persecution of federal LGBTQ+ employees following the war. The development of the United Nations (and the UDHR), the Cold War, and McCarthyism are very common post-WWII topics in high school history classes. This video primes students to connect these conditions to the persecution of the LGBTQ+ community during the Lavender Scare.

Following the introductory video, teachers will guide students through an examination of three key documents. The first document is the Universal Declaration of Human Rights (United Nations, 1948). As described earlier in this article, the UDHR is the prevailing codification of human rights both globally and nationally, and HRE scholars have documented its effectiveness in deepening learning about issues of social justice. Teachers should provide context for the development of the UDHR in conjunction with the creation of the United Nations after World War II. The second document is the complete text of Executive Order 9835. Often called the "Loyalty Order," President Truman signed this authorization on March 21, 1947. Executive Order 9835 includes a preamble that explains the necessity of protecting the United States against the "infiltration of disloyal persons into the ranks of its employees (Truman, 1947, p. 1)." The order's six sections describe investigative procedures for any employee suspected of subversive activities. It is noteworthy, that while communist sympathies and associations are mentioned several times, there are no direct references to the LGBTQ+ community whatsoever. Teachers should guide students through an examination of this concise and accessible document that became central to the Lavender Scare. It is recommended that students examine Part V- Standards, closely, as the Activities and Associations clause in this section was the primary basis for the investigation and purge of LGBTQ+ employees. The third document that teachers should examine with their students as part of the guided practice of this lesson is the first page of the Department of Commerce's Perversion Cases Report (Adkins, 2016). Dated June 15, 1950 this report was filed three years after Executive Order 9835 and five months after Joseph McCarthy's speech in West Virginia. This report describes the Department of Commerce's investigation into its members as part of its compliance with Order 9835. It then briefly details the investigative outcomes of its employees. Each of the five cases reads like a short obituary for LGBTQ+ workers that were either fired, forced to resign, or pushed into early retirement. This document demonstrates how Order 9835 affected LGBTQ+ people in just one of the many departments of the federal government, leading students to get a sense of the systematic witch hunt characteristic of the Lavender Scare.

The student inquiry portion of this lesson involves the examination of three videos that provide historical context for the Lavender Scare, anti-LGBTQ+ discrimination in the workplace (and beyond), personal narratives of individuals targeted by congressional investigations, and contemporary connections. The content in these videos build upon one another and are meant to be viewed in the given order. The first video looks at LGBTQ+ life in post-World War II America (Facing History & Ourselves, 2017). It describes prevailing discriminatory views of the LGBTQ+ community and the manifestations of overwhelmingly negative attitudes. This powerful video allows students to see that the Lavender Scare was one of many oppressive forms of structural homophobia in the United States at the time. The second video develops the connection between the Second Red Scare and the Lavender Scare (Time, 2021). It provides examples, such as Frank Kameny, of LGBTQ+ fired as a result of Order 9835, who later led resistance against discrimination. In his activism, Kameny made clear connections between human rights doctrines and discriminatory practices by the federal government. This video also chronicles the repeals of Order 9835 and Order 10450 under Bill Clinton's administration, and discusses the Trump administration's ban on transgender people serving in the United States military. The third video highlights the immediate and lasting effects of the Lavender Scare on the LGBTQ+ community (PBS, 2019). It provides additional personal stories of those fired under Order 9835 and traces related anti-LGBTQ+ prejudices from pre-WWII to contemporary America. It highlights the resilience of LGBTQ+ communities in the face of homophobia, exemplified by both the Lavender Scare and recent developments. Each of these videos provides excellent commentary by historians and cultural critics, as well as engaging media footage from the different eras covered. The Inquiry Design Model (Appendix B) provides formative learning outcomes for each video, which teachers could use as either post-viewing discussion prompts or questions for students to answer while watching. Since the compelling/essential question asks students to make connections between the Lavender Scare and human rights concerns, it is recommended that teachers ask students to analyze each of these videos with the UDHR.

The summative task of this lesson asks students to create an activist agenda for a contemporary LGBTQ+ rights movement in the United States. The second and third videos mention recent discriminatory policies faced by transgender Americans serving in the armed forces, however, the Trump-era ban was reversed by the Biden administration in 2021. So, students will need to investigate current rights issues faced by the LGBTQ+ community or residual effects of prior policies, and are required to make explicit connections between these goals and the UDHR. Students may choose to take a local, national, and/or global view for this assignment. Locally, students might look at banned books in certain states and school districts, which target LGBTQ+ narratives more than any other minoritized group. Nationally, students could examine issues of safety and expression faced by the LBGTQ+ community across the United States. The inherent community engagement component of this lesson supports an important aim of both social studies and human rights education. The informed action cultivated during this lesson represents a vital, but often forgotten, part of citizenship education. By gaining a deeper understanding of the human rights violations faced by LGBTQ+ people during the Lavender Scare, students' critical consciousness regarding LGBTQ+ discrimination will (hopefully) be raised, leading to increased allyship. Furthermore, the human rights lens offered in this article, including the use of UDHR, provides a framework to guide related activism.

Connections to HRE and Social Studies Standards

The theoretical and pedagogical approaches offered in this chapter align with two sets of K-12 social studies standards created by the National Council for the Social Studies (NCSS). In the first social studies framework, the *National Curriculum Standards for Social Studies: A Framework for Teaching, Learning, and Assessment* (2010), the NCSS outlines ten themes of social studies education. Critical instruction about the Lavender Scare supports several of these themes. For example, *Theme 6: Power, Authority, and Governance*, asks students to analyze how people interact with power structures. The discrimination experienced by LGBTQ+ during the Lavender Scare is illuminated by the resources provided, and coupled with a HRE lens, scaffold instruction about power differentials and the oppression of minoritized groups. These approaches offered in this chapter also support *Theme 2: Time, Continuity, and Change*, which states that social studies programs should include experiences that provide for the study of the past and its legacy. The videos that trace the legacy of the Lavender Scare, as well as the requirement that students engage with contemporary manifestations of anti-LGBTQ+ policies address this standard. Additionally, *Theme 10: Civics Ideals and Practices*, asks students to "evaluate the basic freedoms and rights of citizens in a democracy, learn about the institutions and practices that support and protect these freedoms and rights, as well as the important historical documents that articulate them." The teacher-guided examination of the UDHR, Executive Order 9835, and Commerce Department's Report provides students with primary sources tied to both HRE and critical perspectives on LGBTQ+ rights issues. Lastly, *Theme 5: Individuals, Groups, and Institutions*, asks students to evaluate interrelated structural/institutional phenomena (such as discrimination). The Lavender Scare and Red Scare are certainly clear examples of institutional oppression and human rights violations faced by Americans. This article provides several ways to build content literacy and analytical frameworks for these episodes in United States history.

In the second social studies framework, the *College, Career, and Civic Life (C3) Framework for Social Studies State Standards: Guidance for Enhancing the Rigor of K-12 Civics, Economics, Geography, and History* (2013), the NCSS highlights key disciplinary skills for four dimensions of social studies education. Rights-based instruction that centers critical perspectives on the Lavender Scare supports multiple aspects of the C3 Framework for grades 6-12. For example, an aim of the Civics component of Dimension 2: Applying Disciplinary Concepts and Tools, is to have students "analyze historical, contemporary, and emerging means of changing societies, promoting the common good, and protecting rights (NCSS, 2013, p. 34)." The HRE framework offered in this article addresses this aspect of the C3 Framework. Additionally, the Civics component asks students to "examine the origins, purposes, and impact" of laws and treaties in the United States as well as the intersections of local, state, national, and tribal governments (NCSS, 2013, p. 32)." The examination of the legacy of the Lavender Scare, including recent rights issues faced by LGBTQ+ Americans, addresses this standard. Furthermore, the History component of Dimension 2 asks students to "distinguish between long-term causes and triggering events (NCSS, 2013, p. 49)." The Lavender Scare is a highly textured event that possesses a versatility that allows for both narrow and broad analyses. It could be contextualized in the broader history of anti-LGBTQ+ biases and legislation, which was addressed directly by the Facing History video in the lesson. Or, the Lavender Scare could be approached as a direct consequence of the Red Scare and the zeal of a few aggressively homophobic officials.

Conclusion and Pedagogical Strategies

The blatant human rights violations endured by LGBTQ+ workers that occurred almost immediately after the United States spearheaded the creation of the United Nations and the UDHR presents several opportunities for valuable social studies instruction. Central to UDHR was the right to work, participate in the governance of one's country, freedom from discrimination, and others which were violated by the American government. By approaching this episode in American history with a human rights lens, teachers can historicize injustice in the nation's past and provide a valuable and often neglected perspective in social studies classrooms (see Appendix for lesson plan). Furthermore, within the nascent field of HRE in the United States, issues of social justice specific to the experiences of LGBTQ+ people are less developed than those related to other historically marginalized groups. These critical perspectives of LGBTQ+ history have the potential to promote empathy and allyship. Furthermore, bigotry and rights violations are still a part of the LGBTQ+ experience in the United States and the activism component of HRE, along with the pedagogical strategies offered here, aim to provide focus and avenues of action for current challenges to the human dignity of LGBTQ+ Americans in the workplace and beyond.

References

Adami, R. (2020). The critical potential of using counternarratives in human rights education. In Zembylas, M., & Keet, A. (Eds.). *Critical human rights, citizenship, and democracy education: Entanglements and regenerations*. Bloomsbury Publishing.

Adkins, J. (2016). These people are frightened to death: Congressional investigations and the

Lavender Scare. National Archives. https://www.archives.gov/publications/prologue/2016/summer/lavender.html.

Alter, G.T. (2022). Teaching about LGBTQ+ rights: The importance of elementary education. In Alter, G. T., & Fernekes, W. R. (Eds.). (2022). *The human rights imperative in teacher education: Developing compassion, understanding, and advocacy*. Rowman & Littlefield.

Alter, G. T., & Fernekes, W. R.. (2022). Introduction. In Alter, G. T., & Fernekes, W. R. (Eds.). (2022). *The human rights imperative in teacher education: Developing compassion, understanding, and advocacy*. Rowman & Littlefield.

Amnesty International. (2012). *Realizing sexual and reproductive rights: A human rights framework*. https://www.amnesty.org/en/documents/ACT35/006/2012/en/

Andreotti, V. O. (2014). Soft versus critical global citizenship education. *Development education in policy and practice*, 21–31. Palgrave Macmillan.

Bajaj, M. (2011). Teaching to transform, transforming to teach: Exploring the role of teachers in human rights education in India. *Educational Research, 53*(2), 207–21.

Bajaj, M. (Ed.). (2017). *Human rights education: Theory, research, praxis.* University of Pennsylvania Press.

Banks, J. (2004). *Diversity and citizenship education: Global perspectives.* Jossey-Bass.

Bourke, A. (2024). Exploring child well-being: An integration of children's rights and psychological perspectives. In Mallon, B., Waldron, F., & Cassaithe, C. N. (Ed.s.). *Pushing the Boundaries of Human Rights Education: Concepts, Challenges and Contexts.* Taylor & Francis.

Bullard, R. D. (1993). Anatomy of environmental racism and the environmental justice movement. In R. D. Bullard (Ed.), *Confronting environmental racism: Voices from the grassroots* (pp. 15–39). South End Press.

Corrigan, S. (2022). Martyrs and postcolonial protest: Globalizing the civil rights movement through human rights education. *The Oregon Journal of the Social Studies, 10*(1), 41–8.

Corrigan, S. (2023). Icons, panic, and resistance: Using human rights education to teach LGBTQ+ history. *Iowa Journal for the Social Studies, 31*(2), 33–55.

Corrigan, S. (2024). Human Rights Barbie: Using Critical Media Literacy to Teach About Feminism. *The Social Studies*, 1–12.

Crocco, M. S. (2007). Speaking truth to power: Women's rights as human rights. *The Social Studies*, *98*(6), 257–69.

Dunbar-Ortiz, R. (2015). *An Indigenous peoples' history of the United States.* Beacon Press.

Duncan, K., & Murray-Everett, N. (2022). What's left unsaid: A critical race theory analysis of NCSS position statements. In Vickery, A. E. & Rodriguez, N. N. (Ed.s.). *Critical race theory and social studies futures: From nightmare of racial realism to dreaming out loud.* Teachers College Press.

Facing History & Ourselves. (2017, March 29). *The Lavender Scare: Gay and lesbian life in post-WWII America* [Video]. YouTube. https://www.facinghistory.org/resource-library/lavender-scare-gay-lesbian-life-post-wwii-america

Farinacci-Fernos, J. M. (2018). Looking beyond the negative-positive rights distinction: Analyzing constitutional rights according to their nature, effect, and reach. *Hastings Int'l & Comp. L. Rev.*, *41*, 31.

Flowers, N., & Magendzo, A.K. (2022). The development and practice of human rights education: Historical and global perspectives. In Alter, G. T., & Fernekes, W. R. (Eds.). (2022). *The human rights imperative in teacher education: Developing compassion, understanding, and advocacy*. Rowman & Littlefield.

Freire, P. (1970). *Pedagogy of the Oppressed*. Bloomsbury.

Gaudelli, W., and Fernekes, W. R. (2004). *Teaching about global human rights for global citizenship*. The Social Studies, 95(1), 16–26.

Giroux, H. A. (2007). *Border crossings: Cultural workers and the politics of education*. Routledge.

Grant, C. A., & Gibson, M. L. (2013). "The path of social justice": A human rights history of social justice education. *Equity & Excellence in Education, 46*(1), 81-99.

Grossman, D. (2017). Global Education. In Manfra, M. & Bolick, C. (Eds). *The Wiley handbook of social studies research*. Blackwell.

Hahn, C. L. (2020). Human rights teaching: Snapshots from four countries. *Human Rights Education Review, 3*(1), 8–30.

Ishay, M. (2020). *The history of human rights*. University of California Press.

Kavanaugh, A. (2024). Using Indigenous knowledge systems and stories to decolonise human rights education. In Mallon, B., Waldron, F., & Cassaithe, C. N. (Ed.s.). *Pushing the Boundaries of Human Rights Education: Concepts, Challenges and Contexts*. Taylor & Francis.

Keet, A. (2020). In Zembylas, M., & Keet, A. (Eds.). *Critical human rights, citizenship, and democracy education: Entanglements and regenerations*. Bloomsbury Publishing.

Mohai, P., & Bryant, B. (2019). Environmental racism: Reviewing the evidence. In *Race and the incidence of environmental hazards* (pp. 163–76). Routledge.

National Council for the Social Studies (2010). *National curriculum standards for social studies: A framework for teaching, learning, and assessment*. https://www.socialstudies.org/standards/national-curriculum-standards-social-studies.

National Council for the Social Studies (2013). *College, career, and civic Life (C3) framework for social studies state standards*. https://www.socialstudies.org/system/files/2022/c3-framework-for-social-studies.pdf.

National Council for the Social Studies (2019). *Contextualizing LGBT+ history in the social studies curriculum*. https://www.socialstudies.org/position-statements/contextualizing-lgbt-history.

National Council for the Social Studies (2021). *Human rights education*. https://www.socialstudies.org/position-statements/human-rights-education.

Nelson, J. L., & Pang, V. O. (2006). Racism, prejudice, and the social studies curriculum. In E.W. Ross (Ed.), *The social studies curriculum: Purposes, problems, and possibilities* (3rd ed., pp. 115–35). State University of New York Press.

Oberman, R. & Mallon, B. (2024). The translation and transformation of human rights in picturebooks. In Mallon, B., Waldron, F., & Cassaithe, C. N. (Eds.). *Pushing the Boundaries of Human Rights Education: Concepts, Challenges and Contexts*. Taylor & Francis.

Osler, A. (2016). *Human rights and schooling: An ethical framework for teaching for social justice*. Teachers College Press.

Osler, A., & Starkey, H. (2010). *Teachers and human rights education*. Trentham Books.

PBS. (2019). *Lavender Scare* [Video]. YouTube. https://soptv.pbslearningmedia.org/resource/fp19.lgbtq.lavender/lavender-scare/

PBS. (2020). *The speech that launched the 1950s Red Scare* [Video]. YouTube.

https://soptv.pbslearningmedia.org/resource/amex31m-soc-speechredscare/the-speech-that-launched-the-1950s-red-scare-mccarthy/

Stacy, H. M. (2020). *Human rights for the 21st century*. Stanford University Press.

Tibbits, F. (2020). Contested universalism: Can there be a deliberative hybrid solution for schooling? In Zembylas, M., & Keet, A. (Eds.). *Critical human rights, citizenship, and democracy education: Entanglements and regenerations*. Bloomsbury Publishing.

Time. (2021, January 25). *The history you didn't learn: The Lavender Scare* [Video]. YouTube. https://www.youtube.com/watch?v=2BXaXIAC_sI.

Tolley, W. (2013). Using Competing Visions of Human Rights in an International IB World School. *Social Education*, 77(3), 143–7.

Truman, (1947, March 21). *Prescribing Procedures for the Administration of an Employees Loyalty Program in the Executive Branch of the Government*. National Archives, Office of the Federal Registrar. https://www.archives.gov/federal-register/executive-orders/1947.html.

United Nations (1948, December 10). *Universal Declaration of Human Rights*. https://www.un.org/en/about-us/universal-declaration-of-human-rights.

Appendix A: Lesson Plan

1. Lesson Plan Title: The Origins & Legacy of the Lavender Scare
2. Theme: This lesson asks students to analyze the Lavender Scare through a human rights lens. After building content knowledge about both the Lavender Scare, its historical context, and key human rights concepts, namely the Universal Declaration of Human Rights (UDHR), students are asked to make connections between the UDHR and the rights violations faced by LBGTQ+ workers in the federal government after WWII. As a culminating task, students apply key themes from the Lavender Scare, including workplace discrimination, to contemporary aims of LGBTQ+ rights movements.
3. Grade Level: High School
4. Course: United States History
5. Time Required: 90 minutes
6. Essential and Supporting Questions:
    a. Essential Question: What human rights issues are connected to Lavender Scare?
    b. Supporting Questions
        i. How did discrimination against LGBTQ+ people lead to the Lavender Scare?
        ii. How did the Lavender Scare conflict with stated efforts of the United States to support the human rights of its citizens?
        iii. How has the Lavender Scare affected LGBTQ+ community?
7. Objectives:
    a. Explain how biases and prejudice against LGBTQ+ people in the United States made their way into the workplace after WWII.
    b. Identify the historical context of the Lavender Scare, including its relationship to the Cold War, the Civil Rights Movement, and recent activism.
    c. Describe the immediate and lasting impacts of the Lavender Scare on the LGBTQ+ community, with a focus on contemporary rights concerns.
8. NCSS Standards:
    a. D2.Civ.8.9-12. Evaluate social and political systems in different contexts, times, and places, that promote civic virtues and enact democratic principles.
    b. D2.Civ.14.9-12. Analyze historical, contemporary, and emerging means of changing societies, promoting the common good, and protecting rights.

   c. D2.His.1.9-12. Evaluate how historical events and developments were shaped by unique circumstances of time and place as well as broader historical contexts.
   d. D2.His.14.9-12. Analyze multiple and complex causes and effects of events in the past.
9. Classroom Materials: Computer/iPads, Printed copies of the UDHR (if possible)
10. Instructional Plan (refer to essay and IDM for details/links):
    a. This lesson begins with a five-minute video that establishes the historical context of the Lavender Scare (PBS, 2020). The video uses Senator Joseph McCarthy's infamous 1950 speech in Wheeling, WV to synthesize key sociopolitical dynamics to frame the political atmosphere in the United States at the time. It may also serve as a review of the Chinese Civil War and Communist Revolution, Cold War, discovery of Soviet spies in the United States government, and the moral panics associated with these events. In his speech, McCarthy claimed to have evidence that communists were working in the United States State Department, sparking a hysteria of disloyal employees in the federal government which was soon expanded to include the LGBTQ+ workers. This video demonstrates how the Lavender Scare was related to Red Scare and allows teachers to connect this lesson to prior knowledge.
    b. The teacher-directed instruction portion of this lesson consists of the analysis of three documents: the UDHR, Executive Order 9835, and the Department of Commerce's Perversion Report. To introduce the UDHR, the teachers should allow time for students to read the thirty articles (rights) specified in the UDHR, highlighting specific rights related to the Lavender Scare. For example, teachers may want to focus on the right to take part in the governance of one's country (Article 21) or the right to employment (Article 23). Executive Order 9835, also known as the "Loyalty Order," was signed by President Truman in 1947 to protect the United States against the "infiltration of disloyal persons into the ranks of its employees." Teachers should guide students through an examination of this concise and well-organized document that was central to the Lavender Scare. It is recommended that teachers focus on the preamble and Part V, Standards, as these sections best illustrate how discriminatory policies against LGBTQ+ federal employees were institutionalized. Following the introduction of the UDHR and the Executive Order 9835, teachers may ask students to analyze the contradictions in these two

documents in regards to the rhetoric and actions by the United States government about human rights. Lastly, teachers guide students through a brief assessment of the Department of Commerce's Perversion Cases Report. This report describes the Commerce Department's investigation into its employees as part of its compliance with Order 9835. It briefly details the investigative outcomes of its LGBTQ+ employees (terminations and forced resignations), demonstrating the effects of Order 9835.

c. In small groups, students will view three videos that provide deeper historical context, personal narratives, and contemporary connections for the Lavender Scare. This student inquiry portion of the lesson is organized in a C3 Inquiry Design Model (IDM). These videos are meant to be viewed in order, as their content, and the aligned line of inquiry, build upon one another. The first video examines LGBTQ+ life after World War II and describes discriminatory views of the LGBTQ+ community, including how these negative attitudes led to the Lavender Scare (Facing History & Ourselves, 2017). It allows students to view the Lavender Scare as one of many manifestations of homophobia in American history. The guiding question for students as they watch this video is, "How did discrimination against LGBTQ+ people lead to the Lavender Scare?". The performative task objective asks students to, "Explain how biases and prejudice against LGBTQ+ people in the United States made their way into the workplace after WWII." The second video develops the connection between the Second Red Scare and the Lavender Scare (Time, 2021). It provides personal narratives of both oppression and resistance, including how activists made clear connections between human rights doctrines and discriminatory practices by the federal government. This video also describes the end of Order 9835 and discusses the Trump administration's ban on transgender people serving in the military. The guiding questions for students as they view this video is, "How did the Lavender Scare conflict with supposed efforts by the United States government to support the human rights of its citizens?" The performative task objective asks students to, "Identify the historical context of the Lavender Scare, including its relationship to the Cold War, the Civil Rights Movement, and recent activism." The third video highlights the immediate and lasting effects of the Lavender Scare on the LGBTQ+ community (PBS, 2019). It provides additional personal stories of those fired under Order 9835 and traces related anti-LGBTQ+ prejudices from pre-WWII to contemporary America. It also highlights the resilience of LGBTQ+ communities in facing homophobia. The guiding questions for students as they view this video is, "How has the Lavender Scare affected LGBTQ+ community?" The performative task objective asks students to, "Describe the immediate and lasting impacts of the Lavender Scare on the LGBTQ+ community, with a focus on contemporary rights concerns." Since the essential question asks students to make connections between the Lavender Scare and human rights concerns, it is recommended that teachers ask students to analyze each of these videos with the UDHR.

d. The summative task asks students to create an activist agenda for a contemporary LGBTQ+ rights movement. They are required to use historical and contemporary sources to construct a representation (graphic, poster, artwork, essay, etc.) that discusses the essential question and its current relevance to rights issues faced by their local LGBTQ+ community and/or state. While students may choose to examine broad rights issues faced by LGBTQ+ people across the United States, it is encouraged to have students first investigate local contexts, particularly the workplace.

11. Assessment: The assessment for this lesson lies in student understanding of the historical context and legacy of the Lavender Scare. These outcomes can be assessed by student discourse around the primary source documents, responses to video prompts, and application activity.
12. Community Engagement: The assignment requires student awareness of current rights issues facing LGBTQ+ people in their own communities. This component challenges students and teachers to critically reflect on their own community's status in protecting the human rights of all of its residents. This requirement is a direct response to HRE scholarship that has documented who human rights violations are often framed as occurring far from home (Hahn, 2020), thus diminishing agency and opportunities for critical and transformational citizenship practices (Bajaj, 2011).

Appendix B: Inquiry Design Model, C3 Framework

<table>
<tr><th colspan="3">Inquiry Design Model (IDM) Blueprint™</th></tr>
<tr><td>Compelling (Essential) Question</td><td colspan="2">What human rights issues are connected to Lavender Scare?</td></tr>
<tr><td>Standards and Practices</td><td colspan="2"><u>C3 Framework, Dimension 2:</u>
Civics: Analyze historical, contemporary, and emerging means of changing societies, promoting the common good, and protecting rights.
History: Evaluate how historical events and developments were shaped by unique circumstances of time and place as well as broader historical contexts.</td></tr>
<tr><td>Staging the Question</td><td colspan="2">Students evaluate the origins and legacy of the Lavender Scare, including its context in relation to the Second Red Scare, labor history, and the Universal Declaration of Human Rights.
Video: PBS: McCarthyism & 1950s Moral Panics
Documents: United Nations: Universal Declaration of Human Rights
Teaching American History: Executive Order 9835
National Archives: Congressional Investigations & the Lavender Scare</td></tr>
<tr><td>Supporting Question 1</td><td>Supporting Question 2</td><td>Supporting Question 3</td></tr>
<tr><td>How did discrimination against LGBTQ+ people lead to the Lavender Scare?</td><td>How did the Lavender Scare conflict with supposed efforts by the United States government to support the human rights of its citizens?</td><td>How has the Lavender Scare affected LGBTQ+ community?</td></tr>
<tr><td>Formative Performance Task</td><td>Formative Performance Task</td><td>Formative Performance Task</td></tr>
<tr><td>Explain how biases and prejudice against LGBTQ+ people in the United States made their way into the workplace after WWII.</td><td>Identify the historical context of the Lavender Scare, including its relationship to the Cold War, the Civil Rights Movement, and recent activism.</td><td>Describe the immediate and lasting impacts of the Lavender Scare on the LGBTQ+ community, with a focus on contemporary rights concerns.</td></tr>
<tr><td>Featured Sources</td><td>Featured Sources</td><td>Featured Sources</td></tr>
<tr><td>Video, Facing History:
LGBTQ+ Life after WW2</td><td>Video, Time Magazine:
The Lavender Scare</td><td>Video, PBS: LGBTQ+ Community
Impact of Lavender Scare</td></tr>
</table>

Inquiry Design Model (IDM) Blueprint™		
Summative Performance Task	**Argument**	Construct a representation (e.g., graphic organizer, poster, artwork, essay) that discusses the compelling question using specific claims and relevant evidence from historic and current sources.
	Extension	Create an activist agenda for a contemporary LGBTQ+ rights movement.
Taking Informed Action	Understand: Current rights issues faced by the LGBTQ+ community in the United States. Assess: Persistent and new threats to the LGBTQ+ community, as well as allies in activism. Act: Create a political advertisement/pamphlet/poster that advocates for current rights issues faced by LGBTQ+ workers.	

EduTech Labor: A Tale of Artificial Teacher Assistance and Tech Twists in Online Learning

Andrea Arce-Trigatti, Dorota Silber-Furman, and Aimee Klaschus

Introduction

The introduction of Web 2.0, Web 3.0, and generative Artificial Intelligence (AI) has had several implications for teaching and labor changes in the field of education including the way that students learn and teachers plan, design, and execute their courses. For example, the introduction of Web 2.0 in the early 2000s offered the foundations for what we consider online education today, which provides students the opportunity to receive their education through a virtual setting and a virtual mode that has only been enhanced with the integration of technology from the Web 3.0 and AI (Niewiadomski & Anderson, 2020). More recently, these technologies could mean hosting a class with teacher and students interacting in the online space through a virtual platform (synchronous approach), recording lectures as a lesson and uploading it for students to watch on their own time (asynchronous approach), or posting lessons/modules for students to partake in as part of an expanded learning experience, making the online learning environment more a vicarious platform for interaction and immersion (Niewiadomski & Anderson, 2020).

In this chapter, we explore the impact of technological changes and development (e.g., Web 2.0, Web 3.0, Artificial Intelligence, etc.) on teaching labor changes in the twenty-first century through the lens of students' learning and educators' teaching in this virtual environment. To help investigate this concept, we first present a background supported by academic citations that demonstrate the waves of technological introductions into education. We then focus on the historical context of these technological developments while centering on the social studies common core standards. Specifically, we look at three of the National Council for the Social Sciences' (NCSS) Standards for Social Studies as themes throughout the text: 1) time, continuity, and change, 2) people, places, and environments, and 3) individual development and identity. The research aspect of this chapter introduces a qualitative study featuring postsecondary students' experiences in online learning environments at a two-year public state college. Using secondary data from an institutional study, we leverage an inductive approach anchored in Braun and Clarke's (2006) analytical framework to answer the following research question: In what ways does student learning in the online environment underscore teacher labor changes influenced by this technology? Lessons learned and implications from this study connect back to the three NCSS standards selected for this work. Further, the lesson plan featured in this chapter underscores ways in which students can engage with the NCSS standards and the impact on labor changes due to technological advancements.

Historical Summary of Topic

As noted, this chapter focuses on introducing students to the labor changes affecting them, educators, and teacher preparation programs with respect to the integration of advanced technologies into teaching and learning practices at the K-16 levels. We begin by offering a brief history of these changes with respect to the integration of Web 2.0, Web 3.0, and AI into educational environments. This is followed by a focus on the scholarship that emphasizes the ways in which preservice teacher training has shifted to accommodate these changes. Connections from this scholarship to the NCSS standards are made via key takeaways from the literature shared.

Technological Advancements

With the introduction of Web 2.0, Web 3.0, and generative Artificial Intelligence as a technological revolution, these advancements in technology have been typically painted as a disruptor and possibly a catalyst of human progress whose implications are noticeable in the teaching labor history of the naughts to present day. Scholars define Web 2.0 and Web 3.0 as successive, commencing at the turn of the twenty-first century and advancing the initial iterations of the Web 1.0 of the 1990s (Clark, 2023; Niewiadomski & Anderson, 2020; van Dijk, 2006, 2020). Wherein characteristics of Web 2.0 built the capacities of the internet to move from transactional to interactional communications, Web 3.0 (2010s and beyond) is characterized as a much more decentralized and open virtual space that has lead to innovations including social media, smartphones, mobile internet access, and the development of interconnected social networks (Miller, 2023; Clark, 2023).

Klein et al. (2020) share the following with respect to the advances of technology in educational settings, "Learning analytics is now in its adolescence, having emerged in the mid-2000s alongside the development and growth in capacity for data mining and machine learning" (p. 230). However, they also note that the capacity to leverage learning analytics and the technology that is used to collect comprehensive data from students is still limited (Klein et al., 2020). Specifically, they note that constraints like the lack of infrastructure, alignment to existing technology, organizational culture, and ethical concerns will impact the scalability of any advancements in this area (Klein et al., 2020). To this end, artificial intelligence and machine learning have only expanded what the internet is able to do in terms of human interaction and collaboration in a virtual space, linking assistance and powerful technology to predictive actions that have enhanced virtual capacities (Niewiadomski & Anderson, 2020; van Dijk, 2020).

What we are seeing now in terms of teacher labor changes with respect to technological advancements is the shift from technology as an add-on to education to educational tools as enhancements of exceptional learning. That is to say, with the advancements of technology comes the familiarity of this technology from the changing generations of teachers and educators at the K-16 level. Scholarship in this area, therefore, underscores both pre-service teachers' and postsecondary educators' relative comfort with the use of technology integration in the classroom that was not evident in earlier literature just a decade ago (Schina et al., 2021; Silber-Furman et al., 2023; Turra et al., 2019). Part of this change is due to the pandemic, wherein K-16 educators and students were tasked with learning how to navigate the complexities of an online environment in a relatively short period of time (Arce-Trigatti & Silber-Furman, 2021). However, another part of this change is what remained as best practices in teaching and learning in online environments from what was learned in that rapidly changing context to now.

Pre-Service Teacher and Postsecondary Educator Training

Educational Preparation Programs have also drastically changed the curricular objectives during the past two decades as it pertains to the use of educational technology in the classroom. Pre-service teachers are encouraged more and more to use technology as educational management tools and resources for enhancing learning both in the face-to-face and online learning contexts (Turra et al., 2019; Yu et al., 2016). In terms of the curriculum, pre-service teachers are guided to leverage technology in a way that reflects advancements in artificial intelligence, immersion contexts, and 3D artificial reality to understand the applications of learning theories in different environments, with varying student populations, and with limited resources (Durak, 2021; Santos & Castro, 2021). As noted, after the pandemic, several programs required the integration of educational technology as part of the learning core for most pre-service teachers, as well as support for postsecondary Centers of Teaching and Learning that provide guidance to college-level educators.

Within this space of change, pre-service teachers' and postsecondary educators' integration and understanding of traditional learning philosophies and frameworks has shifted based on familiarity with the technology and shifts in the support of teacher preparation programs (Schina et al., 2021). The scholarship tends to underscore this type of shift with respect to the use of traditional pedagogy with the incorporation of technology. For example, the integration of the TSPACK model, which integrates the use of technological, pedagogical, and content knowledge frameworks to effectively deliver content, has been incorporated into teacher training as part of the educational integrations for the past decade, with significant shifts in the way student learning objectives are framed. According to Santos and Castro (2021), the TSPACK model "... attempts to identify the nature of knowledge required by teachers for technology integration in their teaching, while addressing the complex, multifaceted and situated nature of teacher knowledge" (p. 3) They emphasize that this complex and multifaceted knowledge is further influenced by social contexts, technological use, and access to resources (Santos & Castro, 2021).

When integrated with other, innovation-driven learning frameworks, like the Renaissance Foundry Model, Arce et al. (2022) found that the TSPACK model helps to leverage resources, like technology, to foster innovation-driven learning, prototype development, and interdisciplinary communication. In this work, the authors highlight several case studies where the learning environment spaces are pivotal to understanding the appropriate integration of technology into learning. In one of the case studies, the classroom space that was featured leveraged technological integration to foster collaboration, support interdisciplinary work, and promote design thinking (Arce et al., 2022). This is distinct from traditional learning spaces that are more geared to lecture-style classrooms and individualistic learning styles. Additionally, these trends for the types of pedagogical frameworks that enhance learning through technology applications are visual in pre-service teaching scholarship, as well as the curriculum integrated in their postsecondary programs of study.

For instance, Durak (2021) studied the effectiveness of pre-service teacher integration of technology with different applications in integrated learning and practical activities. Using a mixed-methods approach, this study provided evidence that a significant difference exists between the technology integration exercises performed using different methods, with motivation and satisfaction levels being higher in groups where authentic task-based instruction was used (Durak, 2021). What is a stark contrast between this study and one conducted by Hsu (2012) almost a decade prior is the attitudes and knowledge of pre-service teachers with respect to the integration of advanced technology in their classrooms. In Hsu's (2012) qualitative study, pre-service teachers reflected a level of anxiety and uncertainty with respect to integrating technology into their classrooms, whereas Durak (2021) reflected motivation and enthusiasm in the use of advanced technological tools. However, both studies highlight the appreciation of educational programs that prepared them to use advanced technology from pre-service teachers' perspectives, whether it was the use of Excel in the early aughts or the use of AI in current literature in their classrooms.

In terms of pre-service teachers' knowledge regarding the use of technology for assessment in teaching and learning, the spectrum is vast and reflects a need for further understanding in this area and how it translates to labor markets. For example, Koc and Bakir (2010) first investigated the use of technology for data management in a classroom for pre-service teachers using a survey methodology. They noted that pre-service teachers, at the time, did not feel comfortable navigating spreadsheets or pivot tables as part of their lesson planning (Koc & Bakir, 2010). Current literature, like that of Zhao and colleagues (2021) shows a different perception in pre-service teachers' self-efficacy with respect to leveraging technology in advanced learning and assessment. In their survey methodology research, they found that those pre-service teachers engaged in advanced teaching methods with different technology had more self-efficacy, learning motivation, and learning satisfaction from their students than the control group (Zhao et al., 2021). This study also shows the growth within educational technology and its application in pre-service teaching preparation, as well as the dominant labor changes within the profession.

Overall, the literature highlights a shift not only in the type of technology that is being used for both face-to-face and online teaching, but also the integration of technological advancements in teaching and learning for student learning and growth. These patterns, and the familiarity and comfort of K-16 educators with the use and integration of technology in their classroom, also come with the need for more specialized training (Schina et al., 2021), continued understanding of online educator supports (Arce-Trigatti & Silber-Furman, 2021, 2022; Silber-Furman & Arce-Trigatti, 2021), as well as institutional capacity for resources and access to digital learning frameworks and platforms (Santos & Castro, 2021). From this foundation, we offer connections to larger NCSS standards that help us to better understand in what ways teacher labor has changed due to technological shifts.

Technology and the National Curriculum Standards for Social Science

To connect these patterns in historical scholarship, we reintegrate the social studies common core standards, and three of the National Curriculum Standards for Social Studies (NCSS) as themes as part of this historical summary of these topics including: 1) time, continuity, and change, 2) people, places, and environments, and 3) individual development and identity. According to the National Curriculum Standards (2024),

> The aim of social studies is the promotion of civic competence—the knowledge, intellectual processes, and democratic dispositions required of students to be active and engaged participants in public life. Although civic competence is not the only responsibility of social studies nor is it exclusive to the field, it is more central to social studies than to any other subject area in schools.

Beginning with the first standards in 1994, the NCSS (2024) has offered K-12 teachers a framework for teachers, schools, districts, states, and other nations as a tool for curriculum alignment and development for social sciences as conceptualized in the preceding quote. In focusing on the three aforementioned NCSS standards, this work aims to make connections between online student learning and changes anchored in technological advancements in these areas. Prior to delving into this study, it is beneficial to understand the basic components of the three standards adopted for this work.

Time, Continuity, and Change

The NCSS standard for Time, Continuity, and Change focuses on the study of the past in order to better understand the advances that are making impactful changes in the present. According to the NCSS (2024), this standard emphasizes the importance of,

> The historical experiences of societies, peoples and nations [that] reveal patterns of continuity and change. Historical analysis enables us to identify continuities over time in core institutions, values, ideals, and traditions, as well as processes that lead to change within societies and institutions, and that result in innovation and the development of new ideas, values and ways of life.

In terms of teacher labor history, we can see the continuities over time with respect to the values, ideals, and traditions of exceptional excellence in teaching and learning standards, while also understanding changes in context with respect to technological advances. Looking only at technology, we can see how these changes have impacted teacher labor from the initial understanding of Palm Pilots in classrooms, to Blackberries, SmartBoards, iPads and tablets. Additionally, the training that pre-service teachers have had to integrate into their teaching has inevitably changed the practices and learning that students have experienced, while maintaining similar goals and objectives at the state and federal levels (Dusak, 2021; Lin et al., 2020).

People, Places, and Environments

The NCSS standard for People, Places, and Environment focuses on the interaction of people, places, and environments to understand connections that exist between human populations and the physical world. From the NCSS (2024), this specific standard focuses on the following:

> [the study of] communications and transportation networks that link different population centers, the reasons for these networks, and their impact. They identify the key social, economic and cultural characteristics of populations in different locations as they expand their knowledge of diverse peoples and places. Learners develop an understanding of the growth of national and global regions, as well as the technological advances that connect students to the world beyond their personal locations.

In terms of teacher labor history, this standard underscores the need to understand the connections between pre-service teaching at the postsecondary learning, the integration of technology in teaching and learning at the K-16 levels, and changes in students learning based on technological advances (Schina et al., 2021; Yu et al., 2021). This standard helps to integrate the idea of the digital divide and access in technology in better understanding student learning and teaching practices in various areas, including disparities in rural versus urban settings and postsecondary learning at various institutional contexts (e.g., community college, private university, or public college).

Individual Development and Identity

The NCSS standard for Individual Development and Identity focuses on how different social contexts (including schools, religious institutions, social spheres, etc.) influence individual development and identity. This includes what controls and influences individuals, how individuals control and influence others, and how culture and institutions can be maintained or changed. This NCSS (2024) standard outlines the following:

> Students learn where people and places are located and why they are there. They examine the influence of physical systems, such as climate, weather and seasons, and natural resources, such as land and water, on human populations. They study the causes, patterns and effects of human settlement and migration, learn of the roles of different kinds of population centers in a society, and investigate the impact of human activities on the environment. This enables them to acquire a useful basis of knowledge for informed decision-making on issues arising from human-environmental relationships.

Concerning teacher labor history, this standard emphasizes the growth that accompanies the integration of technological advancements with respect to students' learning and teacher success. For example, the integral growth that occurs in pre-service teachers' self-efficacy, motivation, and satisfaction in teaching has increased with the integration of more refined training and support at the postsecondary level (Schina et al., 2021). Further, student learning is vastly different from what was in existence 5, 10, or 20 years ago. The level of familiarity with flipped classrooms, advanced technology, and online learning has shifted with the influence of the pandemic and has changed the way that students at K-16 levels engage with academia, learning, and student success factors (Arce et al., 2022; Silber-Furman & Arce-Trigatti, 2021).

Research Study and Connections

Building on this scholarship, it is easy to see how these changing objectives are linked directly to social studies teaching and learning at the K-16 level. As noted, social studies goals and objectives, in general, aim to help amplify how technological progress and advancements influence societies in terms of economy, politics, and social change. This was noted earlier in what is evidenced in the scholarship on pre-service teaching and postsecondary educators' expectations with the use and integration of technology in their classrooms, also emphasizing how the labor market for education has changed after the pandemic (Arce et al., 2022; Niewiadomski & Anderson, 2020; Silber-Furman & Arce-Trigatti, 2021; van Dijk, 2006, 2020). For example, the differences in perspectives and attitudes with the use of technology in this field as an integrated part of the curriculum is well noted as an amplification of student learning in online spaces and face-to-face instruction (Arce et al., 2022; Zhao et al., 2021). Yet, there is still a need for educator support, training, and infrastructural understandings in digital learning that influence the ways in which technology can be used. This was noted in Santos and Castro's (2021) study where they indicated that the reality is, "… that there is unavailability and inadequacy of EdTech tools in the public schools" (p. 1). This highlights a digital divide in terms of access and resources that influences to what degree teacher labor shifts reflect the full capacity of technology integration (van Dijk, 2020).

Further, there is an emphasis on how technology, especially advanced technology like AI, is incorporated into state and federal objectives as well as academic policies and classroom guidance (Parnell, 2024). In this way, social studies curriculum provides opportunities for students to engage in a meaningful way with digital tools for tasks that, for example, include data collection, analysis, or ethical reflection. For educators, as part of these standards, the aspect in teacher labor that is emphasized is the need to integrate technological advancements in the assessment of student learning, effective practices, and online learning enhancements (Janssen et al., 2019; Irvine, 2018).

With the following research study, we explore the interconnectedness of the NCSS standards of focus for this chapter and how postsecondary students are experiencing online learning spaces. In this study, we make connections that highlight time, changes, and continuity with respect to online teaching and learning, as well investigate ways in which these challenges and changes may influence students' individual sense of success. These patterns are, in turn, anchored in the scholarship presented above, through the implications they have for teaching and learning and the labor changes that are still to come in the education profession.

Research Methodology

Context

The study reflects data collected from a public, two-year institution in the Southeastern United States. This institution has roughly 11,000 students enrolled with a racial distribution of 40 percent white, 30 percent Black, 25 percent Hispanic, and 5 percent Multi-racial or Asian. The bulk of the student population is 21 years of age or younger (70 percent), with other age ranges fairly evenly distributed at 10 percent each (22–4, 25–39, and 40 and over). Of the students enrolled, roughly 8,000 students were working toward completion of an associate in arts degree, considered to be transfer students to four-year universities at the end of their degree completion. The institution rests in the poorest district of their region, with over 50 percent of the student population considered lower socioeconomic status. Although many students are considered familiar with online content and online learning, there are also non-traditional and first-generation student populations that relate that they are less familiar with this medium.

Data Collection and Sources

This study leverages secondary data from one institutional effectiveness survey implemented in one academic school year of the institution described earlier. In total, the survey asked students 13 questions, with two being open-ended questions. The prompts for these open-ended questions were as follows: 1) Please describe the major challenge you are facing this semester and 2) What additional support or services do you need this semester? During this specific year, the learning experiences of postsecondary students in online environments were captured to address any challenges related to the online shift spearheaded by the COVID-19 pandemic. In this respect, students who were already facing academic success barriers related to their economic and social backgrounds, further faced exacerbating situations concerning the navigation of an entirely digital learning environment (Arce-Trigatti & Silber-Furman, 2021, 2020). In total 210 students responded to the survey and represented the age and racial demographics of the institution.

Research Question

Although scholarship has intentionally explored how the shift to digital learning has impacted diverse groups of students, little literature has intentionally focused on the experiences of low socioeconomic students at a two-year college. In order to help better address the unique challenges and barriers that these students face, it becomes paramount to investigate the experiences and hurdles at these intersections. In this scholarly work, we investigate the research question: In what ways does student learning in the online environment underscore teacher labor changes influenced by this technology?

Methods and Analytical Framework

To answer the primary research question, we adopted a qualitative approach to analyze survey data collected from a public, state, postsecondary institution (Patton, 2010). Participants responded to open-ended questions related to experiences with online learning and their suggestions for areas of improvement. We used an inductive analysis and line-by-line coding procedures that mirror a grounded theory process as recommended by Strauss and Corbin (1990). Inductive analysis calls for data organization and reduction into manageable pieces and structures (LeCompte, 2000). We read and reread thoroughly our data as recommended by Strauss and Corbin (1990).

We also used Glaser and Strauss' (1967) constant comparative methods to seek patterns and codes in data. Inductive analysis calls for data organization and reduction into manageable pieces and structures (LeCompte, 2000). Also, during the analysis process, we used memo creation and, as recommended by Corbin (1990), opening the text to further seek codes. LeCompte and Schensul (1999) explained, "codes are names or symbols used to stand for a group of similar items, ideas, or phenomena that the researcher has noticed in her data set" (p. 55). As part of this study, connections were made to teaching labor changes and technological advancements.

Ethical Considerations & Trustworthiness

This study followed all ethical guidelines for the compliance of human subject data. Institutional Review Board approval was sought and received prior to analyzing the data. All authors completed ethical training as part of the compliance aspects of this study and its respective components. In terms of trustworthiness, we incorporated peer debriefing, rich description, methodological documentation, and reflective processes into the analysis (Ahmed, 2024).

Research Study Analysis

Coding Process

To analyze this data, we adopted the coding and thematizing process outlined by Braun & Clark (2006). Following this process, first we became familiar with the data by reading and rereading through the responses after it was collected. To initiate the coding process, we met, discussed expectations, and then we began identifying codes separately. To ensure that the codes reflected a cohesive process, we conducted a member check and together cross-checked all of our codes (Braun & Clark, 2006; Guba & Lincoln, 1986). Once we came to close on the initial coding process, we began refining the initial 28 codes by reviewing potential connections and overlaps between the initial codes identified. This process led to the identification of 25 refined codes; then we conducted another member check and reflected on the initial coding process before conducting a second round of refinement to the codes. This was to let the connections inherent in the data become apparent after the initial review process and we refined our codes down to 18 codes. To begin the theming process, we adopted Saldana's (2013) axial coding technique and identified six axial codes which formed the anchors of groups of sub-codes: Student Success, Academic Support, Online Student Experience, Performance/Accountability, Strategic/Outcome Tracking, and Motivating Factors. From this process, the final themes were created, which became a reflection of review of various possibilities that converged on the combination that fit the data best (Braun & Clark, 2005).

Refined and Final Themes

In total, six major themes comprised the analysis of the qualitative data for this study. Table 1 features the major components of the themes, as well as descriptions and major codes. These include themes that reflect the connections between the sub-codes and axial codes that form them. All six themes are described in further detail later.

Structures needed for Holistic Academic Achievement. This theme describes the programs and institutional supports within the College that are designed to provide resources to ensure and further the academic achievement of all students. The codes associated with this theme include an axial code of Student Success, linked to the codes Pathways to Persistence, Student Affairs and Advising, and Care for Students. Pathways to Persistence, for example, is an initiative based on a systematic approach to provide just-in-time resources to interventions to ensure student engagement in critical gateway courses. The following quote illustrates the type of resources needed for student success:

> I personally think the more interactive the professors are with their students, the more likely they are to succeed. But then again, it's up to the students to gain their own motivation because they are paying for college but I truly do think that it would be nice if professors are able to encourage students to work hard and don't give up, other than that, THE COLLEGE has shown me a great experience on my first year.

In this quote, we see the initial thought connected to understandings of care for students, in that this online learning student feels that more interaction from professors with their students, may foster the encouragement and motivation needed for students to ensure success.

The other codes, Student Affairs and Advising and Care for Students, speak to other critical aspects of student success, including mental health, sense of belonging, and general well-being, that reflect the holistic aspect of this theme. For example, the following excerpt was associated with this theme:

> Students enter our institutions with a variety of attributes (prior educational experiences, family background, cultural and social preparation, goals/commitments, etc.) which impact their motivation.

This online learning student expresses an understanding of the various elements that play a role in student success including student background, preparation, and motivation. As a connection to this theme, this quote underscores the holistic support needed to ensure student success.

Continual Improvement Strategies for Mastery of Program Content. This theme describes various elements of the teaching and learning aspects related to the course content side of academic programming. The codes associated with this theme include an axial code of Academic Support and related codes of Faculty Professional Development, Academic Independence, and Student Learning Outcomes. The following excerpt was associated with this theme:

> I feel that you can expand when it comes to students who need assistance after hours for networking students. Have something set in place for students who work full time Monday thru Friday. Also it is hard to find evening internships when having a full time job.

What this quote highlights as part of this theme is the need for additional learning supports that could help professional students (those with full-time jobs) readily access additional resources for mastery of program content.

Distinct from the first theme, which focuses on the students and support for student success, this theme focuses on instructors, course content, and student learning metrics, as illustrated with the aforementioned quote. For example, Academic Independence reflects the expertise that faculty bring in creating their course content, which relates to professional development opportunities sought to improve teaching and learning. This student's online learning perspective is helpful for untangling these aspects:

> It is important to assist at the beginning. When the person logs on and helps them walk through the process from finding the right program with the right map to providing assistance to apply and meet deadlines. A person just graduating from High School may not have the skills to navigate through our systems that first time.

Though associated with student success, this quote focuses on content mastery and the skills needed to help students transition smoothly from one educational environment (high school) to another (postsecondary) through additional training and resources.

Elements Related to Digital Learning Design and Success. This theme describes various resources and supports related to student success practices within an online learning environment. The codes that helped develop this theme include Online Student Experience, Resources, and Technical Support, each of which speak to different components of the digital learning space. The following quote associated with this theme emphasizes the connections between these codes:

> As an online student, I think there could be more involvement with online students. For example, maybe having teacher's assistants or designated peers that have already done certain classes to help with questions about courses or assignments. Professors are often very busy, and having assistants or peer helpers could speed up some of the response time. The assistants or peer helpers would be included on Canvas in the "people" link for the course and be easily accessible by email.

As is evident in this quote, the student emphasizes the manner in which online supports could offer a more comprehensive foundation for student engagement, professor interaction, and online direction. This connects to the theme by underscoring design and support infrastructure needed to ensure online student learning versus face-to-face learning.

Moreover, the resources and technical support codes within this theme heavily focused on instructional design strategies that were directed at improving students' learning experiences online. In another example, an online student focused on the following aspects to improve online learning:

> implement intentional class activities that explore the subject matter being covered to enhance learning as well as inviting/stimulating students to apply these concepts to real life events; instill or inspire students to be willing to actively participate in class.

From this perspective, it is not enough just to have static content online. This student is linking to the theme by underscoring design elements in online classes that could inspire, engage, and motivate students to learn within an online setting.

Breadth and Depth of Campus Atmosphere and Interactions. This theme describes the whole range of student experiences on campus, including both positive and negative interactions. The codes included in this theme are an axial code of Performance/Accountability, supported by the codes of Disconnected, Satisfied, Engagement, Unsure, and Student Struggles. Grouped together, Disconnected, Unsure, and Student Struggles illustrate difficulties engaging on campus or in course content. One quote that illustrates this theme is:

Most students today are not focused heavily on that part of learning, because once they step outside of the desired institution of learning, it is not the same as what they learned in their courses to graduate. Each desired field of work has different challenges that are not going to be something you can pull from a manual or a book.

In this quote, we saw the back and forth of students' experiences within an online space. That is, how students navigate what they learn in their course and how they apply it to their work or life outside of the institution matters, because it connects to the breadth and depth of students' experiences on campus. For this online student, the connections made from their online courses needed to have relevant applications to real-world problems to be meaningful for them.

Specific codes in this theme, like Satisfied and Engagement, both illustrate student success stories related to positive interactions on campus and in course content. Interestingly, the Performance/Accountability code is reflective of the vastness of these negative and positive experiences as it describes the level of responsibility needed by students to be successful and engaged in course content and on campus. The following quote encompasses this perspective:

> [My peers] do not understand that they are expected to attend class regularly, or that they do not have all semester to make up assignments, or that they must communicate with their professors, and so forth. I feel that these expectations should be very clear in the admissions process and through orientation.

With respect to academic success, performance and accountability are key to understanding how students integrate themselves into the learning environment. In this quote, we see that the breadth and depth of student interactions even in online spaces involve interaction, or lack thereof, with their peers.

The Inputs and Outputs Supporting the Success of the College Mission. This theme features various processes that are related to different components of a postsecondary institution's mission, including student success and academic quality. The codes that anchor this theme include the axial code Strategic/Outcome Tracking, and the supporting codes Campus Operations/Flexibility, Work-related Skills, Diversity, Equity, and Inclusion (DEI), and Curriculum and Programs. Perhaps one of the quotes that best reflects this theme is as follows:

> Give people with learning disability a chance to learn more about the benefits of the program and how they can improve their skills and improve their skills in the future to become more successful and more productive and better equipped for their lives in their own communities in order for them to become better and more effective we need help

According to this student perspective, if students with a learning disability are given a chance to explore and engage with the resources available to them to help support their learning (i.e., the inputs), then they would also have a chance to improve their skills or be more successful in the class (i.e., the output). Of course, this is one example of many with respect to this theme as student experiences with specific inputs and outputs on campus vary greatly in terms of their learning and success.

Further, specific inputs (e.g., Campus Operations/Flexibility, Curriculum and Programs) have to do with the logistics of campus and programmatic operations, and the outputs (Strategic/Outcome Tracking, Work-Related Skills, DEI) are evidence of the success of the practical steps taken to achieve the college's goal. Several quotes reflect these types of infrastructure or programmatic inputs and outputs. For example, one online student indicated: "Scheduling has been chaotic over the last couple years, and support doesn't match up. When we have to fit a limited schedule it affects our jobs and families." Another online learning student said, "Technology! more AI classes, robotics and cutting-edge coding. Some kind of internship or partnership with Amazon." These show the variety of inputs and outputs, both unique and distinct to programs or experiences mentioned, needed to support online student success.

External Pressures that Influence Academic Engagement and Resiliency. This theme describes external challenges that students face that may mitigate their academic success on campus. This theme included codes like Motivating Factors as an axial code, and Finance/Work and Health and Wellness as supporting codes. In terms of Finance/Work, for example, it was evident that engagement and attendance levels varied depending on the responsibilities of external work for that semester. This was particularly evident in online student learning experiences. For example, one student indicated:

> many many students work and come to class. The lack of evening classes is anti-education for those who work. They were perfect for those who have to work on this current inflation problem in our country and since this was taken away, I know many who have lost hours of work just to make it to class and gain an education. We need evening classes back please.

The perspective of this online student demonstrates the external pressures evident in financial obligations that conflate priorities between real-life responsibilities and academic roles. Another student quote echoed this sentiment:

> Many students need to recognize that working full time and taking a full course load is usually detrimental to their grade-point-average and adds an incredible obstacle to their future academic success. It also adds too much stress to their lives.

Although this quote is from a perspective that reiterates balance to academic, professional, and personal responsibilities, oftentimes for online students competing priorities is a necessity and balance, like the one described in the quote, is a luxury.

Additionally, the other external contributing factor to student motivation and engagement was Health and Wellness, which encompassed both students' well-being as well as their familial responsibilities in caring for spouses, children, parents, and other loved ones. For example, this online student shared:

> [...] first time college students for the current year experienced a lapse in education their freshman year of high school, and a different approach to education due to the pandemic (some learned at home) during their junior year. These are formative years and students as a result are experiencing more anxiety and stress related to things that in the past students could just push through.

Online learning, especially during and after the pandemic, forced students into a learning environment that might have been drastically different than what they were used to before. This is evident in the gaps and lapses that this student is highlighting, especially for first time college students as indicated. Another student echoed the mental well-being related to these types of drastic changes:

> I think that there needs to be more awareness and resources for people struggling with mental health. I struggle with diagnosed depression and anxiety, and I was struggling worse before I got into contact with Student Disability. I wasn't aware of that even existing.

The type of external pressures that could exacerbate the mental struggles that online students face, especially when technology and online environments are rapidly changing, are highlighted in this quote and connected to the conceptualization of this theme.

Findings

In this scholarly work, we investigated the research question: In what ways does student learning in the online environment underscore teacher labor changes influenced by this technology? In the themes found through our analysis, we make connections to the NCSS standards selected for this work and conceptualize the answer to this research question in Figure 10.1. Specifically, we infer that student learning in the online environment underscores teacher labor changes in three ways: Educator Professional Development, Educational Learning Environments, and Student Growth.

Educator Professional Development (Time, Continuity, and Change)

Educator Professional Development highlights the teacher labor changes that were emphasized not only in the scholarship, but also in our study's findings. These professional development opportunities for educators not only emphasize the need for retooling throughout the lifecycle of a technological integration into a classroom, but the need to support K-16 teachers' self-efficacy in the use of this technology and the learning spaces they facilitate. Three themes that relate directly to this finding include: 1) Elements related to digital learning design and success, 2) The ways that technology has influenced student learning in an online space, and 3) Continual improvement strategies for mastery of program content. These three themes connect the instructional design elements of an online learning space with the mastery of the content and the technology needed to share and engage with this content. This finding further connects to the NCSS standard of time, continuity, and change as it highlights lifelong learning, changes in technology, and advancements in educator training.

Educational Learning Environment (People, Places, and Environments)

Educational Learning Environment is a finding that connects directly to the NCSS standard of People, Places, and Environments because it situates technological changes and teacher labor changes within the spaces in which they occur. In this way, our finding addresses the research question in that shifts in technology that change student learning and educator preparation also necessitate changes within the structure of the spaces where this is happening. The themes that relate directly to this finding include: 1) Structures needed for Holistic Academic Achievement and 2) The inputs and outputs supporting the success of the college mission. Both themes speak to the environments and structures that influence student learning in an online space as well as the changes that were needed to help support student learning in these spaces.

Student Growth (Individual Development and Identity)

Student Growth is a finding that emphasizes the objectives of teacher labor changes due to technological growth. That is, student growth is a direct outcome of the changes seen in technological advancements and integration in learning spaces. This was not only noted in the scholarship shared, but also highlighted in various ways within the themes found in our analysis. Two major themes that connect to this finding include: 1) External pressures that influence academic engagement and resiliency and 2) Breadth and depth of campus atmosphere and interactions. Both themes relate to individual characteristics related to being an online student or a student that takes online classes in the postsecondary space, while trying to balance and grow professionally and personally. This finding relates directly to the NCSS standard of Individual Development and Identity as it is a heavily reflective finding that underscores the impact of students on online learning changes as well as teacher labor changes on online learning.

Importance and Implications

As part of this chapter we have learned several elements that impact the teacher labor changes with respect to training, integration, and understanding of the use of new technologies in the classroom. Although technological advancements were steadily being incorporated into pre-service teacher training, the influx of the pandemic forced K-16 educators to quickly adapt to and understand their place in the technological sphere as it applied to education. The scholarship offered in this chapter showed significant changes in educators' attitudes toward technological integration and adoption within the last decade alone, with several new studies now aimed at understanding the ethical implication of the integration of AI into online and face-to-face learning spaces.

To this end, the findings from our study connect directly to implications for understanding teacher labor changes in the context of technological advancements. Looking at three integrated levels, we conceptualize our themes as interconnected concepts that reflect changes in Educator Professional Development, Educational Learning Environments, and Student growth. These three interconnected levels show how teacher labor changes with respect to technological advancements influence the type of training they receive, the institutional changes that need to be made, as well as how these changes impact student growth and learning in these spaces. Implications from these findings connect to how educators and institutions alike can anticipate the types of changes—in training, resources, and supports—that are needed to successfully navigate technological advancements and their implications to student growth.

Conclusions and Pedagogical Strategies

Based on the integration of Web 2.0, Web 3.0, and AI technologies, online learning and teaching have been implemented into schools for over two decades shifting the teaching labor arena (see Appendix for lesson plan). It can be argued that online learning in these different iterations has not only benefited the students, but it also means that teacher labor has demanded a continual retooling of their skills and partaking in collaboration with one another across the globe (Bowen & Watson, 2024; Clark, 2023). Data-driven learning has been amplified as part of the Web 2.0 and 3.0 revolutions, as teachers have more access to educator and student data than ever before. This type of access allows for more personalized learning, more accessible learning, and more up-to-date understanding of student challenges and potential that can be addressed through continual improvement practices (Bowen & Watson, 2024; Center for Teaching Excellence—UF, 2023).

As new technologies are being developed, K-16 educators have new tools, but also new challenges on how to utilize Web 3.0 and AI in the classroom in a positive way. The proper training is a must for the new and more senior generation of teachers. Possibly the new AI tools could be seen as answering a prayer to teacher shortages, too. Some researchers however warn not to substitute AI teaching for human teaching. Understanding these shifts, and how they connect to the social studies common core standards and the three National Curriculum Standards for Social Studies featured in this chapter is vital for students to make connections to their own learning and the changes in their learning environments.

Main Teaching/Learning Strategy

This lesson plan focuses on making connections between the three major social studies themes from the National Council of Social Studies Standards and students' reactions to challenges in virtual learning environments from the data analysis presented in the scholarly essay portion of this chapter. Specifically, we ask students to engage in a reflection and concept map assignment that connects them to their own experiences with virtual learning and the changes in teacher preparation. The following example lesson plan used the following NCSS (2024) standard within as an illustration of lesson design with the incorporation of technological advancements. This standard is as follows:

> Standard D2.His.3.9-12. Use questions generated about individuals and groups to assess how the significance of their actions changes over time and is shaped by the historical context

This standard is encompassed within the NCSS (2024) Time, Continuity, and Change Standard and incorporates active learning and community-based engagement strategies to get students to think deeply about how technology has changed their own learning and perspectives on technological advancements through a historical lens. The lesson plan follows the guidelines offered by the NCSS (2024) and expands to include reflective thinking and collaboration with community partners.

Lesson Plan

1. Lesson Plan Title: Use questions generated about individuals and groups to assess how the significance of their actions changes over time and is shaped by the historical context
2. Theme:
   In this lesson, high school students will explore how technology has played a crucial role in amplifying and reshaping society and history. By integrating research tools and online collaboration, students will gain hands-on experience in understanding how technological developments influence historical events such as labor market changes and their personal lives such as school and work. Students will make connections to both past and present by asking critical thinking questions about technology influence and development regarding school and work.
3. Grade Level: 9–12
4. Course: History
5. Time Required: 60 min
6. Essential and Supporting Questions:
   a. How has technology impacted our societies throughout our history?
   b. How has technology impacted societies and individuals?
   c. How have technological advancements influenced school and work environments through technological impact?
7. Objectives:
   a. SWBAT understand how historical and social context have been shaped by the significance of technology.
   b. SWBAT analyze the roles of individuals and groups in technological innovations and their implications.
   c. SWBAT reflect about the long-term impact of technology on an individual or group in school and work environments through the use of critical questioning.
8. Standards (from the National Council for the Social Studies [NCSS]):
   a. **Standard D2.His.3.9-12.** Use questions generated about individuals and groups to assess how the significance of their actions changes over time and is shaped by the historical context
9. Classroom Materials:
   Access to computers, tablets and/or smart devices
   Access to Internet
   Graphic organizers for note-taking and analysis
   Projector/Smartboard for multimedia presentations
   Online collaboration tools (e.g., Classroom online Discussion Board, Dropbox, Google Slides, Google Docs, Padlet)

10. Instructional Plan:
    a. Entry Task to Establish Context [time estimate 5 minutes—change based on time for class period]

    The teacher will play on the Smartboard a short video clip illustrating a significant technological breakthrough (e.g., Car invention, the first moon landing, creation of the Internet, the first iPhone). The teacher will ask: "How has this technological advancement impacted society? How might its significance change in the future?"

    b. Teacher-Directed Instruction [est. 15 minutes—change based on time for class period]

    Encourage students to think about both short and long-term effects. Encourage students to take into consideration historical and school and work contexts. Teacher prompts the students: What other questions could we ask and answer about these historical events?

    Teacher-directed instruction:

    Teacher presents a brief history of an important technological advancement in a mini-lecture with PowerPoint slides. Teacher will aid in analyzing how technological advancements throughout history shaped the social and historical concepts, especially those related to school and work. Teacher will encourage students to come up with critical thinking questions regarding the brief mini-lecture content.

    c. Student-Centered/Engaged Learning (Student Inquiry Activity/Activities) [est. 30 minutes—change based on time for class period]

    In their groups, students will research another technological breakthrough and create a concept map that visually represents the relationship between the technology and its impact on both the short and long term.

    Students should also create critical thinking questions for group discussion that relate to their research. For example:

    How has this technology changed?

    How has it impacted society and history?

    How did technology influence the school and work environments throughout history?

    Students will create a digital presentation or video summarizing their findings and share it with the class.

   d. Exit Task for Summarizing Answer(s) to Essential and Supporting Questions [est. 5 minutes—change based on time for class period]
      Create a timeline showcasing major technological advancements and their impacts on society and history. Add a critical thinking question to each technological milestone shown on the timeline.
11. Assessment:
   a. Students will use a digital classroom discussion board to write a short post analyzing a specific example of an individual important in the field of technology.
12. Community Engagement:
   a. Students will interview an older member of their family or community regarding technology and its impact during the interviewee's life regarding learning and working. Students will focus on asking questions regarding technological change based on questions that they make in class, with connections made to labor changes.

      After the interview, students will be asked to engage in a reflective activity and they must answer two questions:
      - o What have been their experiences with digital technology and learning?
      - o What would a world look like where they could not use technology to learn?

Table 10.1. Description of Overall Themes

Theme	Description	Codes
Structures needed for Holistic Academic Achievement	This theme describes the programs and institutional supports within the College that are designed to provide resources to ensure and further the academic achievement of all students.	**Student Success** Pathways to Persistence Student Affairs and Advising Care for Students
Continual improvement strategies for mastery of program content	This theme describes various elements of the teaching and learning aspects related to the course content side of academic programming.	**Academic Support** Faculty Professional Development Academic Independence Student Learning Outcomes
Elements related to digital learning design and success	This theme describes various resources and supports related to student success practices within an online learning environment.	**Online Student Experience** Resources Technical Support
Breadth and depth of campus atmosphere and interactions	This theme describes the whole range of student experiences on campus, including both positive and negative interactions.	**Performance/Accountability** Disconnected Satisfied Engagement Unsure Student Struggles
The inputs and outputs supporting the success of the college mission	This theme features various processes that are related to different components of a postsecondary institution's mission, including student success and academic quality.	**Strategic/Outcome Tracking** Campus Operations/Flexibility Work-Related Skills DEI Curriculum and Programs
External pressures that influence academic engagement and resiliency	This theme describes external challenges that students face that may mitigate their academic success on campus. motivation and engagement was Health and Wellness, which encompassed both students' well-being as well as their familial responsibilities in caring for spouses, children, parents, and other loved ones.	**Motivating Factors** Finance/Work Health and Wellness

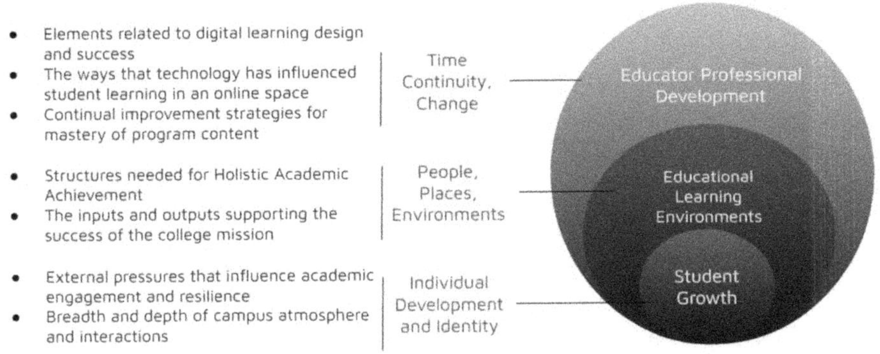

Figure 10.1: Findings and Connections.

References:

Ahmed, S. (2024). The pillars of trustworthiness in qualitative research. *Journal of Medicine, Surgery, and Public Health, 2*(2024), 10051. https://doi.org/10.1016/j.glmedi.2024.100051

Arce, P. E., Arce-Trigatti, A., Loggins, L., Sanders, J. R., Guerrero-Pérez, J. S., Bolaños Barrera, G. E., & Oyanader, M. A. (2022). Universes of Learning (UoL) as creative educational experiences: Exploring the TSPACK and Renaissance Foundry Model as catalysts for learning transformations. Special Issue: International Perspectives on University Teaching and Learning, Spring 2022(169), 65–81. https://doi.org/10.1002/tl.20483.

Arce-Trigatti, A. & Silber-Furman, D. (2021). Riding the Pan(aca)demic Waves: A One Year Portrait of Two Educator's Experiences Teaching in Higher Education through the 21st Century Pandemic. In S. McCarther (Ed.), Snapshots of History Portraits of the 21st Century Pandemic (pp. 1–15). Special Edition of the American Educational History Journal.

Arce-Trigatti, A., & Silber-Furman, D. (2022). "This job is horrible!": Postsecondary Reflections of Virtual Learning Transitions from the Field. Kappa Delta Pi Record, 52(2), 59–64. https://doi.org/10.1080/00228958.2022.2039517

Bowen, J. A., & Watson, C. E. (2024). Teaching with AI: A practical guide to a new era of human learning. American Association for College and Universities Publications. ISBN: 978142449227

Braun, V., & Clarke, V. (2006). Using thematic analysis in psychology. Qualitative Research in Psychology, 3(2), 77–101. https://doi.org/10.1191/1478088706qp063oa

Center for Teaching Excellent—University of Florida. (2023). Harnessing AI for Teaching and Learning: Faculty Learning Community. Retrieved from teach.ufl.edy/wp-content/uploads/2023/08/Harnessing-AI-2023-Booklet.pdf

Clark, H. (2023). The AI Infused Classroom. *Elevate Books Education*. ISBN–9798985137453

Durak, H. Y. (2021). Preparing pre-service teachers to integrate teaching technologies into their classrooms: Examining the effects of teaching environments based on open-ended, hands-on and authentic tasks. *Education and Information Technologies, 16*(1). https://doi.org/10.1007/s10639-021-10511-5

Glaser, B. G., & Strauss, A. L. (1967). *The discovery of grounded theory: Strategies for qualitative research*. Chicago, IL: Aldine Pub. Co.

Hsu, P. S. (2012). Examining the impact of educational technology courses on pre-service teachers' development of technological pedagogical content knowledge. *Teaching Education, 23*(2), 195–213.

Irvine, J. (2018, March 9). Relationship between teaching experience and teachereffectiveness: Implications for policy decisions. Retrieved from ResearchGate website https://www.researchgate.net/publication/331635835_Relationship_between_teaching_experience_and_teacher_effectiveness_implications_for_policy_decisions.

Janssen, N., Knoef, M., & Lazonder, A. (2019). Technological and pedagogical support for preservice teachers' lesson planning. https://www.tandfonline.com/doi/full/10.1080/1475939X.2019.1569554.

Koc, M., & Bakir, N. (2010). A Needs Assessment Survey to Investigate Pre-Service Teachers' Knowledge, Experiences and Perceptions About Preparation to Using Educational Technologies. *The Turkish Online Journal of Educational Technology, 9*(1), 13–23.

LeCompte, M. D. (2000). Analyzing qualitative data. *Theory Into Practice, 39*(3), pp. 146–54. doi:10.1207/s15430421tip3903_5

LeCompte, M. D., & Schensul, J. J. (1999). *Analyzing and interpreting ethnographic data*. Walnut Creek, CA: AltaMira Press.

Lin, Y. N.; Hsia, L. H.; Hwang, G. J. Promoting pre-class guidance and in-class reflection: A SQIRC-based mobile flipped learning approach to promoting students' billiards skills, strategies, motivation and self-efficacy. Comput. Educ. 2020, 160. [CrossRef]

National Council for the Social Sciences. (2024). National Curriculum Standards for Social Studies: Chapter 2—The Themes of Social Studies. Retrieved from https://www.socialstudies.org/national-curriculum-standards-social-studies-chapter-2-themes-social-studies#2.

Niewiadomski, R., & Anderson, D. (2017). The Rise of Artificial Intelligence: Its Impact on Labor Market and Beyond. In Strategic Imperatives and Core

Competencies in the Era of Robotics and Artificial Intelligence (pp. 29–49). IGI Global.

Miller, M. (2023) AI for Educators: Learning Strategies, Teacher Efficiencies, and a Vision for an Artificial Intelligence Future. *Ditch that Textbook.* ISBN - 1956306471

Parnell, A. (2024). *The challenges and opportunities of data-informed strategies: 4 considerations for the future.* Florida Association of Institutional Research, Annual Conference. Virtual, February 24, 2024.

Patton, M. (2010). Qualitative research & evaluation methods. Sage.

Saldana, J. (2013). The Coding Manual for Qualitative Researchers (2nd ed.). London: Sage.

Santos, J. M., & Castro, R. D. R. (2021). Technological Pedagogical content knowledge (TPACK) in action: Application of learning in the classroom by pre-service teachers (PST). *Social Sciences and Humanities, 3*(1), 100110. https://doi.org/10.1016/j.ssaho.2021.100110

Schina, D., Valls-Bautista, C., Borrull-Riera, A., Usart, M., & Esteve-Gonzalez, V. (2021). An associational study: preschool teachers' acceptance and self-efficacy towards Educational Robotics in a pre-service teacher training program. *International Journal of Educational Technology in Higher Education, 18*(28), 1–20.

Silber-Furman, D. & Arce-Trigatti A. (2021) Empathy and Flexibility in Teaching in the Era of COVID-19. Kappa Delta Pi, Teacher Advocate, The Quarterly Magazine for Professional Teachers. Retrieved from: http://digital.watkinsprinting.com/publication/?i=706621&p=10

Strauss, A., & Corbin, J. (1990). *Basics of qualitative research: Grounded theory procedures and techniques* (2nd ed.). Newbury Park, CA: SAGE.

Turra, H.; Carrasco, V.; Gonzalez, C.; Sandoval, V.; Yanez, S. Flipped classroom experiences and their impact on engineering students' attitudes towards university-level mathematics. High Educ. Teach. 2019, 4, 136–55. [CrossRef] 56.

Yu, Z.; Wang, G. Learning achievements and satisfaction of the clicker-aided flipped business English writing class. Educ. Technol. Soc. 2016, 19, 298–312.

van Dijk, J. (2020). *The digital divide.* Wiley & Sons.

van Dijk, J. (2006). Digital divide research, achievements and shortcomings. *Poetics, 34*(4–5), 221–35. https://doi.org/10.1016/k.poetic.2006.05.004

Zhao, L.; Liu, X.; Su, Y.-S. The Differentiate Effect of Self-Efficacy, Motivation, and Satisfaction on Pre-Service Teacher Students' Learning Achievement in a Flipped Classroom: A Case of a Modern Educational Technology Course. Sustainability 2021, 13, 2888. https://doi.org/10.3390/su13052888

Contributors

Andrea Arce-Trigatti holds a Ph.D. in Education with a Learning Environments and Educational Studies concentration from the University of Tennessee, Knoxville. Her research centers on higher education, faculty development, program evaluation, education policy, and critical thinking and collaborative learning strategies. She is an active collaborator and workshop facilitator with the Center for Assessment and Improvement of Learning at Tennessee Tech University. As a founding member of the award-winning Renaissance Foundry Research Group, she has helped to develop and investigate the pedagogical techniques utilized to enhance critical and creative thinking at interdisciplinary interfaces.

Adam I. Attwood is Associate Professor in the Eriksson College of Education at Austin Peay State University in Clarksville, Tennessee. He has experience as a teacher and social studies department chair (grades 6–12). In 2010, he was recognized by the Educational Testing Service (ETS) with the Praxis Recognition of Excellence in Social Studies Content Knowledge. He earned his Ph.D. (2015) in education with specialization in cultural studies and social thought from Washington State University. Also, he holds two master's degrees and a bachelor's degree from Eastern Washington University and did coursework with the Leader's Scholarship at Gonzaga University. In 2018, he was awarded the Richard B. Kobusch Humanities Chair (2018–2019) at Whitfield School. He is the author of *Social Aesthetics and the School Environment: A Case Study of the Chivalric Ethos* (Palgrave Macmillan, 2018) and co-editor of *Teaching the Struggle for Civil Rights, 1977-Present* (Peter Lang, 2022).

Brandon Beck is Assistant Professor of Secondary Social Studies Education at the University of Maryland, Baltimore County (UMBC). He completed his Ph.D.

in Teaching and Learning at Clemson University before coming to UMBC. He teaches courses in social studies education and foundations for preservice teachers. He is the descendant of the first Black department head for the city of Greenville, SC. His identity as a historian, educator, and critical scholar shapes his work within the fields of history, education, and critical scholarship.

Chara Haeussler Bohan is Professor and the Social Foundations of Education unit and doctoral program coordinator at Georgia State University. She specializes in educational history with a focus on gender, race, and biography; curriculum and instruction; and social studies education. She has more than 100 publications, which include books, book chapters, and articles. Her recent research in the *Journal of Social Studies Research* focuses on how the lost cause mythology was perpetuated in "Mint Julep" textbooks. She is the author of *Teaching Enslavement in American History: Lesson Plans and Primary Sources* with H. Robert Baker and LaGarrett King (Lang, 2022) and *Go to the Sources: Lucy Maynard Salmon and the Teaching of History* (Lang, 2004). She was the co-director of three National Endowment for the Humanities Summer Institute for Teachers grants. Bohan was the President of the American Association for Teaching and Curriculum from 2014 to 2015 and served as the editor of *Curriculum and Teaching Dialogue* from 2017 to 2023.

Niklaus Ryker K. Christensen has a Master of Arts in Teaching (MAT) degree and a bachelor's degree in sociology. He taught AP Sociology and German for a year at a Title 1 high school. Previously, he was a combat lifesaver instructor in the U.S. Army. And he was a certified instructor for CPR First Aid AED and EMT-B. For Niklaus, studying sociology informs an understanding of labor history that helps advocate for LGBTQ+ equality.

Sean Corrigan is Assistant Professor of history education at Kennesaw State University, in Kennesaw, Georgia. His current research focuses on critical analyses of issues of diversity and equity in social studies education. Prior to his time in higher education, he taught social studies for 14 years in Compton, CA, Las Vegas, NV, and Vanuatu. He has worked extensively with culturally and linguistically diverse K-12 learners in several countries, in both urban and rural settings. Dr. Corrigan is especially interested in empowering teachers to center social justice and global perspectives in their practice.

Heather N. Hagan is an associate professor and Department Chair of Teacher Education and the Elementary Education Program Coordinator at Coastal

Carolina University. Her research focuses on elementary social studies instructional methods and tools, primarily focusing on inquiry-based instruction and using technology to support teaching and learning. She teaches elementary social studies methods courses.

Tina Lane Heafner is Professor of social studies education in the Department of Middle, Secondary, and K-12 Education at the University of North Carolina at Charlotte. She directs the Ph.D. in Curriculum and Instruction. As a Past-President of the National Council for the Social Studies (NCSS), Dr. Heafner's research and teaching focus on innovative practices in social studies education, with a particular emphasis on technology, online learning, and disciplinary literacy. Her research also examines the intersection of curriculum, policy, and practice in social studies, including issues of civic engagement and social justice, which are key themes in this chapter. Tina has authored numerous publications, including 12 books and articles in leading academic journals such as the *Journal of Teacher Education*, *Theory and Research in Social Education*, and the *Journal of Technology and Teacher Education*.

Alex Honold is Assistant Professor at the University of Mary Washington's College of Education and a former high school history teacher in Dallas and Washington, DC public schools. He received his Ph.D. in Education from the University of Michigan, studying how secondary students develop and frame complex historical inquiries. His works have appeared in publications such as *Social Education* and the book series "Hollywood or History?" He teaches courses in history and social science pedagogy, foundations of education, instructional design and assessment, classroom management, and education research (ORCID iD https://orcid.org/0000-0002-0270-7793).

Aimee Klaschus holds a Bachelor of Science in Psychology from the University of Central Florida and is currently the assessment analyst at the Office of Institutional Effectiveness at Tallahassee State College. She is a quantitative scholar with a statistical focus and her research features best practices in data analytics and data visualization, applications of data analysis in the areas of education and neuroscience, and institutional support for faculty engagement in evaluation.

Meghan Moore-Hubbard is Clinical Assistant Professor of Curriculum and Instruction at Kennesaw State University. She is a proud Appalachian and granddaughter of a United Mine Workers of America (UMWA) member.

Debora V. Saavedra-Winch is a doctoral candidate in Curriculum and Instruction at the University of North Carolina at Charlotte, specializing in Curriculum and Educational Development. She holds a master's degree in Latin American History and has a strong background as a High School Civics Educator. As a first-generation immigrant, she is passionate about intercultural education and promoting cultural diversity and within marginalized communities. Her research focuses on supporting civic engagement among Latino students and enhancing intercultural education practices, particularly through her work with Kuna teachers in Panama.

Adam J. Schmitt is Assistant Professor of teacher education and history at the University of Southern Maine. His research interests include the relationship between elements of social studies teachers' identities and own memories of schooling and their curricular and pedagogical decision-making, as well as the relationship between collective memory and history in how teachers and students make sense of the past, present, and future.

Dorota Silber-Furman is Assistant Professor in the College of Education at Tennessee Tech University (TTU), where she teaches courses connected to English as a second or other language (ESOL), multiculturalism, and literacy. She is a member of the National Association for Multicultural Education and a board member of its Tennessee chapter. She is a former co-counselor of Eta Nu Kappa Delta Pi at TTU. Dorota graduated from the University of Wrocław with a Bachelor of Arts in Romance Languages. She also earned a Bachelor of Science in Multidisciplinary Studies, Elementary Education and a master's degree in Curriculum and Instruction. She holds a Doctor of Philosophy in Education degree from TTU. Dorota's research interests are connected to ELL education, culturally relevant practices, literacy, multiliteracies, international education, and critical theory.

Carolyn A. Weber is Associate Professor of curriculum and instruction and the Middle Level Program Coordinator at the University of Northern Iowa. Her research interests include teaching social studies through inquiry, the history of social studies education, and best practices in middle-level education. She teaches middle-level methods and elementary social studies methods courses.

JoAnn Wood is working toward a PhD in Education Policy Studies at Georgia State University after a long career as a social studies educator. She taught elementary and middle school grades for 25 years before moving from the classroom into curriculum and professional development work with social studies teachers for the past 20 years. Her dissertation research is on the history of early teacher unions and more specifically on Mary C. Barker and her work in Atlanta in the first half of the twentieth century.

Index

TEACHING CRITICAL THEMES IN AMERICAN HISTORY

Caroline R. Pryor, Erik B. Alexander,
James M. Mitchell,
Whitney Blankenship, and
Michael E. Karpyn, and Jenice L. View
General Editors

In the United States, the Common Core Standards, the C3 Framework for Social Studies Standards (NCSS), and the 10 themes of the National Curriculum Standards (NCS/NCSS) each pose challenges for teachers preparing to teach skills, content, and critical issues of American history. The problem for many middle and secondary teachers is that textbooks do not contain sufficient primary source documents and varied secondary literature linked to these standards. The volumes in the Teaching Critical Themes in American History series fill this need by providing teachers with history content, pedagogical strategies, and teaching resources. The series is organized around key problems/issues in American history so that teachers can select which critical topics upon which they might want to concentrate.

Middle and Secondary pre- and in-service educators will find the books in this series essential for developing and implementing American history and social studies curriculum in diverse and complex classrooms. Teachers will find the books in this series valuable as they search for methodologies and material that will help them address the Common Core Standards in the social sciences and history. Community College history instructors can also find the books in this series helpful as supplementary texts in their U.S. history survey courses. The practical—not to mention exciting—implementation of perspectives offered in each title is a key feature of this series.

This series will address topics such as the formation of the American Republic, the problem of slavery in America, causes of the Civil War, emancipation and reconstruction, America's response to industrialization, the New Deal, the fight for Civil Rights, and more. The series editors invite proposals for edited volumes in American history and social studies, along with articles and lesson plans for both the topics above, and other topics of the series.

For additional information about this series or for the submission of manuscripts, please contact the following series editors:

Caroline R. Pryor capryor@siue.edu
James M. Mitchell james.mitchell@csueastbay.edu

To order other books in this series, please contact our Customer Service Department: peterlang@presswarehouse.com (within the U.S.) or orders@peterlang.com (outside the U.S.). You may also browse online by series at www.peterlang.com.

www.ingramcontent.com/pod-product-compliance
Ingram Content Group UK Ltd.
Pitfield, Milton Keynes, MK11 3LW, UK
UKHW021852100926
8556IPUK00020B/1181

9 781636 678917